MW01017001

Ludmila Plett

By Way of Searching

First Edition,
Translated from the original
Russian Language
in May 2011

Edited and Formatted by
Wasser des Lebens Mission, e.V.
Kolomanstrasse 32
73527 Schwäbisch Gmünd
Germany

Unless otherwise noted, all scripture quotations are taken from the New King James Version of the Holy Bible. Copyright© by Thomas Nelson Inc. Used by permission. All rights reserved

Copyright © 2012 Ludmila Plett
Translated by Svetlana V. Shiyka
Corrected by Dr. Peter Rahn, Katherine Rudenya

All rights reserved. No part of this publication may be reproduced, stored in a retrieval system, or transmitted in any form or by any means, electronic, mechanical, photocopying, recording, or otherwise, without the prior written permission of the publisher.

ISBN: 978-1-60383-418-6

Published by:
Holy Fire Publishing
PO Box 1886
DeLand, FL 32721

www.ChristianPublish.com

Printed in the United States of America and the United Kingdom

The Author's Introduction to the English version

Dear Reader, it is my desire to share with you on the pages of this book that, which I had lived through while following a way of painfully long search for the living God and the personal intimate relationship with Him, of which Jesus was saying, "My sheep hear My voice, and I know them, and they follow Me" (John 10:28). Decades of a traditional, formal and ceremonial Christianity that I learned from my early childhood didn't bring any joy or satisfaction to my soul, encouraging me to seek for something that was hidden from me, but what my soul looked for in its longing for peace and harmony with the Lord. I continually asked myself a question, why, in fact, I came to existence and how I should live in order to fulfill the purpose appointed to me from above. Many years had passed before the profound meaning of God's words which came out of the mouth of the prophet Isaiah was revealed to me, "And a highway shall be there, and a way, and it shall be called **The way of holiness; the unclean** shall not pass over it; but is shall be **for the redeemed**: the wayfaring men, yea fools, shall not err therein" (Isaiah 35:8, ASV).

As I began on a way of cleansing and sanctification, I had to re-evaluate my priorities anew; look over my whole life and my walk before the Lord. This led me to a deep inward crisis and consequently, a complete spiritual overthrow, which marked the beginning of my ministry and a new life in Christ. Following God's calling I have encountered many a time some things which we as people only think to be the truth, affirming the truthfulness of the words by the wise Solomon, "There is a way that seems right to a man, but its end is the way to death" (Proverbs 14:12, ESV). All that I experienced in the course of events gradually led me to a conclusion that way too many things presented to us as the absolute truth and "a work of God" aren't such at all in reality. It is so easy while getting carried away in outward "rightness" of something to start serving a man or a cause instead of God; and begin building not on the Rock Who is Christ, but on a "sinking sand" using not the reliable "precious stones" but "hay" and "straw"[1], which will all burn away sooner or later. One can think that he has become a part of something great or has achieved something significant in God or received from Him something special even without suspecting that it is all nothing in His sight. As I look back I can only thank the Lord that while being very gracious He revealed Himself to me, as I have not known Him before although was considered a "good Christian".

Unfortunately, it must be said that the enormous amount of existing religious literature as well as the multitude of views, opinions, interpretations and dogmatisms of a whole host of Christian teachings, in which network of labyrinths you can easily go astray, led to the fact that by losing the sense of direction Christians began to crave a lot more of the new knowledge about God rather than of the intimate relationship with Him. But this is the only criterion which determines the essence and value of our discipleship. As a result of this approach there entered

---

[1] 1 Corinthians 3:12

superficiality, a tendency towards ritualism and formalism of the worship; a readiness to compromise with the world and sin; and therefore, a consequential spiritual coldness of people of God independently of their denomination set in.

The many years of counseling experience reveal a sad picture of the real spiritual state of Christians, practically of all existing Christian congregations and churches. And in spite of the fact that the majority of those who consider themselves children of God are satisfied with their Christianity, which usually amounts to a regular church-attending practice; there is a small number of those who moan and groan within in realization of missing or lacking something important and valuable or may be, even something major.

This is why once finally decided to make known my own experiences on the way of a personal spiritual quest, I am doing it in hope that this reading may bring some sort of help to those seeking souls. Perhaps, in the quiet hours of solitude together with this book they, too, will experience the same illuminating light in their hearts and minds, which the Lord sent to my restless soul during some difficult moments of my life, bringing comfort, peace and desired serenity. My prayer to the Heavenly Father is that it won't be me speaking from the pages you have in front of you, dear Reader, but God Himself, Who alone knows what you need and how to help you.

By narrating my story, sharing my thoughts and things I had lived through in closeness with the Living God;, remembering His mercies and firmness towards me, I in no way want to emphasize my own exclusivity and uniqueness, standing out of the mass of other believers. No, not at all. I know all too well that every individual is unique and exceptional, and there are many of those whose lives were a lot brighter and much more amazing than that of my own, so that if a book was to be written about them it would turn out to be something marvelous. Besides, I am fully aware of the fact that with personal testimony, when you must narrate different events about yourself, it's quite impossible to avoid using ever-present personal nouns and adjectives: "I", "me", "my", which may in itself sound repulsive to some, but I didn't know how else to circumvent them better. There is one hope that I have, though. And it is that if the following lines would be written under the guidance of the Lord and His Holy Spirit, then, in spite of all, they could bring help and blessings. Therefore, as I begin my story, my prayer to the Heavenly Father is that He may glorify His great and holy Name through this account.

Ludmila Plett

⊰⌘⌒

The Opening Prayer

Lord Jesus, You are the One Who knows each and every heart in a way no one else does nor do we know ourselves. You are the One for Whom our life, thoughts and hearts are like an open book. Thank You, Heavenly Father, that You have once made me stop and ponder about my personal relationship with You. Dear Savior, You have once used a mouth of an obtuse she-donkey. In a similar way I am now before You fully aware that if You don't put the right words in my mouth so that they touch another soul, then anything I say here will only be a meaningless sound without the power of Your Holy Spirit. I am asking You to draw closer to every person while he or she reads this book and speak to them the words they especially need to hear. Thank you, Jesus, that with You even the stones can speak. Now that I am about to share my thoughts and experiences, breathe Your Spirit into them and fill them with Your power. Lord, talk to the heart of a reader in a manner You alone can do. Use the written words in such a way that after reading this book, a soul can walk through life enriched and empowered by You. I ask it in Your Name and for the glory of Your Name.

Amen

Table of Contents

*My thoughts are not your thoughts, neither My
ways are your ways, - says the Lord. But as
heaven is higher than earth, so My ways are
higher than your ways and My thoughts are
higher than yours are.*

(Isa.55: 8-9)

Prologue

"*Ludmilka, dochen'ka*[2]! You must get up now, once and for all! You
will be late for your lectures at the institute!"

My mother's soft hand is affectionately petting my head and my
curly hair that lay spread around the table. Her voice sounds very far
off, from a great distance, hardly reaching my sleepy consciousness.
Nevertheless, the last words literally throw me off the chair. Rubbing
my sleepy eyes, I glance over at the alarm clock and am startled. That
makes me completely awake. I have only 15 minutes until the bus I
normally take to get to the institute leaves. Hastily I get dressed,
quickly brush my teeth, rinse my face, and barely hear, as my mother,
deliberately angry, is reprimanding me.

"How many times have I asked you not to stay up late studying
your textbooks? Can't you see your table lamp burned all night for
nothing! Didn't I tell you to set your alarm before you start doing your
homework in the evening?"

I smile back at her knowing very well that she does not really
mean what she says, and deep down in her heart she is in fact
exceedingly happy for her daughter, who chose to follow her footsteps
into the field of medical studies. Giving my mother a big kiss on her
cheek as I leave, I rush out the door into the hallway and seeing that
the elevator is not available (which has mostly been the case) rapidly
run down the stairs from the eighth floor. How wonderful that the bus
stop is actually less than a hundred feet from our apartment building!
The softhearted bus driver graciously steps on the brakes and opens
the bus door again. Almost out of breath, I run inside the bus and on
my way to the only empty seat tell him,

"Thank you!" Real joy is filling my heart.

"Thank You, Lord . . . I made it! Please abide with me throughout
this whole day, I pray. Bless me and keep me to live through
everything with You at my side. Amen."

---

[2] Name format shows mother's affection and "dochen'ka" stands for "my little
daughter" in Russian.

That is how short some of my morning prayers used to be in those early college years.

Ah, how long ago that was! How much had transpired over the years! How many stressful and difficult exams had been left behind. Back then, I considered them my most severe trials of life. Of course, I did not know at the time how often life would have me face very different kinds of problems and hardships, such that I would never have guessed existed. Nevertheless, despite all that has happened, being now well over fifty years of age, having much gray in my hair and having spent decades of my life searching for God and life's purpose, I can joyously say as in the days of my youth,

"Thank You, Lord, that You have so far helped me! Please, be with me further, so that I might reach the goal You have assigned to me while being guided by Your mighty hand."

Chapter 1

Childhood, Youth, The Voice of God.

My parents believed in God and became Christians approximately a year before I was born. Therefore, I can only thank the Lord for His wonderful provision, that being in my mother's womb I was already living under the influence of God's grace. Much later, as I became a young girl who could understand, my mother told me that she was clearly seeing in me their own spiritual flame and searching for the living God as well as their first passionate love toward Christ. Thus, the blessings my parents experienced then, became later my own blessing, something I didn't deserve. This experience often causes me to think about all the mothers and fathers, who by their walk with God and their daily lives determine the fate and spiritual life for their children long before they are born into this world. Along with mother's milk a baby feeds on everything that the mother does and goes through.

In fact, I realized this truth more deeply some years later, when my own quest in search of the Lord had begun. Earlier, my Christianity just like the Christianity of many other children of believing parents presented itself as nothing else but "the faith of my forefathers". As much as I can recall, from an early age, I had kneeled down together with my older sister and four little brothers when my mother and father would pray with us. When our parents were going to a Sunday service they most certainly took all six of us along. In this way, in my childhood and youth my understanding of faith issues and serving God was formed and shaped under the influence of my parents, possibly, without much awareness on their part. Moreover, I must say, that they never forced us to do anything in such matters. Usually, children imitate their parents in the spiritual and physical realm and don't even think about it. As a result, it is not surprising that they become followers of the particular Christian faith group in which they were brought up, because they experience the traditions and interpretations of their parents. So, children of Lutheran parents become Lutherans and children of Baptist parents become Baptists, children of Pentecostal parents become Pentecostals and so on. The same thing happened to me. My parents were part of Christian Evangelical Pentecostal Church, and so, my views and understanding were shaped under the influence of this Christian teaching until I turned eighteen. Unfortunately, as often occurs in many Christian denominations, I was confident that my faith was the only true faith and our church was the only true church. As far as other believers were concerned, I looked down on them in the same way other so-called "spiritual" Christians did, since we considered them to be the ones that hadn't reached **our level** of spirituality. Thus they couldn't have much insight or might even have been deceived. We, as spiritually "advanced," were advised to pray for such people so that God would open their eyes, but were also warned to avoid any communication with them lest we become a prey of their destructive influence. It was astonishing, how Satan deluded Christian people to have distrust, grudges, suspicions and even open animosity towards one another. And all that existed in spite of the fact that we all served the same God and longed to get into same heaven, where only those who are one in God's Spirit can enter. And His Spirit doesn't divide Itself.

And so, being brought up in this particular Christian denomination, I experienced all that characterized that doctrine. One aspect was the so-called baptism of the Holy Spirit with speaking in tongues. Actually, for me that particular gift of the Spirit revealed itself quite extraordinary from the beginning, something I only understood many years later. I experienced spiritual baptism, when I was only 7 or 8 years old. It happened as follows. I was visiting some of my friends. At the house where they lived my girlfriend's father offered to pray for the baptism of the spirit over us. I was absolutely fine with the idea since I had heard about it very often in my own family as well as at our church. With the faith of a simple child I knelt along with other children and after a fairly short time my lips started saying strange words, which I had never known before. I can't remember if I felt anything special at the time. Nobody placed his hands on me, either. I only recall that following the advice of my friend's father I repeated several times the word "baptize". After this prayer some other kids also started speaking in tongues. Later, that man told us that he had a vision concerning each of the children: either a dove was descending on one, or tongues of fire on another. After that we, all the children, continued to play and didn't talk about the event any more. That is how I experienced the so-called baptism of the Holy Spirit, the way it is understood in Pentecostal doctrine, though sometimes with slight variations. In the evening of that same day two women believers asked me to stay overnight at their place. They were Germans by nationality. When I woke up next morning, I couldn't figure out what was going on. Both sisters were sitting by my bedside with faces wet from crying and quietly praying with tears in their eyes. I asked them about the reason for tears and they without any detailed explanation just said to me: "Ah, dear! You will not be able to comprehend that. The Lord kept talking to us all night long in German language using you as His instrument." I recall being dumbfounded by those words. "What do you mean "in the German language"? – I repeated inquisitively. – I don't know any German!" But they didn't shed any light on that to me and in the next few minutes as with most children my mind became preoccupied with other things. I was still but a little girl, and toys and dolls, and games were much more important to me.

Years passed by. I went to school and completed one grade after another. It was easy for me to study. Besides, I was very diligent and patient. And as long as I can remember, in my early childhood years I started dreaming of becoming a medical doctor. My mother who had been educated as a medical assistant and who after the WWII worked as a nurse for over 30 years was able to instill in me the same love of medicine. She kept noticing with surprise how I was sitting in the office where she did the work of a therapeutic nurse and held my breath while I watched a needle prick a patient's vein, the blood appear in a syringe and the administration of carefully chosen medicine to the patient. I watched how she placed cupping glasses on an ill person's back, how the skin was partially sucked into them and its color changed to red or blue. All my dolls had signs of needles all over them because I was always giving them shots. I never had any fear of seeing blood, something normally present in children. My mother used to say that I was born to become a medical doctor. Therefore, being an honor student at school was the first and foremost condition to fulfill my cherished dream. All the teachers at school knew about my strong desire to be a doctor and in every possible way supported me.

Besides classes at school, the usual children's games and books of fiction, which I literally "swallowed up", I had no other interests. Since I had never been an Oktyabrionok[3] or a Pioneer[4] or for that matter, a Komsomolka,[5] everyone at school knew I was a Christian and the other children often called me "bogomolka".[6] Any efforts on the part of Pioneer leaders or teachers and class teachers[7] to talk to me about God and faith in Him didn't get them anywhere, because I usually kept quiet. When they asked me if I was forced to believe in God, I always replied with a short "no" without going into details. More than once I ran home from school in terror and hid behind our tile stove, for some boys from school scoffed at me and called me names because of my faith and even threw stones at me. Such was the godless time and

---

[3] Communist party based organization for small children between 7-10 years old.

[4] Communist party based organization for early teenagers between 11-14 years old

[5] Youth organization a person must become a member of if he/she wants to be a Communist Party member later. Usually it consists of young people from 14 years old and older and is promoted at high school.

[6] Means – "the one who prays to God" but in belittling, mocking way.

[7] A teacher was called "the class teacher" when he/she had a responsibility over an entire class of students during a school year. The class teacher held special meetings, organized cultural events and resolved issues in students lives. Such teacher also taught one of the subjects of the curriculum.

political system in which we lived then. Many children of Christian families had similar experiences, not to mention the parents themselves. Although, I must say, the necessity of standing our ground for our faith and enduring mocking, humiliation and persecutions made all Christians including the children, much more serious and responsible in matters concerned with serving God. That is why I am extremely pleased that my Christianity took shape and form in my childhood and youth during that difficult time of atheism and, therefore, made an impact on my entire future life.

Unfortunately, even though it was important to stand and fight for my faith in God my spiritual life didn't reflect much depth or a search for a closer walk with Him, at least, not until I was 17-18 years of age. At that time, I entered Vladivostok Medical University and took the first step toward achieving my precious goal. It seemed that all was going really well, and I should have been to be extremely thankful to God and rejoiced, while making sure to become the best medical doctor possible, especially, since I thought this kind of occupation was most suitable for a Christian girl. But . . . . There was one "but", that continued to bring disturbance to my soul and forced me to ask myself same question over and over again, "Is this profession the right choice? Does my desire to be a doctor coincide with God's will? Will He back me up in it?"

The thoughts did not bother me in vain. The thing was that when I was still at high school, I heard God's voice for the first time in my life. During the services at the church, in the sermons and the conversations with those who preached I heard that even now God could speak to a person through prophecies and visions. As most people know, Christians from the Pentecostal movement get in contact with God and learn to know His will mainly by means of a variety of spiritual gifts. Though in later years, I have also seen this same type of approach, during the years of my youth it was quite different with me. God Himself suddenly spoke to me in a way that made me stop in my tracks and hold my breath listening to His voice.

It happened when I was fifteen. At the time, I had completed the eighth grade and in conjunction with that event there was a celebration for the students, along with the handing out of diplomas for the accomplishments of eight years of school.[8] Just a few days before the event I was asked to recite a short story, since I loved literature and had good articulation. The idea of the story was directed toward young

---

[8] 8 years of education was the minimal requirement in the Soviet educational system then. Students would be able to continue their studies at technical school or pursue high school education of 10 years, which was equivalent to 12-year school education in United States of America.

people and had to do with matters of abstinence and purity of first love in the context of rude banalities which had started to take hold in the community and which later developed into the notorious behavior of our generation's "hippie" movement. I had really liked the suggested story because it reflected my own understanding and personal opinion. When I was reciting it during the celebration, some of our super-modern girls fled from the auditorium screaming, "No! I can't listen to it anymore!"

Next day after class two teachers came up to me. One was a teacher of Russian and literature and the other a teacher of biology. They asked me whether I would like to sign up for drama class, since I had talents to perform.

"And by the way, Ludmila, who do you want to be?" All of a sudden, the teacher of Russian Language and Literature asked me this strange question. Since she was our class teacher, she knew very well that I was practically crazy about medicine.

I know not why, maybe because I was still under the impact of the previous evening's event or because I just wanted to fool around, but quite unexpectedly, even to myself, I replied:

"Who do I want to become? Oh, perhaps, I will be an actress!" My words were still on my lips when from somewhere above me on my right side there was a calm (yet at the same time unique in its power) man's voice,

"An actress? No. **You will write books.** *"*

It resounded so distinctly and clearly in my ears that I became quiet and stood there as under a spell. In spite of my passion for literature and Russian language and an overwhelming love of reading, it had never occurred to me to write books. Who in the world could have said that? What kind of voice was it? Next to me there were only two women and this was the voice of a man. Utterly confused I looked around trying to spot the One who just spoke to me.

"Ludmila, what happened? Who are you looking for?"

As if from a distance I heard my biology teacher's voice.

"Don't you hear what I am asking you? What about your doctor's profession? Haven't you always said you want to be a medical doctor?"

"Yes, of course, I will be a doctor. This was just a joke," I mumbled in reply still under the impression of the voice I heard. And then, there was that voice again,

"No. **You will write books.** *"*

"Books?!" I thought to myself in bewilderment.

"Books . . . ? What books . . . ?" And then, mischievously following my childish fantasy, notwithstanding what was going on, I finished my reply,

"Oh, yes! I will write su-u-uch a novel about myself!!" At that moment the same voice sounded the third time:

"A novel . . . ? About yourself . . . ? No. You will write about others."

There was silence after that. The voice stopped and repeated nothing anymore. I was totally perplexed. Looking at both teachers, I well understood I couldn't tell them any of that. And they stared at me with amazement having no idea or explanation for my more than strange behavior.

That day as I was going home from school, one thought thoroughly occupied my mind: who had spoken to me? For some reason I didn't think it was God. Being very reserved and secretive during my puberty years I said nothing to my parents. Yet for a long time that night I couldn't fall asleep while thinking,

"Who was it that talked to me? Why didn't I see Him? What books was He talking about . . . ?"

This occurrence might have remained a mystery and most likely been forgotten after a few years if that same Voice had not spoken to me for the second time.

It was in 1966 when I turned 17 and, after high school graduation, was preparing to pass the exams necessary to enter Vladivostok's Medical Institute. Our good neighbors left for vacation and gave me the keys to their apartment so that I could study questions for the exams in quietness. No one bothered me there and I could spend whole days and weeks alone. At times, I interrupted my studies and knelt before God asking Him to help me to pass the exams and enter into this medical school. Once while I was praying in this manner there was again a man's voice which said, cutting the silence in the room,

"It would have been better for you to remain just as you are." Startled by this unexpected interruption, I looked around. There was nobody in the room but me.

"What's this? Who has just talked to me?" I thought in amazement and then remembered that I had already heard that same Voice two years ago. Yes, but what meaning did those words have for me? Why is it better for me to remain **just as I am?** How am I supposed to understand this? Is it really that God doesn't want me to become a doctor? Then, why didn't He tell me about it straight? Couldn't He just say that it wasn't His will for me? But, what if it wasn't the Lord? Then, who was it? I had heard the Voice so clearly. . . .

Pondering over this whole thing, I started praying even more fervently, pouring out my soul again and again expressing my deepest desire to be a doctor.

"Lord," I was saying, "Where else would I be able to serve You and all the people better, helping them in their sufferings and showing them my love?"

So I continued praying with tears, when suddenly above me there was that same voice repeating those same words, *"It would have been better for you to remain just as you are."* Not another word. There was no "yes" or "no", but *"It would have been better for you . . . ."*

I cried bitterly with all my being, for I had no desire whatsoever to reconcile with the thought of not being destined to become a doctor. The following days were filled with utter anxiety and confusion. I didn't know what to do: continue my preparation studies for examinations or take my papers from the institute. But what would I say to my mother who only lived with the hope of seeing her daughter as a medical doctor one day? I repeatedly called upon the Lord, asking Him for some clarity, but no answer came. God was silent. And then I decided to do the following. Since I finished high school with an award for being the best student and had received a medal of honor, I had an opportunity to enter any university or school with only one major exam to pass but only if it would be passed with an "A". If my grade fell lower than "A" I had to continue passing more examinations with all the other students. Since I had received no revelation from the Lord (though much desired), I was determined to get ready just for that one major exam in chemistry. In case I failed or received a low grade I would accept this as a sign of God's will and quit any further attempts to enter this institute.

Passing the major exam was a true miracle for me. I will not go into details about it but can only say that the examiner wrote down "5"[9] and congratulated me for getting to the medical institute. Therefore, I became a student but without realizing the meaning of the words I had heard. Nevertheless, they kept disturbing my soul time and again:

"What could it all mean? And why?"

Just as it had happened the first time, I didn't utter a word about it to anyone.

The next 6 years as a student were filled with many difficult and strenuous studies. Much of my time was spent with textbooks and accordingly, many trials and temptations of youth simply went over my head. Students at the institute and Christian boys and girls at my church enjoyed their youth: they spent time together, dated, loved, and got married. But I was like a white crow among them all. All attempts made by Christian or worldly young men to start dating me always failed. I had no feelings towards them except pity. Dating wasn't for me and I had no time for it, but studied and studied and studied. That's how the best years of my youth were spent.

---

[9] It is a highest score a student can get at any educational system in former USSR for his or her achievements.

Yet, not only had the studies at the institute occupied my heart and thoughts. My student years had also become the years of my first very conscientious pursuit of God. After my entry into the medical institute, a dear Christian woman of about eighty years of age had become my best and closest friend. This old lady had the richest experiences in her spiritual life, derived from many years of suffering and persecutions for Christ's name's sake. But for me her personal relationship with the Lord held something really precious. For hours I could listen to her stories about God's doing in her life and the way He led her through hardships, imprisonment, sorrows and arduous trials to reveal His great power during most difficult times and show other people His grace, holiness and justice. It was unbelievable that in spite of her rather full years this grandmother remembered very well what she told me and practically never repeated herself. My soul was like a sponge absorbing those stories and in response a deep desire to get closer to God grew more and more inside my heart. In fact, that was the time when my quest for God had begun. I had turned eighteen, been baptized with water, and became a church member. It seemed God was observing me very closely and so was Satan.

During my second year at the institute unexpectedly the head of anatomy studies summoned me. When I nervously sat in front of him he said to me without any preamble,

"We have become aware that you are a Christian. Is this true?"

And hearing my affirmative reply he anxiously continued,

"But how are you going to combine faith in God with the work of a Soviet medical doctor?"

"Here you are," I mentally told myself. "This is your hour, Ludmila. Now your faith and your Christianity are on trial." His words mean exactly: "either God or institute".

"Why don't you answer me?" The professor interrupted my thoughts. "Don't you understand what I am talking about?"

"No!" I quietly replied. "I understand you very well. You can expel me from the institute if you have a right to do that, but I will not reject God."

There was silence. I lowered my eyes, but with all my being was feeling his intent, searching gaze directed at me. Minutes seemed like eternity.

"Very well!" The gray-haired man got up interrupting silence. "I know that you are doing excellent work as far as the school program is concerned. You may go now. If necessary, we will call you again."

I left his office walking on air. Fear was gone. My heart rejoiced,

"Thank You, Lord, that You helped me to withstand and remain faithful! This truly was Your grace! Without Your help from above I couldn't have done it!"

18

Another day went by. Then another one. The whole week passed. And then, so did another week. Nobody requested my presence again, and I concluded that the most difficult test of faithfulness would come to me later. When at the end of my sixth year of study all difficulties of learning process had been overcome they could easily tell me,

"God or diploma". Then what?! Would I be able to stand up? Ah, it would have been so much better now, at the beginning of my studies. . . .

Years followed one after another. My soul searched for the Lord and He responded to her quiet callings. By God's grace during those young years of my life I could experience firsthand the words of the Epistle of James 4:8, *"Draw near to God and He will draw near to you"* (NKJV). From time to time some wonderful things happened to me. Our family then lived on the 8th floor on a 9-story apartment building located about 200 meters from the shore of Amur Bay. The windows of our apartment faced the sea and I loved standing by the window late in the evening and looking at the moonlight path on water to think on and on. . . . What is awaiting me in the future? How will my life go? What had the Lord predestined for me? What is His plan for my life . . . ? Once as I was thinking in that direction, I stood by the window. Suddenly, the sky was lit with a soft indescribable glow and right before my eyes a garland of large beautiful flowers was waving. It started moving towards me, then wrapped itself into a ravishing wreath and after a few minutes disappeared. All was dark around once more. Completely amazed I couldn't move from my place. This wasn't a dream. I also didn't possess a visionary gift. I asked myself over and over: what could it be? – But I had no answer. What I had seen remained a mystery to me. I only remember that while I watched that glorious scene my heart filled such a joy that I have never been able to describe. There was something heavenly about it. It was more like a short-lived glimpse into unbelievably wonderful eternity. I knelt and quietly started to pray.

At another time I was soundly sleeping when, in a dream, I saw that an unusual light illuminated my room. In the doorway there was a light figure with His hands stretched out towards my bed and a tender Voice called my name and said, *"Ludmila, get up! Pray."* I opened my eyes. The image was slowly disappearing, but His words still rang in my ears, *"Get up, pray."* I jumped off my bed and glanced over at the clock: half past three in the morning. There was no fear but only indescribable joy. I fell on my knees to pray and had a strange feeling that Christ Himself was bending over me behind my back. After that for many months I would wake up at half past three sharp. Usually, I either heard a softly spoken voice calling my name or there was a light illuminating the whole room or I felt a gentle touch on my shoulder by

Someone's loving hand. Those night vigils became something really special for me and so valuable that I can't compare them with anything on this earth. The words of prayer hardly left my lips as they went straight up to heaven. Such rest, peace, joy and unusual sweetness of God's presence I have never experienced afterwards. After I prayed I would normally fell back asleep and in the morning woke up refreshed and rested as if I had slept undisturbed for an entire twenty four hours.

During that wonderful period of closeness to God I begged Him to reveal His will to me and His plan for my life. Soon after, I had an amazing dream. Surrounded by the total darkness of night I was climbing up a mountain along a stony path. Grabbing the tips of the rocks and seldom seen mountain bushes, with much effort I slowly moved on. Sometimes, a groan was heard from my lips because of fatigue and tiredness. My feet slipped on stones that in turn from time to time began to roll and with resounding echo hurled themselves into abyss below. My heart shrank with terror at thought of the possibility of falling down there myself. Finally, I came to a small even plateau and completely exhausted laid down to rest a little. A dark night sky spread above me and just a quiet half moon and a tiny star adorned it. My eyelids became heavy and I started falling asleep when something huge and shaggy leaped on me. "It's the Devil!" The thought like lightning pierced my mind and a horrifying battle began. He tried to choke me, pinning my body with all his weight to the ground and I tried to get him off me by twisting and turning around. From nowhere, maybe because of my fright, I suddenly felt more strength and power and started fighting like a tigress. However, the devil was stronger. With despairing attempts I tried to free myself from his tenacious clutches, clearly realizing this was my final hour, when a voice inside of me said, *"Why don't you use your armor? Why don't you pray?"* At that moment, overcome by my adversary I laid on my back and my gaze stopped on the half moon. With an effort I pushed back the devil's claws encircling my neck and cried out, "Save me, o Lord! Have mercy on me!" It was a desperate cry of a perishing soul. In that instant the devil seemingly froze. The tiny star in the sky began quickly moving towards the half moon and touched it in front of my eyes. As a result of the impact sparkles flew in all directions and a multitude of bright stars appeared in the night sky and there was a lot of light all around. I suddenly felt a new flow of strength and even thought I was able to overthrow the entire mountains. The Devil though, immediately got weakened and lay like a sack. With ease I threw him off myself and with a rumbling noise he rolled down into a chasm. There was silence. I got up from the ground and looked behind on the path I had climbed. There below were other people who followed the same way with groans and heavy sighs. It was obviously very difficult for them to travel. Then I again heard the voice inside my heart, *"You see, you've made it. Now you must help others. This is My plan for your life."*

When I woke up I laid there with my eyes open not able to fall asleep for a second time. What could that dream mean? There was no doubt it came from the Lord.

But life went on. One session of exams followed after another and with each passing year I was increasingly getting tired. My wonderful nightly awakenings, which brought me so much joy and strength, ceased. Several times I didn't get up for a prayer feeling exhausted. That blessing left me and has never come back even though I asked the Lord for forgiveness and prayed with tears. It left me but it has become a lesson for the rest of my life. Laziness, negligence and carelessness in regards to God's mercies lead to loss of them. Nevertheless, the Lord is good and His mercy towards the ones who fear Him and seek Him is renewed every morning. He found different ways to speak to my heart, comforting, encouraging and teaching me, when I turned to Him with some of my petitions. At that time I was twenty years of age.

As time went on some negative things more often began to occur in our church and in other churches I visited. During the service there were reaching out sermons talking about righteousness, purity, godliness and God-fearing lives, but in reality everything appeared to be the opposite.

At the services Christians acted like angels, but back at home there were many conflicts and quarrels, and disagreements. Brothers and sisters in Christ judged and criticized one another. They had often said things to each other's face that differed completely from what had been said behind their backs. Frequently, members' meetings developed into places and times when people tried to sort out their relationships and decide about ever-present problems to the point that some believers stopped attending in order to avoid losing peace in their hearts. Although, elders had regularly mentioned the importance of God's guidance, they themselves, as I understood, did not hear the voice of their Shepherd. And that's what happened: one day there was a meeting where they raised a question, which had become a problem in our congregation. Opinions divided as usual.

Time went on but there was no unity or progress in making a decision. Observing what was going on I just couldn't understand why they all quarreled instead of praying and asking the Lord to bring clarity. If we were such spiritual Christians, then where truly was the guidance of the Holy Spirit? That evening bracing myself I got up for the first time and turning to our elderly pastor and deacons of the church said, "I don't get it. Why can't we lift up this problem in prayer

My favorite picture of my Mom (in white uniform)

Early childhood: I am 5 years old

Our family in 1964. I am 15 years old. This is the age when for the first time I heard the voice of God which said, "You will write books"

After I turned 18 I started searching for living God and close personal relationship

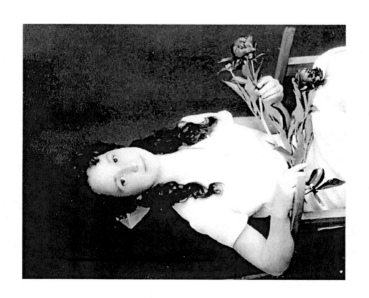

I am 17. The day of my prom after graduation from high school

to God to listen what He would tell us to do? God sends an answer and there will be no need to argue anymore."

Time went on but there was no unity or progress in making a decision. Observing what was going on I just couldn't understand why they all quarreled instead of praying and asking the Lord to bring clarity. If we were such spiritual Christians, then where truly was the guidance of the Holy Spirit? That evening bracing myself I got up for the first time and turning to our elderly pastor and deacons of the church said, "I don't get it. Why can't we lift up this problem in prayer to God to listen what He would tell us to do? God sends an answer and there will be no need to argue anymore."

All fell quiet. Older brothers looked at me with astonishment and I in turn stared at them with no less amazement.

"Well, yes, but we don't have such strong prophets in our congregation through whom we could inquire of the Lord," they finally replied with confusion on their faces.

"But what do prophets have to do with it? Why, we are all God's children and therefore, can come to Him as to our Father personally. That's why it is written, "My sheep hear My voice". What kind of sheep are we if we can't hear the voice of our Shepherd?"

Alas, we didn't understand each other that evening. I left the meeting with complex feelings of uncertainty and despair....

"Why is that? They are ministers who teach us and lead us to God. Why don't they hear God's voice? Why were they startled when they heard my question?"

Having a little bit of experience in fellowship with God I was absolutely sure that such is a necessary part of Christian life and all believers did have the privilege of personal contact with the Lord and therefore, His guidance. But in reality then it wasn't true. But how then should we interpret the words of Scripture about sheep and the Shepherd . . . ? My young head just refused to comprehend it, because at that time I had the faith of a child, who received the Word without any "buts" just as it was written. After that occurrence I completely closed up on the issue. I didn't want to ask elders about anything, since I saw they didn't know much either. (Unfortunately for me, in those years I wasn't able to see myself, but only others.)

In 1970, when I was already in my forth year at the institute, a student from Moscow came to our church. He was studying at the Academy of Arts. This young man used to belong to "hippie" movement but later turned to the Lord in a miraculous way and now was burning with his first love for God. He told us about God's work among believing young people with such passion that I was inflamed with a desire to meet them. Children who are born to Christian families usually automatically practice the Christianity of their parents, which to a certain extent reminds more of a stagnant pond because it usually consists of some settled rules, orders and traditions. But here . . . here was this rushing stream of mountain fresh and pure crystal water! No, I certainly wanted to visit them. But how? I was still a student myself. To take a train from Vladivostok to Moscow would require a whole week of traveling, and an airplane ticket was extremely expensive. Asking the Lord in prayer to do the impossible, I informed my Dad about my desire and... a miracle! My father at once agreed to give me money for the airplane ticket, in spite of our financial hardships as a family with many children. Shortly thereafter at the beginning of winter holidays I flew to Moscow. As I recall that time when I basically arrived as an unexpected guest in a house completely unknown to me I smile at myself even now. How naive and childishly trustful I was then! But, praise God He knew what I needed and sent some young people in my way that understood me and did everything in their power to satisfy my spiritual thirst. Two weeks spent among believing student youth turned into a true blessing and in some ways directed me in my further search. Saying farewell to them at the airport I held onto the flame of first love to the Lord kindled in my heart by these young Christians.

Soon after I came back home I encountered a woman who suddenly appeared in our congregation and through whom, as it was suggested, God moved in a mighty way. As it was revealed later she was a false prophetess horribly deceived by a false spirit. I had never before experienced so closely such false guidance and only a clear warning from the Lord had kept me safe from probably harmful spiritual consequences. Then I realized that any contact with the spiritual world may be quite a dangerous enterprise. The Holy Spirit is only one, but ninety-nine others are false spirits. And this proved to be correct too many times in my life. But just as the knowledge of everyday life comes after so many years so does spiritual maturity. It just doesn't happen overnight.

With the passing years I was also becoming more and more critical about everything that pertained to the Christian life and more often judged my brothers and sisters in the faith. In seeing the lives of others my own life seemed to me so much purer and better. Therefore, I couldn't notice my own failures and sins. Only one thing really bothered me and created much concern. That was the world of my unclean thoughts. Perhaps, I am mistaken, but I sincerely believe that the world of thoughts is the dirtiest area in the life of a Christian person, because things which believers cannot possibly do in real life, they act out completely in their minds. Consequently, the world of our thoughts reflects a true picture of who we are in God's sight. That was what robbed me of peace.

It all started when we purchased a TV set. In seventies television programs weren't the source of such filthiness as they have unfortunately become nowadays. But my young heart was soon attached to it and it really dragged me in. I recall that while sitting in the lecture hall I was hardly able to concentrate because my mind kept going back to the movie I watched yesterday and I couldn't wait to see the next sequence of that film. In those days there were no unethical behaviors, violence, murder or licentious actions, scenes easily portrayed on TV now without any shame or embarrassment. All love related scenes usually ended with a darkened screen conveying a double meaning. Even in spite of my lack of knowledge and ignorance in such issues these scenes when cut short evoked the fantasy of my imagination.

All of my life I had been a romantic type of person. I was drawn to the beauty and inspiration of romance and as a result, my favorite authors were writers such as Turgenev, who wrote about love in an especially noble and pure way. When absorbed in such books I slipped in the realm of unreal dreams. I imagined how things would have worked out in reality and identified myself with the characters in the books I liked without even noticing that with all such harmless dreams I slowly but surely drifted away from the Lord. Sometimes I was tormented and agonized that there was no more former closeness and love toward Him. The world of my thoughts went on defiling my soul and draining it of its spirituality.

During church services I considered it to be my ministry to read out Christian poems. I did it so well that listeners cried tears when they heard my reading, but as I got home afterwards and was left alone I myself bit into my pillow and cried finding no comfort. Why? Simply put, because I felt like a hypocrite and a Pharisee for acting out such a pious spectacle.

From time to time my soul found strength and rose up again to search for the Lord. Our merciful God, Whose grace surpasses His judgment, now and again turned His face towards me, wiped away my tears of repentance and drew me closer to Him. In such moments my heart just melted in my love to Him and I hated myself for my unfaithfulness.

In spite of my reserved character my parents, and especially, my mother, noticed the torments of my soul and were really concerned about it. "What is wrong? Why are you so tormented? What are you missing that you feel that way? You have everything!" They kept telling me, not comprehending my lack of inner peace. But how could I reveal to them things, which I myself was ashamed of? How could I tell them that besides my inward torture I was troubled by questions in regards to the truthfulness of doctrines I had been taught since my childhood? All of this would have stricken them down . . . .

There were other things to confuse me further and even bring me to the point of emptiness. It was the subtle caution and sometimes even open animosity between the Baptists and Pentecostals, two denominations seemingly very close to each other. Baptists thought of Pentecostals as deceived in matters of the Holy Spirit, whereas the latter called Baptists imperfect and under developed understanding the truth revealed to them. I recall in the days of my youth I happened to hear many unflattering comments about the others from both sides. When a young man left the Pentecostal church for the Baptist someone immediately said without much thinking: "It would be better if he went into the world!" In another instance, an older member of the Baptist congregation seeing that his own son had a friendship with a Pentecostal youth, strictly forbade it, announcing: "If you start speaking in other tongues like them, I myself will pull your tongue out!" When I heard it I thought, "Poor Apostle Paul! I wouldn't have envied you had you met such a "brother in Christ" on your way at the moment you said, *"I thank my God: I speak with tongues more than you all"* (1 Cor. 14:18).

From secular point of view one might simply laugh at such extremes, but at that time, I didn't feel like laughing. It was too saddening to watch brothers and sisters in the faith at war, although they all received salvation through the same blood of Jesus Christ, shed for them all on Calvary.

These and other similar thoughts robbed me of peace. In my heart a decision was slowly forming to get away from my home and my congregation as far as possible to try to find different churches and different Christians who would have something deeper and better. Therefore, I started praying about it, asking the Lord to favor me in all this.

More time went by. I was already twenty-three. My final state exams were fast approaching and along with them the anxiety of whether they would become the decisive trial of my faithfulness to the Lord. After years of study all graduates were supposed to do an internship for three years at a place where the institute would send them. Such an assignment occurred prior to the beginning of state exams and I was to be sent to city of Irkutsk[10] to work in the state system as the doctor of internal medicine for VTEK[11]. I accepted it

---

[10] City in northern part of Siberia, Russia

[11] Pronunciation of what should have been abbreviated as All-Union Therapeutic Committee of Expertise – a medical organ in former Soviet Union responsible for dealing with work related illnesses and diseases.

with calmness, rejoicing that I would be living in a big city, where there would certainly be believers and where I would be able to find a church that would satisfy the demands of my soul. But beforehand I had to pass seven final state exams, of which the first was on a subject called "Philosophy and Medicine". Frankly, I was scared that they would force me to make a choice then and there: God or diploma. But my fears weren't confirmed, and the exam questionnaire I got had nothing to do with my faith.

During the examination though, the Director of the State Exam Commission, a professor of urology from Khabarovsk[12] came up to me and said,

"I noticed how unusual your explanation of the theme was. Therefore I am interested in hearing you further. Please, continue."

The exam was passed with an "A" and I sighed with relief, that everything was fine. Nevertheless, it seemed rather odd that on every exam that followed the Director of the State Exam Commission searched for me with his eyes again and again, and as soon as I was seated in front of the examiner, the man would get up from his chair, approach us and attentively listen to my replies. My last subject was Surgery and Urology. That was the subject on which he had been lecturing. When I noticed his reaction and how quickly he got up once again and came to the desk I was sitting at, panic at once overwhelmed me

He told the examiner, "I will ask this student the questions myself." and calmly sat in his place.

"This is the end...," the thought came to my mind as I made every effort to steady my suddenly trembling body.

One by one I answered the professor's questions, some of which were not even related to the questionnaire and derived from absolutely different subjects. It seemed as if the flow of them would never stop. I continued my replies as in a dream and involuntarily noticed the bewilderment on faces of other examiners. I wasn't thinking of my grades anymore. My only desire was that he would stop his "tortures". Finally, the professor was quiet. He opened my grade book and carefully wrote the seventh "5" in the last column.

With a big smile he then exclaimed: "Excellent, girl! I am satisfied. And now I extend to you an offer to become my assistant and to start working on scientific research in Urology at Khabarovskiy Medical Institute. I hope you agree, do you not?"

---

[12] City in the Far East region of Russia

Hardly believing my own ears I sat there as if thunder-struck, trying to figure out what he was saying, when unexpectedly I heard very calm but powerful voice somewhere above my head,

"Tell him – no!"

Startled I turned my head toward the voice – but there was no one. The Voice . . . ! It was that same Voice, telling me six years ago that it would have been better for me to remain as I was. Now it sounded again for the third time and again it happened when I least anticipated it...

"Young lady!" like in a dream the words of the professor again reached my ears.

"Why are you quiet? Do YOU want to be my assistant?"

"No...." I was hardly able to spit the word out. "But we already have our assignments and I must go to Irkutsk."

"Ah! That is nothing!" interrupted the professor. "We will arrange that quickly. What kind of work were you assigned to?"

"I was assigned to the communal system as a doctor-expert."

"You?! Sent to VTEK . . . ?!" he laughed heartily. "No way. We can't allow that! You must go to science . . . . So then, you accept my offer, don't you?"

"Ah, it sounds so wonderful," a thought flashed through my feverish mind. "Graduate study . . . ! The surgery, which I have always loved so much . . . ."

But at that same moment in my ears came the same powerful voice,

"Tell him – no!" Stunned I echoed "no" after the Voice.

"No, dear Professor. I will not go with you and will not become your graduate student. I will go to Siberia according to my assignment."

"Young lady! Do you realize WHAT you are throwing away?? I am offering you a scientific carrier AND a brilliant future! I am repeating myself that I WILL take care of your assignment problem."

"No," I said confidently and firmly, not doubting any longer that I was doing the will of God. "I will NOT go with you to Khabarovsk. Thank you, but this is not my way."

"I don't understand you, girl," shrugged the professor. "I really don't understand you . . . ."

"May I go now?" Taking my grades book I got up from the desk. "Forgive me, please, but I can't explain it to you."

"Very well. You may go. But it's a pity . . . ! It is such a pity . . . ."

His puzzled and confused look followed me even to the door. As I was leaving, I turned my head back and noticed how someone tapped on his temple showing that I was somewhat insane.

"You are a fool!" I could hear mocking whisper of my classmates, who became witnesses to this whole scene. "Such a fool!"

"So what . . . ? Let it be so!" I was repeating to myself while running down the marble stairs. "Let me be a fool in your eyes, but I couldn't do it otherwise."

During the night as I was lying in my bed with my eyes wide open trying to comprehend what had happened, I kept saying in my mind,

"Lord, what is it? I too don't understand You. The third time in my life You are telling me something that is completely beyond my intellectual mind! Oh, please, help me to walk by faith! Help me to trust You like a simple child and follow You no matter where You would lead me. . . ."

Two weeks later my Mother and Father took me to the airport. I was flying to Irkutsk without knowing anyone there. Flying into complete uncertainty . . . .

As we were saying "good-bye" my Mom without restraining her tears said, "You know, dochen'ka, I have a feeling that you will never return to us. All the other children will be with me, but you will live somewhere else!"

My dearest Mom! She hadn't realized then how prophetic her words sounded for me. The foreboding of my Mother's heart would be fulfilled. The rest of my life in the Soviet Union would be lived away from my parents.

Under the wings of my plane my dear land of Primor'ie[13] with its much-loved Japanese Sea spread out and slowly disappeared in the foggy mist. My childhood and my youth remained behind. For me it was the beginning of a new, independent, and still undiscovered way of life. What would it bring . . . ?

---

[13] Far East region of the Soviet Union – spelled "Primorskiy kruy" or lovingly referenced to as "Primor'ie"

Chapter 2

A Christian Without Christ

I was met by the inspector of Social Services of Irkutsk. She addressed me in a rather friendly way, "Ah, that's what you look like!" She measured my small, delicate and youthful figure with her eyes from head to toes. "Frankly, we thought of you as being different in some way. By looking at you I don't think you would fit very well into your future position as a Director of VTEK," and, not even allowing me to recover my composure, continued, "Actually, we have decided to send you over to Leningrad, to the Institute of Medical and Labor Expertise to study some more. Since school only starts in a month, you can begin your work here at the Irkutsk' VTEK for now. You will live in my mother's apartment. She is being transferred to the hospital where she will have to stay for a long time so you should feel absolutely free in there. And after graduation from the Leningrad Institute," she concluded, "You will move closer to Baikal[14], to the town of Tulun[15], where you shall work as the director of the Central Regional VTEK, where due to the lack of trained specialists the work has fallen apart and come to a complete stop. So, as you can see, we place much hope in you and trust you will fulfill our expectations."

So in a few fleeting seconds my future had been determined and I had no choice but to agree. While working for a probationary month at Irkutsk city VTEK I was learning the basics of the medical practice, something that for the most part was unfamiliar to me. Time was passing quickly, and in August of 1972, I came to Leningrad, the city of my dreams, where I had often longed to be. The plans of God are truly amazing and His ways that lead to a destiny known only to the Lord are unexplainable. For the first time in my life I lived in a dormitory filled exclusively with unbelievers. They were medical doctors who arrived there for study from almost every possible location in the Soviet Union. There was much to face and to experience. One of the brightest moments for me was the encounter with one young girl who was also a doctor and who later repented and became a Christian. As a result of my relationship with her I noticed

---

[14] A large and beautiful lake in Siberia that used to be known as a deep lake of potable water.

[15] **Tulun,** city, Irkutsk *oblast* (region), east-central Russia. It lies along the Iya River and the Trans-Siberian Railroad. Incorporated first in 1922, it changed to a rural settlement in 1924 and was reincorporated in 1927. It is a centre for the Azey lignite (brown coal) field and of the wood and forest industry. Pop. (2006 est.) 49,368. Internet Source: http://www.britannica.com/EBchecked/topic/608732/Tulun

one matter that unfortunately has been and is still present in many Christian congregations.

While getting to know this girl and conversing about faith in God, I had never said anything in regards to her outward appearance. Being part of the world she, just like many other women, wore make-up. But God always begins His work in the heart of a person, not with his or her appearance, which will in time change by itself. When I discovered Christians in Leningrad, I took my new friend to their meeting for the first time. Immediately they pointed out to her that she lacked a head covering and was wearing eyeliner. I was stunned and did not know what to do, as I stood by her side and listened to the comments and remarks made by older members of the group.

When we left that house, she threw herself against my chest and with tears welling up in her eyes begged me, "Please, don't bring me here again! Please, never bring me here! It's better if you tell me about God, because here I didn't see Him!"

This incident has become a good lesson for me for the rest of my life and kept me from repeating the same error again. In regards to conversion of a soul you simply must not anticipate God, even if it is as a result of your zeal "to help", a zeal that is really *"not according to knowledge"* (Rom. 10:2). If we behave as those people in Leningrad did, we are more likely to push people away from God rather than gain them for His service. Praise God, that in spite of experiencing bitter disillusionment as a result of her first encounter with believers, that girl nevertheless found the Savior.

My own acquaintance with Pentecostal congregations in Leningrad didn't give me that which I sought either. Everywhere there was the same spiritual hardness expressed in very formal conservative regulations, human guidelines and aged traditions, demands under which my soul moaned and groaned. Usually in the beginning these groups would accept me very cordially when they discovered that I was a doctor and a Christian from early childhood. But when they heard my opinions concerning certain aspects of their group practice they became very sensitive and shunned me. Finally, after I left the city they labeled me as "revolutionary" and sent my parents a letter claiming that I behaved myself "unworthily" while in Leningrad. But in reality I have more than merely sad recollections from those times. One way or another, everything was meant for my own good, even though I was getting a feeling of deep disappointment in Christians and Christianity as a whole. Now many years later, I have noticed the same problem in the lives of many believers and have realized that the devil skillfully uses such moments. In separating us from those who bear Christ's name, he also separates us from God. Too often such or similar frustrations with other Christians lead people to discontent in their

Christianity and, what is especially sad, to dissatisfaction in the Lord. Such unpleasant experiences in the church make us as believers especially accountable, because in eternity God may require the blood of souls, who drifted away from Him, from our hands.

At graduation from the Leningrad Institute of Medical Expertise I received the diploma, Doctor-specialist with Expertise (administrative) and went to Tulun to become a director of the regional VTEK that had really fallen apart. It required a lot of changes and renovations. I immersed myself completely in this new work. At that time the town of Tulun was a small regional center with poor reputation because there were many prisoners who lived and worked there after free deportation or release from a jail ahead of time. In addition, the city jails were overfilled with prisoners. After I found out the history and the way of life in this town I wasn't too excited by the thought of living and working here for at least two to three years. As a young medical specialist I was given what according to the times was a very modest studio, to which I brought my suitcase, a blanket and a pillow. Such was the beginning of my work there, a labor that at times wasn't very safe. Because, for a variety of reasons, many serious errors had been made by the previous administration at this VTEK, it became necessary to take away disability status from many people who had received it unlawfully. Such action, of course, couldn't go unnoticed or without consequences. In my first year there as I was traveling to work by city bus I often heard behind my back someone's malicious whisper, "U-uh, viper! We'll kill you!" Recalling that, I am now amazed at my own intrepidity. But it's as they say: I was still wet behind the ears. And that was true. In youth many things are understood and interpreted quite differently than in later, mature years.

In Tulun doctors were scarce. Hence for several months after my arrival I was getting many calls with second job offers. I was still young and had enough strength and energy for everything. So pretty soon I worked not only as the director of VTEK, but also as a general practitioner at the Therapeutic ward of Tulun regional hospital, translated EKG readings at the town-funded clinic and taught general medicine to future nurses at the local medical college. I was busy 13-15 hours a day and usually got home very late in the evening. Literally, I felt like a squeezed out lemon. The reason why I worked so much didn't have to do with money, since at that time I had more than enough. No, I wore myself out on purpose, hopelessly trying to escape myself. At work I was known as cheerful, energetic, full of determination and wit, a strict and uncompromising woman-administrator, who was described as follows, "This little woman has the energy enough for five men. She is like a tractor – will go through anything."

35

Of course, in saying that people did not know that when I was by myself, upon returning home, I reverted to a weak and helpless creature; for at that time I was no more than a spiritual wreck. Like a worm the pain, despair and disillusionment with Christians and Christianity that I brought from Leningrad corroded and gnawed away at my soul.

There were no believers in Tulun except for a small congregation of Jehovah's witnesses. So for two years I lived completely without the church, only once or twice a year visiting Christians in Angarsk and Bratsk[16]. But to be honest, I wasn't really seeking such fellowship, because it brought me neither joy nor satisfaction. Although subconsciously I realized that such a life style could lead to a bad outcome and to complete spiritual apostasy I did nothing to change the situation. Therefore, slowly but surely I sank into spiritual depression. Morning and evening I forced myself to kneel for prayer, but my prayers had no life, no zeal, no fire, and no love for God. Sometimes I made desperate attempts in prayer "to break through" to the throne of God, but the Lord was silent. While praying I felt as if my words bumped into a ceiling and came back unanswered. Thus I'd become **a Christian without Christ and a believer without faith**. Month after a month passed. Depression and despair reached their apogee. Once I knelt before God and said,

"Lord, I can't do it anymore. I can't continue as a hypocrite and a Pharisee, playing a Christian before men. I don't want to play the role of Your child, but in reality stay so far from You. I know that You exist and so will simply believe in Your existence. Forgive me, but I will go back to the world of unbelievers. It is better for me to be there where I am who I really am instead of pretending to be someone that I am not."

I thought that was the end, but the Lord showed me His mercy. I did not go back to the world. Somewhere deep inside my heart I had a feeling that there was no place for me there and that God has another, but as yet unknown, plan for me.

By that time my popularity as a doctor and a director of VTEK had significantly improved in this town. In a little more than a year the collapsed VTEK has showed great signs of improvement and actually grown. I was now often invited to various conventions and conferences because of my expertise. I lectured many medical doctors, conducted circuit meetings of VTEK and thus was able to visit distant and neglected villages of the Irkutsk region, where there was no electricity and people lived in log huts together with their domestic animals. To reach those remote Siberian villages and logging areas we

---

[16] Towns in Siberia.

36

had to board a small aircraft called a *"kukuruznik"*[17]. We flew above impassable marshy swamps. For one who was born and lived in large civilized cities it was a new view of another way of life. I was highly valued as a doctor, and loved as a teacher, but feared as the administrator. I understood all this and therefore, became more and more confident in my own talents and abilities. My "Ego" grew, fed by the respect and acknowledgment of other people, though I could not see that myself. I really thought I was doing everything right: fighting for fair treatment and the restoration of their rights of others; I loved my occupation and the people I served and dedicated my abilities, strength and time to them; I led a pure and morally upright life; I did not turn young men's heads nor date any of them as was the habit in the world and amongst those who only called themselves "Christians" but were not such in reality. I didn't get married even though I had had many chances and with the exception of one, all the proposals were made by young men who were believers. They were unsure how to approach me and sent their pastors and mothers to me instead, but I kept rejecting their offers because when I was nineteen I vowed to God to marry only the one whom He Himself chose for me as my husband, if it was His will that I should marry. Deep inside my heart I knew if I had made the choice on my own, it would have been the gravest error of my life, one that I would never be able to correct. Therefore, as I brought this matter to the Lord I was at peace even as I was getting older and older. In the Russian mindset an unmarried girl of twenty-five is considered an old maid.

Thus, being very confident that I was doing everything so right, I developed a proud and haughty Self. My life revolved more and more around my Self. That "I", "For me", "To me", or "About me" are what the Lord hates the most. Now as I look back, I fully realize that just like king Nebuchadnezzar I deserved to be humiliated for my arrogant pride; but the Lord, Who was always mindful even of the one whom He rejected[18] had chosen a different path for me and started His work by putting me on the sick-bed.

The fact was that two kids in our family were known to have repeated bleedings and those two were my brother who was two years younger and I. He was diagnosed with Werlhof's disease (poor blood

---

[17] *"Kukuruznik"* – is a folk name for a small 1-motor aircraft widely used in agriculture at the time of massive implementation of corn as a new crop in Russia. It could also be translated as *"Corn craft"*.

[18] ("For we will surely die and *become* like water spilled on the ground, which cannot be gathered up again. Yet God does not take away a life; but He devises means, so that His banished ones are not expelled from Him. – 2 Sam.14:14 NKJV)

At the age of 20-22 I hadn't been thinking about friendships or love, or marriage, rejecting all proposals one after the other. I was only interested in one thing: what was God's will for my life?

After finishing studies at a medical institute (on the left photo, when I was 23) the following three years (on the right photo I am 25) I experienced a complete spiritual isolation during which I understood what it meant to be a Christian without Christ

coagulation). But they couldn't determine my problem and occasionally because of this mysterious illness I was laid up for long periods of time. The same thing happened while I was in Tulun. Due to constant work-related stress and inward distress my health swiftly deteriorated. This condition had become so debilitating that my life was saved twice only because of direct blood transfusions. One weekend while home alone through Saturday and Sunday and without a phone with which to call I fainted and actually bled for several hours. Only on Monday when my colleague at VTEK noticed that I did not come to work, he alarmed everyone. I was saved by a miracle and sent to Irkutsk regional hospital. Only much later did I understand that the Lord had mercy on my devastated soul and undertook to reach it through the sufferings of my body.

Weeks spent in the hospital bed proved to be very valuable to me. My heart hardened and closed up to everything and everyone had been slowly breaking apart. When I returned to Tulun I was quite different. If formerly I could live without praying for two to three weeks, for I thought I should not be saying religious words before God without the full participation of my heart, now I forgot about time while praying on my knees. Soaked in tears I pled with the Lord to forgive my rigidity. I didn't hear the voice of God in me for a long time, but the Bible suddenly started speaking to me in an amazing way. And for the first time in my life I read each page from top to bottom with trembling and respect. In the sufferings of my body and spirit it spoke to me vividly and with wonderful clarity in a manner I had never experienced or could have imagined before. For example, while reading the book of Job I covered it with tears. By anguishing in my own pain I wholeheartedly apprehended his personal misery and torments. And many other passages of Scripture became much clearer, more vibrant and precious.

There for the first time I understood and truly valued Solomon's *Song of Songs*. Frankly, I read it briefly in my youth, but later on I usually only skimmed through its pages because what was written in it served only as a temptation to me. At that time I could not understand why such a love story would even be included in the Bible. Why of all things was there such a stark description of an intimate relationship between two loving people? What spiritual meaning could this possibly have?! But now, when my own soul lost the One it loved so magnanimously, I finally understood the true meaning of the written text. God is love and there would hardly be a better example that would be able to reflect so brilliantly the right relationship between a soul and its Creator than Solomon's description. What else could soul's relationship to God be compared to than an affectionate love of two selflessly loving hearts that could not even conceive of living without the other? What despair and pain fill the words of the Shulamite when she lost the one whom she constantly dreamt of! In the night throughout the city she searches the streets and squares in spite of many dangers and seeks him until she finds him again. The love that they bestow on each other fills their hearts with real happiness. The world with its sorrows and sufferings does not exist for them anymore. In the presence of each other they forget about everything until their love is marred by a letdown. The Shulamite woman lingered when she heard the call of the one she loved, and in response he turned around and left her. How much grief and despair are heard in her words, when she regretfully exclaims, *"I sought him, but found him not; I called him, but he gave no answer"* (Song of Songs 5:6).

After reading those words I just wanted to cry. My soul that gone astray from its Lord, was seeking Him now with agony and groans, but being grieved by me He no longer answered my call. God's silence and His apparent absence are the things that the soul cannot bear and are especially strongly experienced by those who had previously heard God's voice and, in having a close relationship with the Lord, had tasted the sweetness of incomparable communion with Him. Once you have known that, your soul becomes simply unable to be satisfied with anything less. It will cry and moan and search until it finds that communion again or it will perish. Laziness, carelessness, slackness and negligence may have very harsh consequences. It is dangerous to make the Lord wait for you when He stands by the door of your heart and knocks. Because when you finally consent to get up and open the door to Him, He may turn around and leave. The Holy Scripture tells us not in vain, *"The Spirit who dwells in us yearns jealously"* (James 4:5). To grieve the Lord and to drive Him away is pretty easy; but to get Him to return may be an extremely difficult task. I have really suffered when I sought out with tears and groaning the One Whom I lost because of my own negligence.

Then, in 1974, being foolish, young and spiritually inexperienced I was unable to understand the true reason of my loss. Only with the passing years, gradually, did the Lord help me to realize that the real reason for the loss of His presence was not only my pride, but first and foremost, my criticism and judgment of others, that led me to bitterness, which in turn emptied out and destroyed my own heart. During those days God scrutinized and exhaustively worked on my critical and judgmental disposition that was rooted so deeply in my heart. Only several years later did He declare war on my pride and conceited, bigheaded "Self". My desire now is to share with you the lessons I learned from that.

Christ forbids us to judge, period. But amazingly enough, criticism and judgment as a spiritual illness among Christians occur most often.

The ability to critically evaluate is one of the most common inherent abilities of a human being. But in the spiritual sphere you cannot achieve anything by criticizing. It only undermines the strength of the one who is being criticized while depriving the critic of a close walk with God. Only the Holy Spirit has full rights to critical evaluation, because He is the only One Who really can point out something negative in the life of a believer and not offend or hurt the person at the same time. Someone who holds onto the spirit of judgment in himself cannot keep the fellowship with God, because such a spirit makes a person hardened, vengeful and unforgiving. It instills in a person's mind that he or she is better than everyone else, especially than those who are being criticized, and it pleases his or her self-loving nature. We should flee from anything that feeds this kind of attitude or similar ideas that we may somehow be better than others.

You can't really escape from God's penetrating and imminent character. He sees and knows everything. If I see the sliver in my brother's eye, it means I've got a beam in my own eye. Whatever bad I notice in somebody else, the Lord sees in me. Every time I judge someone, in reality I judge myself. The Jewish aphorism goes like this: "A man sees his physical flaws in a mirror, but his spiritual ones – in his neighbor." A mirror does not soil you nor does it cleanse you. It only gives you a chance to look at yourself with the eyes of others. If a man notices a fault in his neighbor, it translates into this – he himself has the same flaw. In the letter to the Romans (2:17-21) it says the following, "*Indeed you are called a Jew, and rest on the law, and make your boast in God, and know His will, and approve the things that are excellent, being instructed out of the law, and are confident that you yourself are a guide to the blind, a light to those who are in darkness, an instructor of the foolish, a teacher of babes, having the form of knowledge and truth in the law.* **You, therefore, who teach another, do you not teach yourself?**'

Often we don't want to believe that the thing for which we blame or judge others, we do to a high degree ourselves. But this is the bare truth. The reason why we recognize the hypocrisy, pretense, falsehood and many other iniquities in others is because all of that is found to some degree in our own character. If it wasn't there, we wouldn't have been seeing it in others. The greatest sign of the saint is his humility. He thinks in himself: "Yes, all that I detect in others, I also have. And it would all be expressed in me if not for the grace of God. Therefore, I have not the smallest right to judge." The Lord says, "*Judge not, that you be not judged*" (Matt. 7:1). But, if we judge then with the measure we use towards others we ourselves will be measured. Who of us would dare to stand before God with the request such as this: "God, judge me the way I have judged others"? We judge our neighbors as sinners. And if God had judged us in a same way we would all be in hell. But instead God judges us through the wonderful redemptive work completed by His Son Jesus Christ. That's why we should be merciful in our judgment towards our neighbors, remembering that we ourselves are what we are only by the grace of God. The Lord when He begins our nurturing process, first of all starts with a major cleaning-up inside us, after which not even a drop of spiritual pride is left. Later on, when I saw myself the way I might have been if not for God's grace I could never find a single person, whom I might consider as a hopeless case.

In saying that I do not mean to make a statement that a healthy, sober, critical assessment of certain areas of life and of spiritual questions and things is a sin. Certainly, the Bible teaches us to test and to search out things. Nevertheless, criticism, judgment and condemnation along with pronouncements of our verdicts of others have a different motivation at its root, one that for the most part is our own "I" or "Self," an attitude that God hates. Grace granted to us by the costly blood of Jesus Christ shed on Calvary, makes us all equal in the eyes of God. Whoever I am or whatever I experienced with God does not give me any right to encroach upon someone, for whom Christ had died just as He did for me. The Bible reminds us, "*Who are you to judge another's servant? To his own master he stands or falls. Indeed, he will be made to stand, for God is able to make him stand*" (Romans 14:4).

Malicious criticism and judgment does the most harm specifically to the one who does it. While taking care of somebody else's errors and sins, the person quickly looses the ability to notice himself and to critically assess his own words, deeds and actions. He takes upon himself the role nobody gave him because there is only One Judge – God, Who is being insolently pushed out of His lawful place. When we judge our neighbor without sympathy we call down upon ourselves God's judgment. But if God becomes our Judge, then nothing good can come out of it, because it says, "*For judgment is without mercy to the one who has shown no mercy*" (James 2:13). And the first thing that He does – He departs from us leaving us to ourselves. Without the Lord a soul immediately loses its sense of direction, wonders blindly in the dark and at the same time looses many other things. Such a person has no more peace, rest, or joy in his heart, for he or she begins to resemble the ones of whom it is written by prophet Isaiah, "*But the wicked are like the troubled sea, when it cannot rest, whose waters cast up mire and dirt*" (Isa. 57: 20-21).

The loss of peace means the loss of the Lord Himself. The soul remains alone, without its Guide and in that state starts sliding backwards. The indispensable companions of disillusionment and judgment are feelings of hurt and bitterness. These two literally consume the person, and slowly lead him **to animosity and revenge**.

The soul gets hardened and as a result the work of **God's grace** is discontinued. And where would we be without the grace of God, if it's the only basis for our salvation? This heartbreaking process is well described in the Scriptures,"[. . .] *looking carefully lest anyone* **fall short of the grace of God**; *lest any root of bitterness springing up cause trouble, and by this many become defiled*" (Heb.12:15). Without having the abiding grace and mercy one cannot expect the revelation of the power of God.

That was exactly what happened with me. When full of disappointment with and judgment of other Christians I lost the Bridegroom of my soul, was weakened and impoverished spiritually, and was transformed into a parody of a child of God – a Christian without Christ. Thankfully, God did not punish me for my apostasy in the way I really deserved it then. By allowing me to live through that He taught me a very significant lesson, namely, that God forgives us just as much as we forgive others. **The tragedy often is in our inability to forgive the hurts and forget them.** In allowing any sin to rule inside our hearts, especially criticism and judgment, we, first of all, break ourselves and cause ourselves all kinds of illnesses and troubles, which perhaps we would be able to avoid if we were more careful and attentive. But we have a wonderful God! He is able to change our errors and oversights into something extremely good for us and often achieves that through suffering and sickness. Suffering, no matter of what sort, physical or spiritual, urges us to seek the Lord and always bring spiritual renewal i.e. exactly what we need. After experiencing that myself, I could say it with King Hezekiah, "*Indeed it was for my own peace that I had great bitterness; But You have lovingly delivered my soul from the pit of corruption, for You have cast all my sins behind Your back*" (Isa. 38:17).

My dear reader! I am retelling this to you for the sake of your own relief and comfort. Perhaps, by turning aside and making an error you are going through a similar school of suffering. It is not an easy thing to go through, but afterwards, it will endow your soul with something good. God leads us in the way of sorrows and allows sufferings in our lives especially for the purpose of achieving something with us or to accomplish something through us. Sorrows and sufferings are the greatest factors of human life, because through them a multitude of unnecessary petty things are being burned out of our soul and our proud and haughty "Self" is getting destroyed. A person who has gone through the fires of suffering and been revived has something precious about him that makes him a blessing for others.

Recently, I happened to hear a story about the birth of a precious pearl. A mollusk that dwells inside its hard shell lives on the sea floor and breaths with its lungs or gills, and periodically sucks in a tiny water stream which brings oxygen diluted in water to its little body. Sometimes "the accident" happens and together with the water stream the mollusk sucks in a grain of sand or a miniscule stone. This foreign object causes extreme pain and suffering to its victim, but the poor thing cannot rid itself of the irritant. Nevertheless the Creator of the Universe had given an amazing ability to this small creature. In response to the severe pain in its gills, the mollusk starts producing a special kind of liquid which gradually envelopes the little stone or grain of sand until it stops causing pain. In this way the prized pearl is born, as a byproduct of pain, sorrows and sufferings. Isn't it a wonderful lesson for all who suffer? If because of our own slackness we err, have made a mistake or even sinned we endure suffering as a consequence. However, if later we repent of our failures, our graceful God in His incomprehensible love and mercy transforms our fall into something good, changing us into something better. No wonder it is said that people who suffer a lot, usually have a tender heart.

We are all humans and therefore, are inclined to fall and err. The question, though, remains, "Have we learned to rise after the fall?" In the Old Testament the Lord in His desire to teach and encourage His wayward people said through the prophet Jeremiah (Jerem.8:4), "*Will they fall and not rise? Will one turn away and not return?*"

In these words of the Heavenly Father we see His hand stretched out to us at the moment of despair and gloom. Even if we fell and went astray by choosing a false path it does not mean that God forsook us. But it is important for us not to lie there spiritually speaking because we have decided that it is over now and we are finished. Rather in reaching for the grace of God and relaying on His help we must do all we can to rise up again quickly. In such circumstances some people lose heart and quit, but others take courage and, trusting the grace of God, struggle to the uttermost to find the presence of God again. The two years that I spent in Leningrad and Siberia, spiritually speaking, were the dark times for me. Nevertheless, in spite of everything that was negative, there the Lord helped me to understand the danger of criticism and belittling others and to learn a significant lesson: **never quit, no matter how hard things are!**

Chapter 3

The Voice of the Shepherd is Heard Again

As my heart had been melting and I was getting closer to God I clearly began to experience a real loneliness in my life. I missed the fellowship of believers so much. One evening while I was praying to the Lord, I said, "Father, I don't know what my soul needs. I went through so many churches and congregations looking for it, but did not find it. Is it really that in the whole Soviet Union there is no place where my soul would find its desire satisfied?"

When I spoke those words, deep inside my heart there was suddenly a gentle voice that sounded in a new and unusual way, "*What if it will not be in the Soviet Union?*" I stopped awe-stricken. This was that same Voice I had heard two and a half years ago, but now it came to my conscience, not audibly from outside, but somehow inwardly.

"Lord," I said after a minute of silence. "But what good is that, if such a place is in some other country?! I do live in the Soviet Union!" But the answer never came.

Totally bewildered I meditated on the meaning of such words. The fact that the Lord heard my prayer and replied filled my heart with unceasing joy. That actually meant that He had forgiven me! I was forgiven for my infidelity, apostasy and hardness! This was more that I could ever have desired at that moment.

It was September of 1974. I was granted a vacation leave and upon the recommendation of an acquaintance from Leningrad, I flew to the Black Sea, to Crimea, where some of her friends lived and where I could rest and restore my health a little. Crimean beauty really charmed me. I visited quite a few spectacular places that still preserved the ancient traces of the amazing history of the peninsula. Two weeks went by. When I was getting ready for the return trip, fully enthralled by new discoveries, like a bolt from the blue sky I suddenly heard the words, "*I have given you time, but you spent it for nothing and did not seek My fellowship*". That was true. I was so fascinated with the excursions that I didn't think much of anything else.

"Lord, what must I do?" I asked with trepidation.

The answer came at once, "*Leave immediately and fly to Leningrad. There I will tell you what to do.*"

When I announced my sudden departure to my kindhearted hosts and said that I had to go to Leningrad right away they tried to persuade me not to do that. They told me that there were too many tourists at the airport that couldn't leave because all the tickets were sold out.

"Please, take me to the airport," I said, nevertheless, and decided that if it truly was the voice of God then a miracle was bound to happen. My perplexed host only shrugged his shoulders and agreed to take me there. In a half an hour we left their house.

As I entered the airport building I unintentionally exclaimed, "Oh!" Everywhere imaginable, on the floor, the benches and the radiators tired and exhausted people were sitting or lying. It looked like they had been there for days on end. Many cashiers' windows were closed.

"Well, didn't I tell you?!" The brother turned to me with displeasure. "You see, we came here for nothing."

"Lord!" I called in my heart. "If it was You, then tell me what am I to do now?"– And in that instance I heard the clear answer in my heart, *"Go to the military cashier's window and ask for a ticket there."*

"What . . . ?! Go to the window for military officers?!"

I swiftly looked around. That window was open and no one was standing by. I asked my host to watch my luggage and quickly walked there.

"Hello, miss?" I inquired looking inside the small window. "I urgently need to fly to Leningrad. Please sell me a ticket."

"Are you crazy??" The cashier was flabbergasted. "Don't you see how many people are wandering around unable to leave? Moreover, why did you come to me? You are not the military pers . . . ."

She didn't finish her speech and suddenly stopped part way through her reply and giving me a strange look, hastily said, "Give me your passport. Quickly, please."

And in the meantime while I was extracting the document from my purse, she was already telling someone over the phone, "But I need the ticket now, don't you understand . . . ? Yes, it's a special case . . . . What? The departure is in 10 minutes? Good. I'll take the ticket."

Then, reaching with her hand for my passport through the window, she told me,

"Your flight is in 10 minutes. You have to go to the gate right now."

When she finished filling out my ticket and took the money, she all of a sudden swept her forehead with the back of her hand as if awaking from a dream and whispered faintly,

"What am I doing . . . ? Who are you? " But then, glancing at her watch she stopped and added, "Run to your gate!"

As I was leaving the counter I still sensed her surprising stare. A miracle had happened right in front of my eyes! I rushed to the man waiting for me. Showing him the ticket I took my suitcase and in a few fleeting moments took my place inside the airplane, still hardly believing what had just happened.

"What does it mean?" I wondered looking at the clouds passing by my window. "How can I understand all of this?"

My acquaintance in Leningrad was surprised at my sudden arrival.

"You should have at least called," she reprimanded while ushering me to the table. "What is it? Has something happened with you . . . ?"

"Maria," I said surprising myself at what I was about to say. "I need to see that woman you introduced me to a year and a half ago. She lived in Gatchina[19] then."

"Yes, she still lives there. But I have not seen her since. Why do you need her?"

"Why . . . ? Oh, if I could only know that myself!" Only then, at the table it became clear to me that I must go to her, but what and why I understood not.

"Ludmila! What is it with you? Can you explain to me what is going on? I don't understand anything."

"Neither do I, Maria. I only know that I must find that woman. You probably have her address, don't you?"

"Yes, I'll try to find it. I had it written somewhere." Maria went to search for the address.

I got up and approached a window asking inwardly, "Lord, what do You expect from me?" But there was silence in reply.

The next morning I took an electric train to Gatchina, a small town in the Leningrad region. When I found the house I was looking for, I knocked on the door but there was no answer. A neighbor came out and said that the woman I was seeking was at work. She couldn't tell me how to find her, but she did know that the woman worked at a store called *Bereska*.[20]

Walking out onto the street I hesitated, not knowing what I should do. Then the voice in my heart sounded again, "*Go. I will guide you.*"

Deep in my thoughts, I wandered at random for a long time not even trying to inquire of anyone. Then, as if because of a jolt, I stopped abruptly. There was a store sign right in front of my eyes that said *Bereska*. Full of amazement at what was going on I entered the store and right there, by the door, behind the cashier's counter was the lady I had been looking for. I took a shopping basket and walking toward the end of the store finally came to the end of the shoppers' cue that led to the cashier. I stood there and wondered what I was going to say to her and whether she would even remember me at all. It had been over a year since we first met. Finally, it was my turn in the cue. The woman looked inside my empty basket and then inquisitively looked at me. Immediately her face became pale.

---

[19] A suburban town of Leningrad or St. Petersburg

[20] Common name for a gift store for international tourists visiting Russia, translated as "a birch-tree"

"Is it you?" She whispered with strong agitation that immediately transmitted itself to me. "So, it is you . . . !" She tried hard to collect herself and after a minute of confusion continued, "I don't even remember your name. We have met only once. Please, wait a couple of minutes, while I find someone to replace me at the cash counter."

As I moved aside I leaned against the wall in anxiety. I had a feeling that something was about to happen. Then like lightning a thought bolted through my mind, "She will come and say that in such and such town the Lord told a young brother that He recognized a wife for him. And I am to become that wife." My feet became heavy as if filled with lead. And in my heart there came a gentle voice, *"Remember what you promised Me, when you were nineteen? Well, this time has come. I have chosen him for you."*

I grabbed the wall with my hands as I saw Nina approaching and just had enough time to tell myself, "That's it, Ludmila. Your boat has just moored to the dock."

"I am still struggling to recall your name. I think you are Ludmila," Nina said when she came up to me,

"When I saw you at the cashier's counter I definitely realized it was you. Sorry, but I will speak plainly. Several months ago I visited a small congregation in Estonia. There was a young brother to whom the Lord had spoken and had asked him if he was ready to accept the one whom God had chosen for him, and the young man had replied affirmatively. At the same time the Lord revealed that He would bring the girl to me. Upon my return from Estonia I had been waiting and waiting, but nobody came. In our area there are no Christian congregations, not even a small group of believers. I had even started doubting and decided to go to Ukraine hoping to meet "the girl" there. However the Lord stopped me and sternly said, *'Have I told you to look for her? I will bring her to you in My time.'* It was several months ago. And now you are here. Therefore, "the girl" is you, right?"

What could I say? I would not have ever come to her if not for such extraordinary guidance. Everything was so obvious that it was really impossible not to believe in God's providence and direction. I was speechless. In the evening when we were sitting at the table of Nina's home I asked her if she could share with me a little bit more about that young brother living in Estonia.

"Truthfully, I don't know him that well," she said."He is German by nationality. He is tall, swarthy and has thick black hair. He also plays a guitar. That's about all I can tell you."

"And how old is he? What does he do and where does he work?"

"I know nothing about it. Are you doubting, Ludmila?"

"It's not doubting, Nina. But I will not take a single step until the Lord confirms to me personally what His will is in a way that I will ask

50

of Him. Now I will start praying about it. Here, this is my address in Siberia. Give it to this young man and to the pastor of that church. Let them pray about me, because humanly speaking, it is impossible for me to move to Estonia. You see, after the institute I must work at least for a year in Siberia. According to the existing law they will never allow me to leave before that. Yet, if it's really God's will, the miracle will take place."

The following morning I returned to Leningrad and from there flew to Irkutsk. It was October and that meant winter in Tulun. I plunged again into what seemed my never-ending work. But in reality I was happy to be occupied, for otherwise my thoughts would have tortured me. There was peace and quiet in my heart. I committed all to the hands of the Lord while beseeching Him for clarity. And He reassured me three times that all that was happening with me was, in fact, His will. I won't describe it in great detail. But I can tell you that in a dream He showed me my bridegroom as well as the path we were predestined to share from now on.

I saw myself standing beside high city walls that resembled those once used to surround old cities in medieval times. Not far from the wall there was a large beautiful house with white colonnades and marble steps. There on the steps a young man was sitting with his head resting against his right arm, so that I could only see his fluffy, thick black hair. I stood there in hesitation not knowing what to do next. As if awakening from a dream the young man got up and slowly walked down the stairs towards me. Then for the first time I noticed his face. When he came near he took me by the right hand and without saying a single word led me to the city gates which opened up of their own accord before us. We stood on a road which looked very strange. It was straight as an arrow but for its entire length was covered with ruts, grooves, pits and bumps. However, most amazingly the road was very white as if covered by a fresh snowfall. It ran very, very far away to the horizon, where it sharply rose to heaven and became golden. After I awoke, for several days I thought of what I had seen. I realized that it was from God and had a certain meaning. In a few days I received a letter from Estonia. It was from Heinrich and his picture was enclosed. It was the face I had seen in my dream.

Dear reader! I am sharing with you something that is as precious to me as a rare pearl. And it's not for you to trample it under your feet. It's not a product of human fantasies nor a story concocted by my girlish imagination. God has been, is and will always be the God of miracles. In working His will in the life of one person or another, even today He can accomplish that which seems impossible to a modern Christian. The Lord does not consult anybody nor does He interest Himself in people's opinions. He acts as the Sovereign God, Who is not dependant on anyone or anything. Such being his nature He can certainly perform something quite unusual in my life or in anyone else's. When we read the Bible we find that men and women of God had unusual visions and received orders which they had to carry out. These directions were often accompanied by some supernatural interference that normally served as a kindling fire. God often comes in unusual ways beyond what our human mind is frequently able to grasp of His deeds. Moreover, that which we cannot understand as normal, we frequently question or simply reject.

The year 1974 was coming to its end. The time for my annual report at VTEK was rapidly approaching, and I had to go to Irkutsk, where I was going to tell about my intentions to get married. Of course, I knew too well that another miracle was bound to happen in order for me to be released from my duties before the designated time. And that day came. The main medical or administrative expert of Irkutsk region, a tiny, energetic, dark-haired woman, met me with a friendly smile on her face. She didn't even hide her satisfaction over the annual report I submitted. All the numbers of Tulun's VTEK had brought her real joy.

"You know what, Ludmila Mikhailovna[21]!" she addressed me. "I think it is time for you to begin the scientific research on the subject of your expertise. Start preparing all you need for your Candidate Dissertation. You probably have enough of your own material. If you need anything else we will gladly help you. No wonder they said about you in Leningrad that you were an expert with the bright future. So, get on with it!"

My heart started pounding feverishly. I felt it was the decisive moment. I could not do any kind of dissertation! Silently, in my mind, I prayed and committed myself into the Lord's hands. Addressing her also by her first and middle name I said,

"Thank you . . . very much, but unfortunately I can't accept your offer, because I am planning on getting married . . . ."

"Really!" Her eyes sparkled. "Well, perhaps, it's about time. And who is he? Have you met him in Tulun?"

"No. My future husband lives in Estonia and I will have to move there."

"What?" There were notes of barely concealed anger in her voice. "Never!!! I will NOT let you go!"

She agitatedly got up from her desk and walked around it. It was obvious that my declaration had stunned her. No doubt she had had

---

[21] This is the proper way to address a person in Russia if he or she is older or has a high-ranking position, or just out of respect. Such an address would always consist of the first and middle names.

entirely different plans for me. Then, calming down a little and composing herself, she continued,

"You have to understand . . . . I have been looking at you as my successor, with every intention of transferring my position to you. Certainly, I wish for you to be happy in your personal life, but in this case according to the law I just can't allow you to leave. You haven't worked the assigned time after studying at the institute! We have made a highly skilled professional out of you in order that you might fulfill our hopes, but you . . . !"

I looked down at the floor and listened quietly. What could I say? It would be unrealistic to try to explain to this lady, a member of CPSS[22], that it was God's will for me. In my heart I fervently prayed, "Lord, if it's really Your will, please perform this miracle!"

For the longest time the chief expert tried to explain to me why it was impossible for me to leave, even given my situation. Her voice changed from pleading to angrily and indignantly demanding and back again. I remained silent. Suddenly she stopped and softly said,

"No, I can't . . . but I have to let you leave. Fill out your application for resignation."

I thought I had not heard correctly. Still not believing my own ears I sheepishly lifted up my eyes and looked at her. There was a different person in front of me. Her face radiated with something gentle and motherly sweet.

"I hope you have been smart enough to bring his picture, right?" Her voice sounded tired and somehow reflected a feeling of doom. "At least show me what he looks like."

"Yes, of course. Here!" I offered her Heinrich's photograph that luckily I had recently received. She took the picture and for a long time looked in his face. Then she returned it to me with the words,

"Yes. What can I say . . . He is very handsome. Well, if this is your destiny, I wish you happiness."

As I was leaving the building of the Irkutsk Regional Department of Social Welfare I beamed with joy. The Lord had heard my prayer! Once again He confirmed the truth about His will for me! He had performed a miracle, indeed! Oh, what a Lord we serve! There is nothing impossible for Him! He can do anything! Now I had no doubts at all that He would also help me with the relocation. If He started something, He would certainly finish that as well. I just needed to entrust myself completely into His hands.

That was how the Lord had lifted me up not only from the pit of spiritual defeat, but also provided me with His blessing. Yes, He is really the God, Whose mercy is far beyond judgment!

---

[22] Abbreviation for The Communist Party of the Soviet Union.

During the following month with God's help I got all the paperwork together, packed my belongings, sent off the container and took care of the apartment rent. It was surely done in an extraordinarily short period of time considering that I lived in Tulun by myself and had no one who could help such a physically weak girl as I was. But when God becomes the major Helper, then the improbable happens almost by itself.

It was February 8, 1975 when I entered the airplane that followed its flight path from Irkutsk to Leningrad, where I was supposed to meet my fiancé for the first time. The duration of the flight was several hours and in all that time I was fearfully thinking that I was not ready for this important change in my life. When there were about 2 hours left till the arrival of my plane I started begging the Lord to delay the arrival for at least 20-30 minutes so that I would have enough time to prepare inwardly. But this prayer wasn't answered. The airplane landed 20 minutes earlier than scheduled. Later Heinrich told me that while waiting at the airport he had been asking the Lord to hasten my arrival. God granted his request then, not mine.

When late that Saturday evening we arrived at the town in Estonia by train where our destination was, I felt drained of almost all of my emotional strength. I was received by friends of Heinrich. Seeing my condition they didn't question me much but put me to bed. All night long I was hearing the most incredible, unique and beautiful angel songs that filled my heart with unspeakable joy. The next day was Sunday, and I went to the church fellowship there for the first time. One sister in Christ quietly asked the pastor who I was and where I was from, and he stated briefly: "This is Rebecca from Mesopotamia[23]."

That is how I got married.

---

[23] Referring to biblical Rebecca who hadn't seen her bridegroom until she arrived with Abraham's slave in the land where Isaac, her future husband, lived.

Our wedding day March 30, 1975

This is how I saw Heinrich for the first time in my dream.

Chapter 4

Questions....Questions....Questions...

The small church in Estonia that I had become part of was very peculiar. Its pastor came originally from the Baptists, a man used by God, who in the past had spent many years in prisons for preaching the Word of God.

While serving his sentence there, he had met Christians from the Pentecostal movement, who impressed him a lot. Thus, his method of preaching and teaching had been influenced by both denominations. Members of the fellowship also presented a very colorful picture in a spiritual sense. There were new converts amalgamated with Baptists, Pentecostals, Methodists and people of other confessions; I don't exactly remember all of them now. My husband was born into a fundamental Baptist family and was spiritually brought up in that same teaching. Several months of life in Estonia had passed and as a result I began to understand certain things that had not been apparent to me before. Basically, when one remains in one Christian confession for a long period of time and suddenly comes across another one and starts communicating with Christians of different denominations or, so to say, moves within the Body of Christ by crossing denominational barriers, then to one's own surprise one notices that other groups are not so much in error as one had previously thought. Moreover, perhaps one's own insights had not been so right after all.

Oh, how we lack tolerance and flexibility in spiritual matters! How fiercely stubborn we can be in clinging to our own understanding and opinions! The first person, who belonged to Baptist doctrine and literally shocked me, was my own husband. When he told me how he heard the voice of God and received His guidance in seemingly very simple everyday situations, I listened to him dumbfounded.

"How could this be?" I thought to myself. I had always been told that this was our (the Pentecostals') privilege, and that those Baptists could not have any of that because they didn't have the baptism of the Holy Spirit with the sign of speaking in tongues. But here was this Baptist who had such an intimate relationship with the Lord, one that was not often found among Pentecostals! Therefore, God must also enter into an immediate contact with members of other Christian confessions. But how could a person be lead by the Holy Spirit if he hasn't experienced spiritual baptism? It appeared that the fact of the baptism of the Holy Spirit did not really determine the spiritual status of a Christian. Then, what did it mean to be a spiritual person? Was it enough to go through the baptism of the Holy Spirit and speak in tongues? As a matter of fact, what was really meant by "baptism of the

Holy Spirit"? Was this baptism just a moment of emotional experience followed by speaking in tongues afterwards or was it something infinitely more that the person could obtain, one whose presence was obvious by the fruits of the Holy Spirit which were revealed in a person's life?"

Such and other questions then more often popped in my head and prompted me to turn to my Bible. Concerning the Holy Spirit one can find there many varied and seemingly unmatched descriptions. The first that caught my attention was that the Lord Jesus Christ Himself characterized the Holy Spirit as "Spirit" and "the Helper"[24], and described His manifestation in peoples' lives as "*And when He has come, He will convict the world of sin, and of righteousness, and of judgment [. . .]*" (John 16:8). According to this definition, first and foremost, the Holy Spirit manifests Himself not in the sign of other tongues, but in opening a person's spiritual eyes, condemning his sin and revealing God's truth to his mind while reminding him of judgment which is ordained not only for the Devil but also for the ones who serve him in one way or another. It is interesting that the first area where the Holy Spirit starts working in a sleeping Christian is in the matter of sin and the absence of the true faith in the Lord. For, it is clear that the Holy Spirit is called "Holy" because He cannot tolerate anything unclean, i.e. first of all, any kind of sin. Otherwise, He would not be the **Holy** Spirit. With this in mind, why is there among Christians who claim they have such a Holy Spirit within them so much open and hidden sin? In verse 13 of the same Chapter of the Gospel of John (16) it says the following, "*However, when He, the Spirit of truth, has come, He will guide you into all truth [. . .]*" A similar thought is confirmed by another verse from the same Gospel of John, "*But the Helper, the Holy Spirit, whom the Father will send in My name, He **will teach you all things**, and bring to your remembrance all things that I said to you*" (John 14:26). But, if this is true, if the Holy Spirit indwelling in a believer leads him to the truth in all questions, matters and problems, then why are there so many unresolved issues and problems in the midst of Christians who have the Holy Spirit? Even though I was a young member of the church I was too often faced with the fact that elders, leaders and pastors couldn't find a way out of the dead end caused by this or that problem.

While growing up in the Pentecostal doctrine I had always heard about the baptism of the Holy Spirit in direct connection with speaking in tongues. However, in the Bible it is not always interrelated. For example, John the Baptist was filled with the Holy Spirit in his mother's womb and worked with the great power of the Spirit, but nowhere in the New Testament will you find a single mention about

---

[24] In the Russian translation it says: "the Comforter"

him speaking in tongues. Jesus Christ Himself had the Holy Spirit descend upon Him in the shape of a dove during His baptism at the Jordan River but never spoke in other tongues except for that one occasion on the cross. There, on the cross of Golgotha, He cried out, *"Eloi, Eloi, lama sabachthani?"* But even this wasn't said in some heavenly language, but in Aramaic, which was understood by many onlookers there and meant, *"My God, My God, why have You forsaken Me?"* (Mark 15:34). Indeed, we do run into speaking in tongues in different passages of Scripture in connection with the filling of the Holy Spirit, for instance, in Acts 2:4, 10:46, 19:6. However, not in all the cases of a similar spiritual experience is there any mention of speaking in tongues.

While listening to my husband and observing his life, which generally was much better than and far surpassed my own, I involuntarily kept questioning myself: who in reality was more spiritual? Was it I, who had had the spiritual baptism in my childhood, or was it he, who knew nothing about it, but was brought up and grew in a true fear of God? What were these "other tongues"? **Were they the sign confirming the fact of the baptism by the Holy Spirit**, according to the statement of Pentecostal Christians **or** were they just **one of the many gifts of the Holy Spirit**? In the Word of God it seems you can find the corroboration of both opinions. Such is the passage in the Gospel of Mark (16:17-18) that says, *"And these signs will follow those who believe: in My name they will cast out demons; they will speak with new tongues"*, but in 1 Corinthians, chapter 12 it says about speaking in tongues as one of the gifts of the Holy Spirit, *"There are diversities of gifts, but the same Spirit… For to one is given the word of wisdom through the Spirit, to another the word of knowledge through the same Spirit, to another faith by the same Spirit, to another gifts of healings by the same Spirit, to another the working of miracles, to another prophecy, to another discerning of spirits, to another different kinds of tongues, to another the interpretation of tongues"* (12:4, 8-10).

If you carefully and thoughtfully read Chapter 14 of First Epistle to the Corinthians where there is frequent mention of gifts of the Holy Spirit, and particularly, of different tongues, you could think that the Apostle Paul talked about them not in the sense of a sign, confirming the filling with the Holy Spirit, but as one of many gifts of the Holy Spirit. Several of the last verses of Chapter 12 validate such an assertion, *"And God has appointed these in the church: first apostles, second prophets, third teachers, after that miracles, then **gifts** of healings, helping, administration, **varieties of tongues**. Are all apostles? Are all prophets? Are all teachers? Are all workers of miracles? Do all have gifts of healings? Do all **speak with tongues**? Do all interpret?"* (1 Cor.12:28-30).

Here is the enumeration of gifts and the claim that not everyone has all of the mentioned gifts, a list that also includes tongues along

59

with the others gifts: of interpretation, for example, or healing, or prophecy and so on. But if this is so, if not everyone has one and the same gift, then why was I taught otherwise from my childhood? Why was I trained that all who had the Holy Spirit must speak in tongues without fail?! Had this really been a true statement? Did it correspond with the Holy Scriptures? Can you really press the Third Person of the Triune God, namely, the Holy Spirit, into one of His gifts – the different tongues? Wouldn't that be equal to taking the air which fills the whole Universe and trying to cram it into a small matchbox? Isn't there something infantile in such an understanding of this issue? Addressing Corinthian Christians who according to their views could be considered the Pentecostals of their age, the apostle Paul makes them listen to reason by saying, *"I thank my God I speak with tongues more that you all; yet in the church I would rather speak five words with my understanding, that I may teach others also, than ten thousand words in a tongue. Brethren, do not be children in understanding; however, in malice be babes, but in understanding be mature"* (1 Cor.14:18-20).

It is interesting that by speaking such words this great man of God wasn't afraid to grieve, quell or even worse, to blaspheme the Holy Spirit, apparently implying in regards to Him something substantially greater than just different tongues. I still remember how several older Christians among the Pentecostals carefully observing us, the youth of the time, had kept asking us with anxiety, *"Do you still pray in the Spirit? Try to pray more often in tongues. Otherwise you will suppress and grieve the Holy Spirit, Whom you received at your baptism."*

The Apostle Paul who had given us so much instruction and explanation in connection with this matter, considered it to be a necessity to put up certain borders and orders concerning the manifestation of this gift. And he did this in spite of his own extensive ability to speak in tongues. Unfortunately, his orders are not followed by any of the Pentecostal or Charismatic churches. For example, he **forbids the speaking in tongues simultaneously by a whole group** during the worship and requires the **avoidance of praying in tongues if there is no interpreter present** (1 Cor. 14:27-28). If speaking in tongues, in fact, is a sign confirming that a person is filled with the Holy Spirit, then why does Apostle Paul establish such strict limitations, which in the teachings of the Pentecostals, can grieve and suppress the Holy Spirit?

Truthfully, it had always been a confusing fact to me, that the first mention of speaking in different tongues was connected with the events that occurred at the Tower of Babylon and had an imprint of God's judgment. Centuries had passed before the speaking in tongues reappeared, though in a different form, at the Day of Pentecost. Then all by-standers were able to understand what was being spoken and all of them heard about great works of God, a feature practically absent nowadays in connection with modern glossolalia. However, why would God use the tongues of assorted peoples? Perhaps, on **the Day of Pentecost it served as a symbol** given by God **to the Jews** who had come there from fifteen heathen nations of the world, and were familiar with their languages. During that time **unbelieving** Jews staying in Jerusalem **had resisted God's election of Gentiles.** It is possible that by using many other languages that were "foreign" for them or "other than" their normal everyday usage, God had shown that **His election belonged to everyone** and was offered to all of His creation.

In harmony with the First Epistle to the Corinthians 14:22 the tongues of that time were not **a sign** for believers but **for unbelievers.** If such statement remains true to this day then why does glossolalia still continue to be widely spread during the meetings of **believers?** Yet Paul had not only discouraged such practice in the churches but sternly reproached it. If his admonitions and restrictions in this matter are indeed applicable in the modern day, then how should we evaluate speaking in tongues among the congregations and churches practicing such occurrences even today? Is it in obedience to the Word of God or in disobedience?

A tree is known by its fruit. What about a Christian? How do we determine the spiritual status of a believer? What signs would indicate the presence on the Holy Spirit in him? Is it by the gifts of the Spirit or by His fruits, which are described in the letter to Galatians 5:22-23? If a man has no love, joy, peace, longsuffering, kindness, compassion, faith, meekness and self-control, can we really say that he is baptized with the Holy Spirit only because he speaks in other tongues? Can, in fact, the speaking in tongues alone prove the filling with the Holy Spirit?

In Chapter 13 of the First Epistle to the Corinthians it says that all spiritual gifts including the speaking in tongues are **nothing,** if there is no love. Absence of love among Christians, unfortunately, is an incontestable fact. However, much more attention is paid to the gifts. How are we to understand that?

When reading the history of Christianity you get the impression that speaking in tongues was present only during the times of the early apostolic church after which it practically ceased to exist for an unbelievably long period of time embracing more than **eighteen centuries!** What does such a long silence mean? Could it be the evidence of the words of the Scripture where it said, "[. . .] *whether there are prophecies, they will fail; whether there are tongues, they will cease* [. . .]" (1 Cor. 13:8). If speaking in tongues is indeed a biblical symbol of the baptism with the Holy Spirit, then why had God hid such a great and

61

significant truth from His children for more than eighteen centuries? And yet, there were innumerable multitudes of His faithful and loyal servants prepared to suffer any torment including martyr's deaths for their Christian faith. Are we Christians of the twentieth and twenty-first centuries any better that we have been favored to become part of this "mystery"? But it's not a secret for anyone that we in particular are living during the time of the global spiritual cooling-off, when we can rather expect the deviation from the truth than the receiving of a special divine revelation about it. Can we really believe that during the eighteen centuries when speaking in tongues was not practiced, the Holy Spirit did not do His work, but in April of 1906, the birth date of the new movement of speaking in tongues He resumed His work?!

Perhaps, speaking in tongues is only an invaluable relic for us and nothing else, just like the bronze serpent which Moses made according to God's order, but for whom the Israelites started burning incense as if to God. Under a mask of its relevancy to God the bronze serpent changed into an idol and became a substitute for the true God. This was the reason why it was destroyed by King Hezekiah (2 Kings 18:4).

With time I discovered and was shocked by the fact that glossolalia became a characteristic of not only Pentecostal, Charismatic, partly Adventist and some other denominations of Christians, but also of other people having nothing in common with Christianity, for instance, representatives of some eastern religions, spiritualists, Satanists, people possessed with evil spirits and followers of various dangerous sects. Of course, prior to my marriage I knew nothing about it and was pretty much satisfied with the explanations given by many ministers, who tried to convince believers who doubted and hesitated the authenticity of their tongues by quoting, *"If a son asks for bread from any father among you, will he give him a stone? Or if he asks for a fish, will he give him a serpent instead of a fish? Or if he asks for an egg, will he offer him a scorpion? If you then, being evil, know how to give good gifts to your children, how much more will your heavenly Father give the Holy Spirit to those who ask Him"* (Luke 11:11-13).

The story of the origin of "the speaking in tongues" movement also puts us on guard. According to the eye-witnesses, "the fire from heaven came down" during worship in one of the houses in Los Angeles, California "to mark the beginning of a new era of Pentecostal, and afterwards, of the Charismatic movements and the likes of them. When reading the account of the phenomenon and events that occurred, you get seized with a mixed feeling of amazement and uneasiness. Unwittingly you ask yourself a question: "What was it really? Was it a great revelation of our age that came from God or a great fallacy of the last days?"

Possibly such question had never created a big problem for many Christians, but for me, who was brought up in the Pentecostal movement, it was very important to understand such events correctly. Moreover, I had other questions. There were still too many aspects of my spiritual life where I came to a dead-end street. For example, how should we realistically fight against sin? How should we resist the devil's temptations with a firm faith? How could we live a life of victory? What do the words of the Scripture mean when they say, *"For this is the will of God, your sanctification"* (1 Thess.4:3). How are we supposed to sanctify ourselves and is it really possible to be holy while living on this sinful earth? If it isn't possible, then why is it written, *"Be holy, because I am holy"* (1 Pet 1:16)? Surely, God would not ask something of us that we cannot practically accomplish.

Such thoughts repeatedly came to me in connection with the new congregation of which I became part because of my marriage. There they talked much about sin and sanctification by way of confession. Those sermons were something completely new to me. I had heard casually about it before, but couldn't recall any of the preachers devoting whole sermons to the subject. We had always been convinced that we were all cleansed, washed and saved and all we had to do was to thank the Lord for our election and the act of special grace we received. But it was one thing to hear that everything was good, and quite another to feel and know that your condition was far from perfect.

Does it make any sense to try and persuade me that Jesus is the Victor over Satan, if Satan regularly has victory over me? What does it help to know that the Lord took my sins upon Himself if those sins continue to have power over me? How do I implement that which is written in the Bible into my own life? In his Epistle to Philippians (2:12) the Apostle Paul says: *"work out your own salvation"*, which means "to realize", "to implement", and "to put into practice". Well and good, but how do you do this in real life? I had always felt I was lacking something. Perhaps, now I was very close to finding that "something". What did sanctification mean and how did the confession of sins occur? Was it not enough that I brought my sins in the private prayer to God?

And then I suddenly remembered something. It happened with me in Siberia, in Tulun from where I had recently come. On one occasion I knelt before God for a long time and in tears confessed to the Lord the sins that weighed heavily upon my soul and oppressed it. During my prayer, I can't exactly say how, whether in my heart or in my mind, the words were spoken, *"Who are you confessing to? I know it all."*

Unexpectedly, I shut my mouth and remaining on my knees continued to reason, "How am I supposed to understand this? Shouldn't I confess my sin if I committed it? And if I can't do it before God, then where do I go? On the other hand, He indeed already knows my transgression, because He sees through me."

In that instance as if echoing my thoughts, the voice in my heart went on, "*Think of Cain. He hadn't yet sinned, only thought about it, when I came to him and asked: 'Why are you angry? And why has your countenance fallen? If you do well, will you not be accepted? And if you do not do well, sin lies at the door. And its desire is for you, but you should rule over it*" (Gen. 4:6-7). *You see, Ludmila, I do know everything.*"

I recall that I was much confused after what I had heard. I couldn't figure out why it was said to me. Was it to stop me from confessing to God, since He knows it all or had the Lord wanted to tell me that there was another way of doing it? If so, then what kind of way was it? Surely, I was not about to go to the Orthodox Church to confess my sins there to *bat'ushka*[25]. I had heard about it from other people, but, having been being brought up in a different tradition, I was skeptical towards such confession. After thinking all of it through and without having made any decisions, gradually I simply forgot about it; but now it all came back to me when I listened to sermons about confession. So, maybe it was right nevertheless, to confess sins in the presence of another person. If so, then, who should I confess them to? Does it say anything about it in the Bible? When I started looking for an answer I found the following words in the Epistle of James 5:16, "*Confess your trespasses to one another, and pray for one another, that you may be healed. The effective, fervent prayer of a righteous man avails much*". (If we were to translate that from the German version of the Bible, this verse sounds like this: "Confess your sins one to another and pray for each other in order to be healthy. The prayer of the righteous man can do much, if it is serious"). But what does it mean "to confess to one another"? Who it that "another"? Is it my friend or a confidant? Is it my husband or wife? Is it the pastor of the church or some other minister? Can you really reveal your sins to anyone whom you trust or should it be a special person ordained by the leading elders or called to such ministry by God Himself?

In the Holy Scriptures it says, "*fervent prayer of a righteous man avails much*". But what does "fervent prayer" signify? What is implied here under the word "fervent" (or "serious", as it says in German language)? Does it mean that the prayer must be repeated a few times, or persistent and long, that is, over a long period of time? Perhaps, it is

---

[25] The name stands for a loving way to call someone "father" in the old times. Usually, it was used to call priests in the Orthodox Church in Russia.

meant a prayer with fasting. If that, then how long should the fasting last? Moreover, that's not all. That prayer should have been raised up, not by just any believing person or any Christian, but by a **righteous** person. But who will dare to call himself "righteous"? Doesn't it say in the Bible, *"There is none **righteous**, no, not one [. . .]."* (Rom.3:10), even though the word "righteous" is used repeatedly throughout the Bible? Is it possible to amalgamate the two religious views? Who is considered righteous according to the Holy Scriptures? For example, in our day, are there people of whom one might say that they are righteous, whose prayer freely ascends to the throne of God? Ones to whom one could open one's heart without fear while revealing one's innermost being? In my sub-consciousness I felt that my soul had been longing for such an experience. It has been almost ten years since the death of my old friend (grandmother) and all these years I had not met a single person whom I could have trusted wholly and who could have helped me to move forward spiritually. Where were those mature souls who had treasuries of wisdom, endowed by God with the ability to help others? I had so much missed such fellowship that could have spiritually enriched my soul...

Paying attention to the words of our pastor I kept thinking, "Isn't this the man who might be able to help me?" When he preached his words had power. You could feel that what was being preached in the service he had experienced himself or at least had pondered it a lot. I was drawn to his spiritual depth and the wealth of his soul (which I felt subconsciously). Once (it was not long before my marriage) I confided a sin to him, which had laid on my soul very heavily and after a joint prayer I received a complete freedom from it. Later, he prayed for my husband twice when he was ill and after that he felt significantly better and healing followed.

I was told that KGB agents, who constantly kept the pastor under observation, had said with great respect that he was the only man before whom they were ready to take their hats off. Earlier in his life while he was serving a sentence for preaching the Word of God, he fearlessly continued to do so even there, in spite of the ban by the prison authorities. He was severely beaten for this, so that his blood splashed on the walls. Because of his testimony and sermons behind the bars several criminals repented and turned to God. One of them came to our church after he was freed from prison and became a member.

Knowing that the pastor used to be a very zealous Baptist preacher I asked myself a question, "What had made him abandon that teaching? What didn't satisfy him? What had prompted him to lend his ear to Pentecostal ideas and to slightly change his views on some things?"

At the time I knew about the Baptist doctrine only by hearsay and was at a loss how a man who had been there for so many years could leave the place where he was spiritually born and grew up. What attracted him there, where I had personally experienced, to say the least, a few disappointments? Which of the two doctrines was true? Judging by stories told by others, those two groups were pretty much alike, except for a difference in understanding the matter of the Holy Spirit. But if that was the only source of disagreement, then, why could they not be together? Why were there cases when Christians transferred from one teaching to the other, and, as was known, more often the change was from Baptist to Pentecostal? What failed to satisfy such people in the Baptist congregations? Was it the spiritual coldness, dryness or mere formality? What seemed to be so attractive in the Pentecostal fellowship? Or on the other hand, why did some Pentecostals leave their congregations behind and search for Baptists in order to join them? Did they take such a step for personal motives or did they have some sort of spiritual basis to support their move? If, as the Pentecostals think, they have something infinitely better, then why would some of them leave that "better" part behind only to satisfy themselves with less? Did they see some discrepancies with the Bible in the Pentecostal teaching and practice or, confronted with various spiritual revelations, lose faith in the genuineness of the movement and thus came to a decision to stay away from such guidance? Perhaps, the Baptists had a much more reasonable approach to spiritual truths and had a better grounding in the Word of God, since this was all they had to rely on.

How can it be generally explained that there is such a dissociation or even animosity between Christians of different confessions? They all bear the name of Jesus Christ, worship the same God and strive to enter into the same heaven! How are they going to see each other in eternity, if here, on this earth they want to have nothing to do with each other? How can they call themselves disciples of Jesus, if Jesus Himself clearly said, *"By this all will know that you are My disciples, if you have love for one another"* (John 13:35). Moreover, not only Christians of different confessions suffer from lack of mutual understanding and oneness, but the same thing sadly occurs among those who belong to the same confession. So the Baptists are split into two types: registered and unregistered (separated) Baptists, Pentecostals are divided into those who wash their feet as a ritual during the Lord's communion service and those who don't. There are other reasons for divisions and separations between the Seventh-day Adventists, Mennonites, Methodists, Lutherans and other members of the Protestant family. And yet this is not enough. Even the members of one church have no like-mindedness. How do we comprehend this and align it with the

Bible, the same book we all have in our hands? The Lord had only one name for all of us, God's children, for whom Jesus shed His blood on the cross of Calvary! Why do the children of One Father humiliate each other and live with each other even worse than half-brothers?

While asking myself question after question I did not suppose that there were many more people who were busy doing the same as I. They looked for an answer and did not find it; they asked but could not get a specific or plain reply. True, I learned about it much, much later, after many years, but back then I thought I was the only one "crazed" about such matters. So I just brought all my spiritual problems and needs in my prayers to God. In turn, He gradually dotted my "i's" and crossed my "t's" during not just several years but several decades of my life. He is Sovereign and acts the way He prefers. He never rushes when we are in a hurry, and is never late even though we often think otherwise. More often than not, God answers in a way that causes another question to arise. Nicodemus experienced that when he had come to see Christ late at night. I had gone through something similar as well. One question gave birth to another and my search went on. I suppose, it is typical for all people to pose questions, but for Russians it is especially strongly pronounced. One thing I did realize with time. The Lord's silence in fact can also be His answer, and a very significant one. He knows too well if an inquiry was a short-lived curiosity and a superficial desire to find out something new or if it is really an important matter of life. That's how the answer comes. However, no matter what, God always remains for us a God Who listens.

Chapter 5

From Delight to Disappointment

As I have mentioned earlier, the congregation which I attended together with my husband, and where he had started attending less than a year before our wedding, consisted of people who belonged to a variety of Christian denominations. These were souls who found no spiritual satisfaction in their own traditional churches but searched for a close relationship with the Lord and personal communion with Him. Therefore, we understood each other very well in our quest for God. The first two years I spent with them were the years of pure delight and admiration. It seemed that finally I had found what I had long been looking for. In particular, I was charmed with the openness and sincerity of their hearts, as well as the mutual love and unity between the church members. In spite of persecution by the local authorities we met in different houses several times a week for worship. In fact, some of the members, including my husband and me, rode by one or two buses from other towns covering a distance of 50 kilometers or more one way. Often we had to return home that same evening or even late at night so that in the morning we could get to work. Our fellowship was so precious to us that we forgot about sleep and tiredness.

I want to repeat that our pastor even though coming from a Baptist church, while in prison, had accepted much from the Pentecostal doctrine. He valued spiritual gifts and as a result, there were many prophecies, interpretations, visions and other revelations that occurred so often that even I, who was brought up among Pentecostals, was constantly amazed. Nevertheless, as unfortunately it sometimes happens in such cases, when people indulge in revelations, they usually stop being watchful and spiritually sober. That in turn creates good soil for the invasion of a wrong teaching. And it all started when a false prophet presented as a ministering brother entered our fellowship. With his stories and revelations he succeeded in convincing the pastor as well as many other members of the necessity of immigrating to America.

Since in the past I had already encountered somewhat similar suggestions and the problems that they arise, I received this message with great caution. However, everyone tried to persuade me that this revelation was from the Lord and that God wanted to lead His people from this godless country to give them freedom in a new land. While listening I unwillingly recalled how in the years of my childhood and my youth, Christians who received visions of this type moved from place to place to the so-called areas of exodus for God's people, from where God would lead them to other countries. How much embarrassment and slander the believers suffered, when they followed such "revelations" with childish faith without testing and checking them out first! Concerning this new tide rolling over our church I decided to pray and ask the Lord for clarity in this matter.

Soon after, I had a wonderful dream, which even now, after so many years vividly remains before my eyes. Somehow, as if from the great height, I saw a very large field separated into big lots. On every lot there were people laboring hard and everyone had his own work to do. Suddenly, a huge tractor appeared on the field and began moving back and forth destroying the boundary paths and trampling the fruits of their labor under its tracks. People stopped their work and as if going mad rushed toward the tractor. In a short time there was complete chaos everywhere. Almost everything was wiped out. Many people lay on the ground, crushed by the machinery. Others wandered about the field blinded, not knowing what to do anymore. Still others simply disappeared from view. Then the picture of this dream faded away, and I saw a huge barn for storing the grain that was empty. No doubt, it was built for the harvest that was supposed to be reaped from the field bulldozed by the tractor. Now sinister desolation reigned in this granary. The wind blew flapping the shutters and half-torn boards. There were thick spider webs on the walls and in the corners. Mice and rats scurried everywhere and snakes crept on the floor. All over the place there was trash and old sheaves of hay lay scattered around. Standing in the middle of the deserted barn I heard a rolling masculine voice: "See! Your house is left to you desolate!" Awaking from my dream I realized with fear that it was the answer to my prayer.

When I shared the dream with the pastor and some members of the congregation they took it in very cautiously. A train calling for immigration was already on its rails and to reject this alluring idea was really impossible for most of them. It was 1977. At the time some Christians who were Germans by nationality had already left the country for the Motherland of their fathers – Germany. But the immigration movement to America had just begun for the Russian Christians. In different spots in the Soviet Union there came to existence groups of people who actively undertook to work through the immigration process, prompted not so much by prophecies but by the version of the International Declaration of Human Rights publicized in those days. Prophecies and all kinds of revelations occurred later and unfortunately, happened to be very inconsistent.

The history of immigration of 70s and 80s of the twentieth century is rather complicated and muddled. It could take another volume to describe it. But that is not my task, especially, since the immigration tide carried along many of my own relatives and friends, whom I wish not to cause any grief. A lot of them have already suffered the consequences and, very likely, to the full extent. It is no secret that there was too much fraud, exaggeration and obvious lying, all of which perhaps served as a reason for all the troubles, quarrels and misfortunes that followed those who were ready to leave the Soviet Union by **any means whatever**.

One way or another, the desire for immigration swept over our congregation just as much as over others. The results didn't take very long to appear. A spiritual atmosphere was replaced by an immigration mood. More and more attention and time was devoted to this endeavor. All chats, conversations and dialogues revolved around this subject. Letters were written; documents were produced and special trips were undertaken. Everything was done because of and for the sake of immigration. Even all prophecies and revelations turned in that direction. It is quite embarrassing now to say things like that, but then it was something that stood to reason. Finally, I surrendered and agreed that it was the will of God, and I gave in to the power of the immigration movement. I do not wish to evoke the memories of what we had gone through as an aftermath. It only serves as a bitter lesson, not as a pleasant recollection. From time to time the voice of our conscience broke in from the depth of our hearts into our minds whispering: "But we are Christians, we can't do that!" However, it was soon muffled by a voice justifying particular behavior as the only possible way and indicating that all who wanted to immigrate were behaving in a similar fashion.

"God knows the reasons why we are doing that." Yes, indeed! God knew and saw everything and certainly had nothing to do with what we had striven to see as His will.

The immigration tide didn't just go away traceless. As a result of spiritual cooling-off, sin had slowly crept into our congregation. In the beginning it wasn't very noticeable, but later on it took its apparent shape and form. Lies and all kinds of untruthfulness lead to disagreements and divisions. Not even a trace was left of the former unity and love that had characterized the church members. It was replaced with mistrust and suspiciousness that with time intensified even more. After submitting documents for immigration to the USA a year passed by, then another one, and one more, and so on, but our congregation remained in its place. Our worship services had long ago lost their power and charisma. We were now united by the idea of immigration more than by faith and the search for God. People's souls languished and suffered, but sin continued to gain its foothold.

Once our pastor advised Heinrich and me to accept the offer by Heinrich's parents to send us an invitation for moving to Germany, where they had already lived for several years. With prayer we committed this matter into the hands of the Lord and decided to comply with pastor's advice. However, it took another four years until we received a permission to leave the country. It certainly was an extremely difficult time full of anguish for me. Only the former blessings helped me to keep my head above the water, spiritually speaking. In the depth of my heart I had a feeling that somewhere, somehow I had deviated from the way of truth and wandered from the Lord, even though all the prophecies and revelations affirmed that God was with us and that we just needed to remain faithful to our decision during this time of trial. We were afraid to doubt such statements in order not to blaspheme the Holy Spirit. Sometimes, good sense suggested that there was something terribly wrong in all that was going on. But the fear of displaying disloyalty paralyzed any ability to critically analyze events.

During the services we still heard the sermons with their emphasis on sin, purification and sanctification. And people continued to cleanse their souls wanting to be ready for departure into another country and for serving God there. Some of them revealed their sins and secret thoughts openly, in front of the whole congregation, unable to endure the tedious and poignant inner struggle. Those actions bore very bad fruit. But for the most part we tried to speak about these matters with one of the ministers in private. That is how I did it too. I usually went to one of the deacons of our church. Seemingly, his desire to help me was really sincere, but the more I confessed, the heavier I felt within my heart. After a while I noticed that I was becoming increasingly dependent on my counselor and the counseling. At that time I had no experience with it whatsoever and it looked like neither did the ministers. They stewed in their own juice, so to speak, as for the first time they gathered the knowledge of how to conduct this ministry. Finally, I got so entangled spiritually that I was very close to despair. In spite of all my attempts to break through to God's light, darkness reigned inside my soul. I couldn't grasp anything anymore, not being able to tell the difference between a lie and the truth, right and wrong and whether revelations were from God or man. Sometimes I wanted to scream because of the mental pain and hopelessness. Once when I was in such condition I went to the bathroom to clean it.

I felt so heavy in my heart that my lips yielded a cry, "Lord! What do You want from me? I don't understand You anymore! I don't understand anything at all anymore!" This was a direct challenge thrown into the face of God. In fact, it was filled with anger, rebellion and demand.

What happened with me at that moment I know not. Standing in the middle of the bathroom I yet didn't see it any longer. An amazing picture developed in front of my eyes. It is hard to describe how it was, but I saw an ocean with the seashore and also a vast space of dry land.

72

At the place where water separated from the earth there stood an indescribably huge figure of God. His one foot stood on water and His other rested on the ground. His head touched the sky and even though it was way up there, somehow I was able to see His face and, especially, His eyes. They looked at me with sadness and at the same time, sternly, almost in wrath. Then, my gaze was fixed on His foot standing on the seashore, which I could observe so clearly that it enabled me to distinguish billions of separate sand grains forming on the shore. Suddenly, one of the sand grains started moving and transformed into a tiny human figure, which lifted up her minuscule fist toward God and began yelling, "Lord! What do You want from me? I don't understand You anymore! I don't understand anything at all anymore! You are cruel! Yes, You are cruel!"

I shuddered in fear. Those were my words! I recognized myself in the puny human grain of sand figure. Yet there was so much power, glory and majesty in the figure of God and just as much nonentity in my own tiny body. And that nonentity dared to challenge the great God! Getting confused on my own I blamed God for that. It was such madness!

I came back to my senses by hearing my own heart-rending scream. I don't know how it was that my vocal cords didn't break from the extreme pressure. Again, I was in the bathroom with a rag in my hands, but I wasn't the same anymore. Something had happened to me. Or rather, something had happened inside of me.

Throwing aside my cleaning rag, I ran into another room; fell on my knees and drowning in tears repeatedly cried out, "My dear Lord . . . ! My Father and my Savior! Forgive me! Oh, if You can . . . please, forgive me!!! How could I . . . . How could I even do that?"

This was an hour of my spiritual sobering as if something had turned inside of me. I started seeing things differently, comprehending them in another way, perceiving them from a new perspective. In cutting off this confession business I came to the conclusion that never again would I pour out my heart before any human being. From that day on the healing process in my soul slowly began. It was 1979. Working as an internal medicine doctor at the town's clinic I was also elected to be the Chairman of People's Control Committee[26]. Being actively involved in that work dragged me into a lot of trouble and in the end I was compelled to quit my job. I stayed at home for a whole year. In a spiritual sense it was a blessed time, but at the same time I

---

[26] Organization in Russia, which used to be regarded as a very powerful organ among common people. It related to different spheres of life, but mostly to job matters checking on correctly followed procedures, rules and regulations compliance, etc.

was still drawn to the clinic. At this juncture, medicine still remained an idol to me and I "served" it no less than I did God.

On one occasion while kneeling in prayer I addressed God with the following words, "Dear Father! You know how much I love my work and how much I desire to serve people with my profession. I studied for seventeen years to become a physician and You had always helped me in that. Please allow me to continue my work and to find another place . . . ." I haven't finished my sentence when other words sounded in my heart amazingly clear,

"Ludmila, I need a different kind of physicians."

"What?" I asked again instinctively, "A different kind of physicians? What sort of different?"

"I need physicians for soul." I heard a reply, and the voice grew quiet.

Thunderstruck I remained on my knees, pondering the meaning of this *"physicians for soul"* phrase. Although I had already become familiar with the counseling I had no idea that those two definitions were somehow connected. I had to leave these thoughts because I didn't fully understand them and the spoken words were soon forgotten.

Shortly after I got a job as a district physician at the clinic situated near a small workmen's settlement and enthusiastically started my duties. The premises needed to be expanded, remodeled and re-equipped. All of such tasks demanded much strength. But all I had lived through within the past five years took its toll. My health abruptly declined. My newly started incidents of repeated bleeding put me down on a hospital bed once again. In the meantime the diagnosis of my ailment had not yet been determined, and the doctors were lost trying to treat only the symptoms of anemia. But the moment arrived when even the multiple transfusions of donor's blood couldn't help anymore. I was losing blood from my stomach, intestines, kidneys and other organs. It was obvious that this was a generalized sickness, yet all the tests and observations at the city hospital did not shed any light on my condition. Because of my weakness and feebleness I could barely move my legs while clinging to the walls. The specialists held a conference but did not come to any certain conclusions. They transferred me to a small private room in the hospital. I was wasting away like a candle. I remember when one evening pale and helpless I looked through the window to the snow falling outside and thought of death. Frankly I, indeed, had no desire to live at that moment. Being a doctor myself, I realized that my case was hopeless and without the right diagnosis death was inevitable. Suddenly, I became afraid. "Lord!" I pleaded with God, "Please, heal me . . . ." And immediately I heard an answer, *"Physician, heal yourself."*

74

Instantaneously these few words recorded in the Gospel of Luke 4:23 tore a blindfold from my eyes. My memory brought back the haughty thoughts of my ability to help others by treating their diseases. I recalled how pride overwhelmed my heart when the next patient who had already been rejected by other doctors was "back on his feet" because of **my** efforts and persistence. It wasn't only the doctors and patients who regarded me as an expert but I also believed that. And now this body where my "Ego" lived, helplessly lied out on a hospital bed. With all my abilities to treat others I could not heal myself.

A feeling of shame for my arrogance and haughtiness overpowered me to such an extent that it seemed my face was burning. Now I understood for what reason this sickness was allowed and why I had ended up in such critical condition. I sensed myself being at a dead end. How much it had required of the Lord to bring me to this realization and how patient He was with me!

With remorse I reiterated while swallowing my tears, "I have understood everything, Lord! Now I have understood everything. You are just. I deserve these sufferings but if it is possible, please forgive me once more and heal me, if You want."

I continued praying for a long time and cried until peace entered my soul. It got dark outside. I was lying down with my eyes closed, enjoying the indescribable inner peace when the voice inside said, "*Ask your current doctor now to let you go home for the weekend. There I will tell you the diagnosis of your illness.*" I was still trying to interpret what I have just heard when the door silently opened and I saw the doctor in charge of my case, who had a night-watch that day.

She sat down on my bed edge and anxiously said, "Well, what are we going to do with you, my dear colleague? I must admit that I am reduced to complete despair. None of the examinations conducted thus far indicated the source of your bleeding. A Physicians' conference hasn't made any progress either. One thing is clear, it's impossible to keep giving transfusions of someone else's blood to you. Something must be done, but what? What do you think about it?"

"Doctor," I quietly answered, "Allow me to go home . . . ."

"What?" She interrupted and didn't let me finish. "Do you realize what you are asking for? You are almost non- transportable! I see how you are hardly able to move even when holding to the wall! What 'home' are you talking about?"

"Doctor, please. I beg you . . . ." I repeated my request. "Please, allow me to leave for Saturday and Sunday. I promise that I will tell you my diagnosis when I come back here on Monday morning."

"Ludmila Mikhailovna!" searching my face the doctor exclaimed in awe. "You are saying some really obscure things. Why in the world do you need to go home to diagnose your sickness? If you suspect what it is why don't you name it right now and we will start examinations in that area. But to let you leave now in such condition – it is a huge responsibility! What if . . . ."

"Doctor, please!" I pleaded with her again. "Only Monday will I be able to tell you my diagnosis. But it is necessary for me to get home."

"You really surprise me, doctor Plett." The physician shook her head in bewilderment. "I would never allow that to any other patient, but you have certainly intrigued me and I will let you go. I will put you in a car to ride home. However, if anything happens, immediately call for the ambulance and come back. I am allowing you to go on your own responsibility."

I don't remember how many times I stopped to rest until I got to the fourth floor and then completely exhausted fell on the couch.

"What does it mean?" I wondered after catching my breath. "Lord, what should I do now?" My wandering gaze stopped on the bookshelf where there were all kinds of medical books.

At the same time deep inside my heart a voice spoke. *"Take that book on hematology and open it."* I stood up in obedience, took the stated book and opening it saw in front of my eyes the description of a very rare disease of small blood vessels, accompanied by periodical profuse bleeding. I was reading and not believing my eyes. It was the exact account of my sickness, which would be familiar only to a narrow circle of particular doctors/hematologists. During all my years in medical schools and at work I had never heard anything about this disease.

I fell on my knees and thanked God for His mercy. When my husband got home from work he was astonished not knowing what was happening. Monday morning I came back to the hospital with this book on hematology, informed the doctors about the diagnosis of my sickness and asked them to send me over to the hematological ward of the Estonian Republican Clinical Hospital in Tallinn. They sent me there immediately. I certainly dared not tell my own doctor or answer a question of a main physician-hematologist who received me in Tallinn: Who diagnosed me and Who I was so much obliged to for help. Had they discovered the truth they would probably have considered me insane. In those years the Soviet Union was the country of militant atheism.

Several weeks later after thorough examination at the hematological clinic I was discharged with the fully confirmed God-revealed diagnosis. Many years afterward while getting into all kinds of everyday situations and problems I often recalled those words, *"Physician, heal yourself."* It is a good lesson for all of us, is it not? Too often it happens that while trying to help others we are powerless to help ourselves. Comforting, admonishing and teaching other people we often are too weak to solve our own problems.

An old wise Russian proverb goes on saying, "I can handle anybody's problem with bare hands, but to take care of my own, I have no mind."

After coming back from the hospital I returned to my job. Life went on filled with everyday worries and work, which with passing years had been bringing more and more disappointments. In the healthcare system I had come across too many things that weren't good; with scandalous lawlessness and unfairness against which I could do nothing nor change in any way. My favorite occupation was gradually losing its nobleness in my own eyes. During my night watches at the hospital there were occasions when patients died in my hands because there wasn't enough medicine or because there wasn't anything else we could do. I looked into their faces exhausted from agony and saw the fear and anguish of their souls, foreboding the eternal peril, and suffered from the realization that I wasn't able to tell them about the most important thing – the possibility of their salvation through the repentance from their sins. I hated myself for it and... kept silent. After night watches like that I used to return home all utterly shattered and kept thinking about my futile efforts to help man's body while doing nothing to save his soul. Of course, the reasoning was justified by all the atheism and bans to witness about God, so I just simply couldn't do it. But I was not able to quiet my conscience. It was racked and tormented. During those years, more and more, I remembered the words I had heard in the days of my preparations for the exams for admission into the medical institute, "*It would be better for you to remain as you are.*" Only now I was getting their meaning. Well in advance God had known much of what I couldn't even assume.

In that period of time as I had been clarifying certain things in my personal quest, often, all of a sudden another topic would pop up and trouble me. For instance, I once prayed in my solitude about something that had long been bothering me. Abruptly, a voice spoke inside my heart, "*I will set you as a block for offense and stumbling and many will stumble over it and fall*". When the meaning of these words finally reached my mind, I cried out in horror, "No, Lord! Not that! This cannot be Your will. I don't believe this is Your voice, because it's inconsistent with the Holy Scripture . . . !" I remembered so well the Word of God that said, "*Whoever causes one of these little ones who believe in Me to sin, it would be better for him if a millstone were hung around his neck, and he were drowned in the depth of the sea. Woe to the world because of offenses! For offenses must come, but* **woe to that man by whom the offense comes!**'" (Matt. 18:6-7). That's why it couldn't be God Who would make any man a snag for stumbling over and causing offense to other fellow men! Surely, He would not destroy souls! Therefore, this voice must have come from the devil, who always seeks to kill and destroy.

It was certainly easier for me to reject the voice than to accept it as being from God. I convinced myself in all kinds of ways that what I had heard was a pure temptation that must be renounced and forgotten. And so I prayed and asked the Heavenly Father to help me to do just that. But time went on and the spoken words didn't disappear from my mind, surfacing time and again and intimidating me with their distinctness. One day I just gave up and falling on my knees pleaded with the Lord to make it lucid for me, since I simply couldn't believe that God could have said anything like that.

The answer to my prayer came in the form of a reminder about the passage of Scripture from Gospel of Luke (2:33-34), "*And Joseph and His mother marveled at those things which were spoken of Him. Then Simeon blessed them, and said to Mary His mother,* **"Behold, this Child is destined for the fall and rising of many in Israel, and for a sign which will be spoken against [. . .]"**.

Frankly, as I read the verses of the Holy Scriptures, I was awe-stricken because never before had I paid much attention to these particular words. Therefore, if God the Father destined His own begotten Son for the falling and rising of many in Israel, then why couldn't He use another human being for the same purpose? Much later while reading the book of the prophet Ezekiel I came across the following words again, "*When a righteous man turns from his righteousness and commits iniquity,* **and I lay a stumbling block before him,** *he shall die; because you did not give him warning, he shall die in his sin, and his righteousness which he has done shall not be remembered; but his blood I will require at your hand*" (Ezek. 3:20).

It's a rather shocking word, isn't it? Unwillingly, you start realizing that we evidently don't know our Lord. We tend to simplify Him according to our own very limited human mind, and try to interpret this or that passage of Scripture as it fits our own understanding. However, if you accept the Word of God as it is, the way it was written, then at times, it, indeed, is capable of stunning you. I don't know how, why or for what reason, but from what it says it becomes apparent that **God Himself, with His own hand**, sometimes places a stumbling block before someone to cause his fall. What is it? Is it a judgment, punishment or retribution? Only eternity will answer that question. Our human brain is incapable of containing such thoughts. One thing is obvious though, that only the Lord can place and remove such a stumbling block. Nobody else, including the block itself, can do that.

To return to the interrupted story about our church in Estonia, I want to say that sin in all shapes and forms including fornication and adultery was gaining more and more foothold in that formerly blessed fellowship in which I had previously found so much delight. But in spite of all this, many prophecies, filled with promises, and encouraging sermons continued. Was it only the human mind attempting to put support under the disintegrating "work of God" or was it the action of a false spirit? One can only guess. One way or another, the members of the congregation were now more united by the idea of immigration than by Christian love but went on with their meetings, even though their souls were in fact groaning within.

In the meantime, four years passed after we had submitted our petition for the immigration to Germany. And in December of 1983, at the moment we didn't expect, the permission came. I can't say that the news brought us no joy, but we were leaving our fellowship behind with heavy hearts. In a short time our ways totally parted. To leap ahead for a moment to four years later, after we had left for Germany, all the members of the church who wanted to immigrate got out of Estonia, one family after another, and scattered across the United States of America. As a result not even a trace of our congregation was left. From time to time we heard sad rumors about them, but soon the ties were completely broken. At the end of 1989 we received information that our former pastor had passed away in poignant sufferings from a severe disease. We can only hope that at his departure into eternity the Lord had opened his spiritual eyes and given him realization, repentance and forgiveness. Nevertheless, I retain many good reminiscences of him. In loving the Lord he made a wonderful beginning and was full of desire to be faithful to Him, but was enticed onto a false path by trusting excessively revelations and prophecies he erroneously considered to be true guidance from God.

How important it is though, in our own walk with God and in service to Him to remind ourselves continuously of King David's words, *"Search me, O God, and know my heart; Try me, and know my anxieties; And see if there is any wicked way in me, And lead me in the way everlasting"* (Ps. 137:23-24).

Not without reason, the Word of God warns us, *"Therefore let him who thinks he stands take heed lest he fall"* (1 Cor. 10:12). No one is insured against falling, no matter how great one is in the eyes of God or men. We are all capable of deviating from the way of truth and making an error, but much depends on our readiness to admit it, for then the Lord is allowed an opportunity to correct us. We, humans, can be absolutely positively sure of something, build a foundation on such a belief, and make it grow strong and even convince others of that which may not be the truth at all.

Our first years together in Estonia

December 1983. Before leaving for Germany

This was exactly the case in this church in Estonia. Our pastor lost his way, but he did it wholeheartedly, thinking he was walking in the right direction. Once he accepted the idea that revelations and prophecies received from others were true, he lost cautiousness, soberness and watchfulness (the elements most in demand, especially for those who lead God's people). His failure to be watchful led to severe repercussions: personal sin, destroyed family life, loss of his children, two deaths in the house, years of torment, weary anticipation of departure for America, unrealized hopes for an extraordinary ministry awaiting him there, bitter disappointments in those he trusted, severe disease and as a finale – agonizing, perhaps, untimely death. Who knows? Maybe everything would have been different if it had not been for his unreasoning credulity.

I have shared the story about our former congregation with one purpose only, because, unfortunately, such a case is not an isolated one. Similar things happen all too often. It is no secret to anyone that the devil can come in the form of an angel of light. However, when he comes in that way to us personally we usually are unable to recognize him and tend to accept him as the messenger of truth. It is especially dangerous when the ministers of the Gospel succumb to the influence of the spirit of falsehood. In a situation like this the aftermath of delusion is literally devastating. And subsequently Satan succeeds not only in turning the leader's life into ruins but also the lives of many who followed him without doubting his infallibility. Usually the souls of such trusting people carry the consequences of this trauma for the rest of their lives. They are broken apart inwardly, spiritually disoriented, unable to trust anyone anymore, disappointed in everything, searching for peace and obtaining none. This is a true tragedy that occurs much more often than we would like to think. And it is quite impossible to avoid it because for as long as humanity has existed, there have been human errors.

Dear Reader! Perhaps, you have already noticed that in describing all that happened in Estonia I did not mention the name of the city or the names of the people involved. I intended to do just that, so that the names of those who have been dear to my heart even up until now would not be dragged through the mud. I cannot understand people, who in matters like this, always look for a scapegoat. Although, this familiar term may sound a little rude, nevertheless, it is an exact description of a situation equivalent to this one. In Old Testament times "a scapegoat" in Israel was a real male goat on whose back the Jews symbolically laid all their sins and then drove the unfortunate animal into the chasm where it finally fell down and died, so to say, together with the sins it carried. For the Israelites it was a part of their religion and a very suitable tradition, which actually found its place

81

among us, Christians, to become a convenient form of self-justification. After getting into some kind of error and realizing it, we attempt to find the guilty one who brought us there and was the main leader in teaching something that was not the truth. Such people we make fully responsible. They are blamed for all kinds of errors, sins and every sort of deviation for which I, the poor human being, must pay. But I have really failed to consider that I have my own head on my shoulders and the Word of God in my hands, which is supposed to be *"a light unto my path"*. I also ignore the detail that I used to admire and agree with everything, thoughtlessly doing all I had been taught but now deem myself a poor, ill-fated victim who had been seduced and mislead. I believe such treatment of the daily events is unworthy of an honest and devoted Christian. If we slip up we should have enough courage to admit it and not to make someone else our "scapegoat". Certainly, it is much easier and more pleasing to blame somebody else. But the question is – will we really be able to justify ourselves one day as we stand before the throne of God?

I cannot blame anyone, not the former pastor, or any other church member, because I myself was guilty for **accepting** that, which was a delusion. During all the years I had lived in Estonia the Lord tried to get my attention numerous times. It should have alerted me to think more seriously about what was being said and taught. But, no, I had chosen the easier way of passively following another person's ideas and I deserved to be punished for that. However, no matter how bitter the realization of this mistake had been, there was still something good that I could learn from this experience. First of all, it was a spiritual experience, which unfortunately, can only be derived from a collection of personal mistakes. The falling we suffer, no matter how painful and how deeply hurtful to one's heart, later becomes a beautiful lesson that helps us to avoid repeating the same kinds of errors again. That's why the Lord put the following words into the mouth of the prophet Jeremiah, *"If you take out* **the precious from the vile**, *you shall be as My mouth"* (Jerem.15:19).

Chapter 6

Encounter with Revival

Those who think that life in the Western world is like living in clover are terribly mistaken. I recall how during our first months in Germany one man upon seeing my admiration of beautiful houses and lavish villas said casually, "If you only knew how much grief there is under these wealthy German roofs."

I couldn't understand him then. How is it possible that people can be miserable while having so much abundance and prosperity? Now, after more than twenty-five years of life in the West I only smile at my own former naivety. Behind the gorgeous exterior there are hidden problems that we couldn't even conceive of in the Soviet Union. Quite radical and sharp re-orientation awaits a person who resettles from one country to another. Not many can endure it. Suffice it to say that during my first three years in Germany I cried more than I had ever cried in my entire life. And who knows, I might have gone blind from all the tears I shed if not for the strict voice that resonated once again in my heart, "*I forbid you to cry!*"

My tears dried up in an instance. I finally understood that I grieved the Lord with my misapprehension of His plans. All the ways back were cut off. And I had nothing else to do but to consent. East of the German border I left not only my relatives and friends but also my place in the social scale, my work and my profession. Without knowing the language, I certainly could not pass the exam to support my diploma and therefore, was not able to work as a doctor. My two diplomas are still in the closet as two of my most precious souvenirs. My higher education meant nothing anymore and I was transformed into a common homemaker. After ten years of rigorous professional work, everything was reduced to house cleaning, meal cooking and washing dishes. I was thrown to the ground from the heights of recognition and trampled under many feet. My entire being resisted and rebelled against it. But the Lord knows how to humble the ones "*who walk in pride*" (Daniel 4:37). And so He started to decrease what had grown into a very large "Self" that had sat on the throne of my life for too long, in order to prepare me for the future ministry and to prove the indisputable truth, "God creates all things out of nothing, and everything that God wants to use, He first turns into **nothing**."

From the start, my husband and I had intended to move from Germany to the United States of America in order to help the rest of our congregation that still remained in Estonia, with their immigration. But that was not as easy as it seemed to us. All the doors there were shut before us. At that time we wept in despair but now, so many years later we understand that it was a great mercy of God for us. Unwittingly one recalls the words of the Scripture, *"For My thoughts are not your thoughts, Nor are your ways My ways,"* says the LORD, *"For as the heavens are higher than the earth, So are My ways higher than your ways, And My thoughts than your thoughts"* (Isaiah 55:8-9).

However, I had better tell everything in sequence.

When our airplane landed in Frankfurt and we entered the huge airport terminal, the first sentiment that hit both of us was one of complete freedom. No one was watching us and no one demanded anything from us. The usual passport and custom controls were finished in no time and we were wished well and sent on our way. We were now surrounded by this incomprehensible, mysterious and absolutely unknown world to which we were unaccustomed. When our relatives who met us at the airport drove a car at a speed of about 190-200 kilometers per hour while having a lively conversation, I felt sick to my stomach. Yet, we could hardly catch our breath not only because of what seemed to us an unbelievable speed limit, but also because of the sea of lights from the ever-moving stream of cars. Now there was much we had to get used to: people's behavior, their relationships, life styles, diverse points of view on subjects of daily life, approaches to the problems and their means of resolving them. Often I had a feeling that I had gone not only to a different country but also to a different planet altogether. Everything was interesting and new, but in less than three months, I started having nostalgia for my Motherland and could not have peace until after three years I went back to Russia, to Leningrad, in order to meet with friends and my parents. Prior to that visit, I looked at the socialist system, at the Russian people and at my formerly favorite city with a fresh eye, since now there was something else to which I could compare my earlier life. My heart ached for simple Russian folks, and for their hard life, in which they were deprived of many things people in the West took for granted. However when I returned, I saw everywhere disorder and filth that I had basically never noticed before. One way or another the trip cured me of homesickness and made me believe that God in His grace had given us something infinitely better.

Upon returning from Russia my husband and I were able to fulfill our long-standing dream to fly to Kwa Sizabantu mission station in South Africa. Understanding of and close ties with the mission occupied the following seventeen years of my life, the story that I would share with you next.

The first time I heard about Kwa Sizabantu in Estonia was in 1979, when my mother-in-law sent us a letter from Germany and enclosed a post card depicting a group of smiling black people. On the backside of the card I read, "Mission station Kwa Sizabantu, South

Africa." Mother's postscript where she reported that she attended a service where Erlo Stegen, the mission's director, had preached was the first information we had ever received about it. I will not forget how long I stared at the picture bewildered by the particularly amazing light reflected on the faces of the black Christians. It is hard to find the right words to describe what I saw in their appearance then. Studying the photo I wondered: what was making them so magnetic?

That evening I sat for a long time holding the picture. And when I finally retired to bed I had a wonderful dream. I saw myself at the mission, standing across from the group of Christians, shown on the postcard. A road separated us. A pleasant breeze was lightly stirring their clothes.

I stretched out my hands and was repeatedly saying, "I want to be with you so much! I must understand where that light I see on your faces is coming from!" In reply they only smiled back and shrugged their shoulders letting me know that they could not help me with that. And while I stood there I started helplessly crying.

Suddenly above me on the right side there was a loud voice saying, *"Don't you cry! You will be there. But first, you must walk this road."*

I turned my gaze downward, looked at the path that separated us, and woke up. I stayed in bed with open eyes pondering the meaning of all of this. Surely, I could not get to Africa if I still lived in the Soviet Union, the country behind the iron curtain, from which you could practically go nowhere. (We had not yet submitted the immigration papers at that time.) Well, perhaps, it was just a dream. One might see anything in a dream. And so I tried to put it out of my mind, period. But I couldn't forget it. At that moment I couldn't even imagine that exactly seven years later that dream was predestined to come true.

When we arrived to Germany at the end of December 1983, I was knocked off my feet by a severe flu. That day I stayed in bed with high fever of almost 40 degrees Celsius, when unexpectedly a woman called. She used to send us letters to Estonia describing her long trips to Kwa Sizabantu mission in South Africa.

"Ludmila," I heard her voice in the receiver. "Do you want to get acquainted with Stegen's family? They are now in transit visiting on a farm. I am going there and can take you along."

"Now?" I hesitantly asked her again. "Yes, of course, I do, but I am in bed with a high fever . . . ." However, the desire to see these people was so great, especially after just two weeks of being in Germany, that I've made a decision right away, adding, "Sure, I'll go with you. I just need to change and will be waiting for you." The infirmity was literally holding me down, but my mind was on a different subject. I simply could not allow myself to miss the opportunity.

When we got there, there were many people gathered together besides the South African guests. Everybody was cheerful and carried on a dynamic conversation. Many of them wanted to speak directly with the Africans and therefore, they were extremely busy. Thus in the beginning I saw only one of the Stegen brothers – Haino, who was available at that moment. With an interpreter's help, I was introduced to him and explained that I had come from the Soviet Union only two weeks before. He became very interested and began a conversation with me. Fortunately, there was an older man nearby who had moved from Russia many years earlier who was able to help our communication by playing the role of translator. The way my talker carried himself, listened, and inquired – somehow made me feel very comfortable and sincere. Immediately I experienced kindly and trustworthy feelings towards him and confidently revealed to him the innermost recesses of my soul, tormented through years of searching. Pointing at the familiar postcard of the co-workers group from Kwa Sizabantu mission, which was hanging on the wall of the room I finished my story with the dream I had in Estonia four years earlier. Haino Stegen smiled with understanding and expressed his hope for its fulfillment in the nearest future and that he would like to see me together with my husband at their mission in South Africa.

The arrival of the oldest brother of Stegen's family named Friedel interrupted our conversation. It looked like he had already been told about me, because as he entered the room he addressed me as if I was his old friend with the words, "Well, do you feel good here with us?"

"Good?" I asked again and shaking my head, specified, "No. Not just "good", but very good!" ("Gut? – Nein. – Sehr gut!"[27]) That was the extent of my German vocabulary that I had collected in two weeks of our residency in Germany. Friedel Stegen heartily laughed at my words and proceeded to another room. That was my first encounter with the Stegen family during which I was able meet four brothers and a sister of Erlo Stegen. Unfortunately, the latter was absent at that time.

What happened afterwards I remember as if in a fog, because my flu condition certainly made me aware of its presence. I recall a noisy dinnertime. Everybody talked in that, still very much unknown to me, German language, and everything I looked at floated in front of my eyes as a result of weakness and high body temperature. I wanted only one thing, to get to bed and close my eyes.

Several months had passed after that encounter. Winter faded away. Spring had just begun. On one occasion, friends of ours informed us that there would be worship services in churches of

---

[27] In German language

86

various German towns where Erlo Stegen would preach. Certainly, it made us very glad, since we had longed to hear him speak. It so happened that during the past few years he had been touring his forefathers' Motherland – Germany twice a year, in spring and fall as well as visiting other Western European countries on missionary trips. A young brother had volunteered to help and agreed to interpret into Russian for me. At the first opportunity we went to one of the church meetings that made a permanent impression on my soul.

Behind the pulpit there was a tall, well-built and slender, middle-aged man who spoke with unusual inspiration in a loud, perhaps at times, even shrill voice. I looked intensely into his resolute face and, while listening to the interpretation, thought to myself that perhaps never in my life had I felt like that while hearing the Word of God.

At that service for the first time I realized the meaning and the depth of the passage of Scripture, *"For the word of God is living and powerful, and sharper than any two-edged sword, piercing even to the division of soul and spirit, and of joints and marrow, and is a discerner of the thoughts and intents of the heart"* (Hebrews 4:12).

While paying attention to the words of that preacher I repeatedly asked myself, "Where does that power come from? Why does all that is being spoken by him reach to the depth of the soul and literally turn it inside out, and reveal the concealed things and disclose all that is in secret? How is it that the Word of God in his mouth becomes alive and active, in a full sense piercing to the division of soul and spirit, and of joints and marrow, discerning the concealed matters known only to one's heart?" The more I listened, the more I was amazed at his knowledge of the depths of the human soul, especially in the question of sin. I was surprised at the boldness with which Erlo Stegen called things by their real names. Even our former pastor in Estonia had not dared to speak about sins that openly.

I left the service profoundly stunned and with every intension to hear him again at the first opportunity. My wish soon came true. Later, on two more occasions, I sat holding my breath as I listened to the stern and sometimes even wrath-filled words of the missionary that mercilessly exposed and condemned human sins, one by one.

At that point, I did not question, why sin was the main theme of his sermons and why practically everything was directed to that subject. Evidently, during that time my soul needed exactly that, as4 it searched for the way out of stagnation and spiritual impasse. Under the influence of what I had heard, I remembered less and less spiritual wounds caused to me by other people and more often thought about my own sins. Our first year in Germany was followed by the second and then, by the third. My husband and I wasted no opportunities to attend the services conducted by Erlo Stegen. Nothing could stop us even, if the town where the service was held stood afar at a distance of 200 to 300 kilometers or more.

His sermons had been making more and more impact on me. Often it seemed as if I was placed in front of the mirror of God's Word, where I saw myself as a dirty pig. It dispirited me but at the same time prompted to act. For the first time in my life, I had a desire to mend my relationships with other people whom I had offended some time ago. As a result, I sent out letters in which I asked friends, acquaintances and former colleagues at work to forgive me, as I recognized my wrong words, deeds and actions. Frequently there was silence in reply, but sometimes I received responses full of astonishment, admiration, encouragement and a mutual request for forgiveness. However strange it may seem, those from whom I expected to receive complete understanding, knowing them as spiritual people, replied with letters full of malice bordering on hostility and harsh judgment. However, those who outwardly seemed weak, carnal Christians displayed real love and readiness to forgive and forget wrongdoing. In the matter of dealing with sin and being willing to humble oneself and to forgive others, the souls of people began to reveal themselves in an unexpected way. In time, it became clear that this was when real spirituality made itself known. Yet, no matter what the reciprocal reaction of my addressees was, my own step towards reconciliation brought relief and some unknown bliss to my soul. With delight, I shared all that was happening to me with my friends who remained in Estonia, but, to my disappointment and surprise, they did not understand my joy. Gradually, our close heartfelt ties with them weakened more and more until, after their immigration to America, our connections altogether ceased.

Once in the fall during the next missionary trip brother Haino with whom we had had a long conversation three years earlier, accompanied Erlo Stegen. When my husband and I came to the church service at the neighboring town and approached him there to say "hello", he asked us if we were planning to visit them at Kwa Sizabantu in South Africa. Of course, it was my long-standing aspiration but there were too many obstacles (financial ones were among them; that kind of trip costs an arm and a leg for such a trip to become a reality). When brother Haino heard our reasoning, he smiled and said, "Well, in that case we, in South Africa, will pray for you that the Lord may bring you to us."

In few months all the problems took care of themselves and on December 18, 1986 we boarded an airplane for our trip from Frankfurt to Durban. After 14 hours of a tiresome flight we landed in the huge city of Johannesburg and for the first time touched the ground of South African Republic.

The black continent met us with the fiery sun forcing us immediately to forfeit our winter garments and put on light clothing and shoes. Then, there was another short transfer flight from Johannesburg to Durban, where we were welcomed by Kwa Sizabantu co-workers whom we had informed of our arrival ahead of time. On our way to the mission station, while sitting inside a comfortable minivan, I couldn't stop turning my head left and right, to view the changing scenes behind the window. Everything was unusual, the amazing tropical flora with its lavishness and abundance of bright colors, the strange (to the eyes of a European) landscape with grass-roofed huts of the black residents scattered on the hilly slopes and, everywhere, huge plantations of sugar cane. However, most wonderful of all were the black people themselves, wearing their stunningly dazzling clothes. Calm and unhurried, they often walked along the roads or even expressways, on which oddly (in our opinion) one drove on the left side of the road. When I looked into their faces and watched their movements and reactions I unwittingly thought that they somehow differed from us, the white people, and in spite of all, was determined to find out what it was.

Swollen from the long flight, my feet ached with a dull expanding pain. The sleepless night on the plane had filled my eyelids with a lead weight. My whole body demanded rest. We really wanted to sleep but the van continued its course, taking us deep into Natal province.

Dozing off I was suddenly jolted awake by someone's exclamation, "Look, there ahead of us on the right side you can see the Kwa Sizabantu mission!" Among seven or eight fellow travelers, there were few who were not visiting these places for the first time. As I looked in the indicated direction I saw in the distance a row of buildings and many round huts standing in a half circle.

"Oh!" I thought to myself. "This missionary station is like a real small village!" In the meantime the van came to a sign "Kwa Sizabantu", turned right and in a few minutes stopped at the central mission building where they had a small house with a reception room for incoming guests.

Forgetting my fatigue I got out of the van and, looking around, noticed the landmark and the road I had seen in my dream in Estonia seven years before. My heart loudly pounded inside my chest as I had a presentiment that something unusual was about to happen. It seemed I again heard the words in my ears, *"Don't you cry! You will be there. But first, you must walk this road."* The lengthy road of seven years had been left behind. I stood on the path beaten by hundreds of feet in front of the building that was depicted on the postcard I had seen a long time ago. Finally! Finally, my wish has come true!

"Lord, what have You prepared for my soul here? Is this what I had unsuccessfully sought for twenty years?" By then I had already turned thirty-eight, but my spiritual quest had begun when I was only eighteen. "Am I really on the threshold of my target?" For whatever reason the words spoken to Moses came to my mind, *"Take your sandals off your feet, for the place where you stand is holy ground"* (Exodus 3:5). What if something like that was due to happen to me here? Would I really at last come into the presence of God in this place? No one could hear when I whispered with lips trembling with apprehension, "I've been waiting for this moment for so long, Lord . . . ! Waiting for so long . . . ."

From the first minutes of being at Kwa Sizabantu my heart was filled with the anticipation of something extraordinary occurring, but day after day nothing unusual happened. Life at the mission station was steadily moving on. Co-workers living there were occupied, each with his or her ministry, whether of a spiritual or practical nature. There was a flow of visitors coming and going from different regions of South Africa and from other countries. They were received, housed in the rooms and huts, fed and cared for without charges for the services. Every morning and evening there was a regular worship service where mission workers had preached. On Sundays Erlo Stegen or one of the other leaders of the mission preached. During the services I had never heard anyone speaking in tongues or prophesying. No one had ever told the congregation about a vision or any other kind of revelation. From the outside, the form of the worship meeting looked as it would if conducted in a Christian Baptist church. Perhaps, the only difference was that they had always had one preacher at the pulpit and if anyone else got up to say something, it was just to add to the theme of the sermon[28] already delivered. Meetings went on in a quiet atmosphere. The main factor that moved one was the authority and depth of the sermons that reached out to the minds and hearts of listeners. No one remained indifferent and each one received enough food for thought, for further personal meditations. Several hours after the service I would usually catch myself still thinking about what I had just heard. The Word was becoming ever more living and powerful for me.

Our fellow travelers from Germany socialized with mission co-workers and went around visiting friends, things I couldn't do due to the language barrier, since I didn't know any English and was only able to speak a very limited German. My husband, on the other hand, spoke

---

[28] In comparison with Russian-speaking churches, the latter usually have two or even three preachers speaking on different subjects for the nourishment of the congregation during Sunday services.

rather fluent German and therefore, his social circle there was much wider. Because of that, I often stayed in the hut by myself or walked on the premises watching the routine of daily life, and the children's behavior at the school and in the kindergarten that belonged to the mission. As I applied myself to helping with the washing of dishes in the kitchen, I also noticed the relationship between those who worked there. Frankly, it was the ordinary life and associations between people living at Kwa Sizabantu mission that served as the greatest blessing to me. There was no hassling and bustling, no grudges or exasperation. Peace, quiet and amazing harmony reigned everywhere.

"How strange it is!" I thought to myself. "These people act as if they were programmed to do only good. Don't they have any problems? Surely, they can't always perform a pious spectacle here in front of so many mission guests. It is possible to do that for a period of time, but not for one's entire life spent at the mission station" (since I had heard that there were many co-workers who lived here for ten, fifteen and even twenty years).

By the time we came to Kwa Sizabantu the revival had celebrated exactly twenty years. In a normal course of human life, people that are forced to live within a restricted area quickly get tired of each other and that becomes the root of difficulties in inter-personal relationships. As a result there is an ever-increasing pressure, which more often than not, turns into hostility and animosity. However, it seemed that either there was no such problem at Kwa Sizabantu or it had been craftily masked. One way or another, this was a very attractive picture to which onlooker was exposed. As a doctor with years of medical experience, I had gotten into a habit of analyzing things, which I, of course, pursued in my observations at Kwa Sizabantu mission. However, if I may say, even I didn't have anything to say against it. Except for a dubious mixed feeling that people living there seemed almost surreal with their ever present kindness, courtesy, politeness and readiness to serve others. Nevertheless, this notion had only bothered me for a few days, and then disappeared never to return, because within my own heart an intensive work had been begun.

The first ten days of our visit to Kwa Sizabantu were ending. During evening services, it was becoming more striking to see that after the sermon many of the attendees did not leave the sanctuary but stayed in their seats as if glued to them. Gazing into their faces, I noticed the reflection of the inner fight occurring inside their souls. Shortly afterwards these people got up and walked towards the light construction next to the service center. It seemed odd to me, and so, on one of such evenings, I followed them to find out what they were doing there. My eyes saw a remarkable scene in the long hallway. Along the walls by the closed doors, there were chairs with black and white people sitting on them. Hard-to-hide tears welled up in the eyes of many. I felt very uncomfortable because their sad and dispirited faces mirrored the expression of despair and pain.

I stood to the side and began to watch what was going on. You could have guessed that these were people suffering from various kinds of problems. A lot of them, it seemed, talked to themselves inwardly while in tormenting thought process. At times they were obviously fighting tears that welled to the surface and had to turn away to conceal them. Others got pen and paper out and quickly wrote something down, as if anxious to forget that which was in their hearts. Occasionally, one of the doors opened and a person walked out allowing another one to enter. It shocked me to see the look of those who exited from those mysterious rooms. Even though there were still traces of fresh tears on their cheeks, their eyes sparkled, shone and radiated joy and inexpressible happiness. As some of them were leaving the room, they breathed out a sigh of relief. Their whole appearance conveyed a pacification and serenity that I could not comprehend.

"What are they doing in those rooms?" I wondered. "Why do they change so much after twenty to thirty minutes of being inside?" I continued to stand there and waited until those whom I had watched earlier sitting on the chairs crying came out. That's it. The same thing recurred. Recently de-spirited and despondent faces now smiled and tearful eyes beamed and shone. Oh, how similar did they look to those people I saw in my dream seven years ago! Was it really something that happened within those rooms that made people so happy and radiant?

On the next day, I carefully probed the situation and asked my translator about **what** was happening behind the closed doors of those strange rooms. He smiled and explained that people went to those rooms for counseling. There they could open up their hearts in the presence of a counselor who afterwards prayed with them. That which I heard and especially, what I saw the previous day with my own eyes ignited an interest but the thought never crossed my mind to do the same. Apparently, my soul had not yet been ready for this step. Nevertheless, the Lord has His own plan for everything and He brings it to life in His own time.

Chapter 7

Wrecking of My Ego

As I had already recounted, the concept of confession of sins in front of another person was not anything new to me. When I had had the experience in our former fellowship in Estonia I was at last so very disappointed that I promised myself never in my life to open my heart to another human being. My previous confessions had left me only with pains of frustration, and not the blessings of joy and freedom. Why, then, have I become a witness of something quite different? What difference was there between what I had been through and what those people experienced here? Even though it awoke my interest, I remained firm in my decision not to do this anymore.

One day I noticed a change in my husband. When I asked him what had happened, he answered that he went to counseling and told me how they did it here. After listening to him, I walked out of the hut feeling the rebellion rising up inside my heart.

"No way," I repeated to myself. "Never and under no circumstances will I do this again! I can trust only God and to God alone will I ever confess! I had suffered enough grief in Estonia when I went to a man for my confessions! I don't want this anymore! What is a man, whoever he may be that I should confess to him? I am not going to have any mediator between God and me!"

It was amazing that resistance and hardness against counseling grew within me so rapidly, although nobody had told me about it, nor forced me or urged me. My tough, fierce "no" seemingly screamed out of each and every cell of my body, making me look like an angry, rumpled sparrow.

In this moment of emotional anxiety and bitterness, a quiet calm voice spoke in my heart, "*You will have to do it. You need to cleanse your life in the open confession and you shall go to Friedel Stegen with that.*"

The words still rang inside as I almost yelled out in reply, "No! No! A thousand times "no", Lord! I will not do it and moreover, will not go to Friedel Stegen! It might have been someone else, but not him! And You know why I don't want that!"

I had absolutely no doubts it was God's voice, because by then, I knew it very well. However, even that couldn't restrain me. At the time, not willing to obey, I wasn't afraid to shout my malicious "no" into the face of God!

That evening at the worship service, I could barely hear anything. My heart was shut and deaf to the Word of God. In my frantic zeal, I totally lost control of myself. Muttering to my husband that I wanted to take a walk alone before going to bed, I nervously began pacing among the huts until it got very dark outside and I returned home all shivering from the cold air. My husband went to bed, saying "good night" and not at all suspecting my terrible condition, quickly fell asleep. I restlessly tossed on the bed fretting, because sleep escaped me. It was extremely dark inside my soul, darker than the African night, when you cannot see you own stretched out hand. Now, when my fingers are writing out these lines I realize with horror how evil and hardened the heart of a Christian can become, when the Lord touches the spot that serves as the devil's foothold. I remember that just the phrase "to cleanse and put your life in order" provoked my anger and a burst of indignation. But all my life I have been considered an exemplary Christian! Oh, how much evil and all kinds of uncleanness often hide behind external piety! If I had not discovered it within myself I would never have believed it. In essence, we do not know ourselves; do not know what we are capable of doing. And without realizing that, we constantly play our roles, thinking this is what we are in reality. It goes on and on until God in His mercy exposes the place that has been Satan's bulwark for the longest time.

The same thing happened to me that night. I could not recognize myself. The flame of hell burned within my heart, hardened beyond limits. I felt no fear before the Lord, no respect for Him, either. But God always brings His work to completion. The fight had begun. And in that battle He fought not me but him, who occupied me and was now warring for his possessions. It was the devil himself.

As his captive I tossed on the bed as if in hell, when the words clearly reached my heart, *"You will go and reveal your sins, naming your thoughts as your deeds."*

"No!" I raged as a mad woman. "No, I will not do that!"

"I am telling you, you have to do it," the voice sounded again.

"And I am telling You, Lord, that I will not do that!"

"Ludmila, I am telling you for the last time, that you must confess your sins."

"I said that I am not going to do this and will not change my mind!"

"Then, I will take My protection from you."

"So what, take it!" I blurted out harshly, not realizing what I was saying, and in an instance something extraordinary took place. In some strange way, I perceived a huge wall surrounding me, which suddenly, in a blink of an eye, shook and tumbled down. Behind that wall with my own eyes, I saw the devil, which jumped on me like a beast of prey and we were clutched in a ferocious battle. I do not know if it was a spiritual experience. But I recall seeing it all with my physical eyes and felt the heavy weight of the attacking body. It is rather difficult to describe with human words how Satan looked, but it was a sinister picture and because of it every hair on my skin stood up. His trunk was all covered with black bristled skin. Hanging right above me was his frightful snout breathing out a foul odor. His hooked fingers with claws had encircled my throat and were choking me so that I was instantly out of breath. I wriggled on my bed trying with all my strength to throw him off, but it was all in vain. Our strengths were too unmatched. My glance fell on the bed standing next to mine, where my husband was sleeping peacefully like a baby. Oh, if only he could have prayed for me now! I opened my mouth to scream, but couldn't do it. Only a weak hissing came off my lips. I wanted to call upon the Lord, but that too, was impossible. My lips opened up once and again, as if they belonged to a fish thrown out of water onto ice, but I was unable to make any sound. Suddenly a thick darkness enveloped me and flames of fire appeared in front of me. At the same moment the hell yawned right before me and I saw the words written by someone as if on the side. They were, "*Blessed are the pure in heart, for they shall see God*" (Matt. 5:8). The entire Gospel of salvation was concentrated for me in those words.

I cannot even begin to describe the feelings of horror and despair that swiftly gripped me. I, a Christian from birth, who received a water baptism as well as a spiritual baptism the way I understood it, was walking straight into hell with all my gifts and blessings, simply because I did not have a pure heart . . . .

Involuntarily, such an experience makes one ponder the wide-spread theory of a guaranteed salvation. It is easy to convince someone of something, which you yourself have never experienced. To all who are convinced of the authenticity of this theory I want to say that nobody would had been able to assure me that I was saved that night, since I saw with my own eyes that I was going to hell. In the light of eternity everything seems quite different.

But I should continue with my story. In that second when I saw burning hell and the words, "*Blessed are the pure in heart, for they shall see God*", a silent cry formed inside my soul, "Lord, if You can, forgive me! Save me from the devil! I beg You, please, give me one more chance for salvation! Just one chance! If I don't use it, then may I be thrown into fire of hell, for You are just and righteous! I do not ask for more! Give me only one chance and I will do all You will require of me! I will serve You where You want to send me, whatever it may cost me! I promise You, Lord!" I repeat that this cry did not proceed from my lips, but from within my heart, because I had no voice.

As soon as those words were silently emitted, I noticed a large hand in the air to the left of me that reached down to my bed, and grabbed the devil still lying on top of me, who somehow instantly went limp, and cast him on the ground. I heard a muffled knock as if from the fall of a heavy sack and everything grew quiet. There were no more flames, nor the words of the Scripture inscribed on the wall. In the calm of the night there was heard only the serene breathing of my husband. My body felt as if made of sponge. My night gown was so saturated with sweat that it could have been wrung out. My throat and neck were really hurting so that I was hardly able to swallow any medication. The breathing was hard. I painfully stretched my hand to turn the night light on. When I looked at the clock, it was quarter to four in the morning. I don't know how long this battle with the devil went on, but it seemed like an eternity to me.

I do not wish for anyone to experience a night similar to that one. My stubbornness had been broken, but at what cost! I stood on the edge of obliteration. There was no more turning back. I had been given one more chance. Only one chance . . . .

Often now, when I talk with people and notice how they become sour or argue with God and spiritually make a fuss over something like little children, I think with sadness that they are not aware what it means to have only one chance. It looks like they regard God's patience as something they can tamper with forever.

Meanwhile, the day was just dawning on the other side of the window. After all that had occurred, my head felt as if it was on fire and seemed to be encircled by an iron hoop. But it didn't matter any longer. It was terrible to recognize, though, that my husband as he awoke could have found only a breathless corpse in my place. I quietly wept, thanked God for His bestowed mercy and realized how unworthy of it I had really been.

Figuratively speaking, after that night my "Ego" was like a squashed worm. Not a trace of hardness or resistance was left. Now I was prepared to do anything my Lord would have asked of me. Impatiently I waited until morning to find Friedel Stegen and go to him for counseling. I certainly could not sleep anymore. My nerves were completely on edge, and I only prayed to the Lord asking for enough strength to accomplish all I was supposed to do.

While waiting for dawn I began to recollect the events of the past night, and only then realistically understood what pure madness it was to tell God, "You can take away Your protection!"

In front of my eyes images of the past went by, when the Lord had clearly displayed His protection in saving me from inevitable death. In the days of my youth He had saved me from disgrace three times. A few times I was in danger of being killed. Twice in my life I was close to being torn to pieces by dogs. The first time it occurred when I had just turned seventeen. I had graduated from high school and that night was returning home all alone from the school graduation party. It was one o'clock in the morning. In the pitch-black darkness my dress stood out as a beacon. Deep in thought I was walking past dark barracks when suddenly I heard a fierce growling next to me and a large German shepherd watch dog flew at me. It stood on its hind paws and pressing against my chest knocked me into a roadside ditch. I couldn't gather my wits as I was lying with my back on the grass. And I don't know where that almost inhuman strength had come from but I was able to throw it off me several times. I can't recall how long this fight continued, but at some point drained of all power I whispered, "Lord, help me!" At the same moment I heard quickly approaching heavy steps. A muffled kick sounded, and the huge dog flew to the side as a small puppy.

"Miss," I heard a compassionate voice. "It has not bitten you, has it?"

A man in a white shirt leaned over me and giving me his hand tried to pull me upward. Alas, my body was like rubber and my legs just couldn't support me. Then he lifted me up and carried me to the closest barrack where there was a dim street lamp, barely lighting the house number.

He examined me and soothingly said, "Everything is all right. It didn't even tear your dress. I will walk you home. Where do you live?"

"Here, after a few blocks, at the end of the street."

Having said the number of our house, I attempted to get on my feet but wasn't able to do that, and again helplessly sank to the ground. Seeing that, the man bent over and carefully took me in his arms and carried me like a little baby.

"Is this your house?" he asked, putting me down on the porch and knocking loudly on the door. Notwithstanding the late hour, the door immediately flew open and my Mom was peering through the opening.

"*Dochen'ka*, what's happened?" she exclaimed noticing my pitiful, disheveled appearance and my white prom dress soiled with dirt and grass.

"Who did that to you?"

"It was a German shepherd. It jumped on me, but this man came in time and saved me." I turned around to thank the man in a white shirt, but there was no one there.

"What German shepherd? What man?" My mother began crying. "What are you talking about? There was no one with you! Tell me the truth, what had really happened?"

"Everything is fine, Mama. It really was a dog, but a man saved me. Don't you see? It didn't even bite me," I tried to persuade her while holding onto the doorpost to avoid falling.

"But, where is he?"

"He stood on the porch until the last moment when the door opened. Have you not really seen him? He couldn't have just disappeared, could he?"

"There was nobody with you," Mom repeated. "When I opened the door, you were standing alone. You are probably delirious. Your Dad and I couldn't sleep. We were on our knees praying for you until we heard the knock on the door. What's wrong with you? Can't you walk? O, my God, your facial expression has changed! You are white as a sheet! At least, let's go inside the house! Let's go!"

"Where is that man? Where is he?" I agonizingly scoured my mind, trying to comprehend what had occurred.

"I know for sure that I could not walk and he carried me in his arms. I remember him very well and will certainly recognize him if I meet him again. Perhaps, he lives somewhere nearby. I ought to find him and thank him." But days, weeks and even months went by and yet, I never met that man, no matter how carefully I looked into faces of every person who crossed my path. Whoever he was – a man sent by God or an angel in the shape of a man – I do not know. Maybe only eternity will reveal it. One thing is clear, though. In all that happened there was the definite hand of God and His merciful protection.

Several days later as I walked past the cafeteria, I saw that dog behind the bars of the fence and was shocked by its unusually large size. In a rage, it could have torn me to pieces in no time and bit my head off. But God did not allow it by performing a true miracle. Ever since then, I began to be afraid of dogs. However, twenty years later when we were already living in Germany, another incident happened that I consider nothing other than another miracle.

Once as I felt overcome by nostalgia for my Motherland and all my friends and relatives left there, I went to a distant park with my needlework. I just wanted to be alone and give myself to thinking while enjoying nature. As I sat on the park bench I traveled to Russia in my thoughts and recalled all I had experienced there. Suddenly, I heard a voice within my heart.

"*Leave this place, because there is danger awaiting you!*" I started and lowering my gaze saw a small creeping snake nearby. Knowing that actually there were no poisonous snakes in Germany I followed it with my eyes and decided that the voice was simply my imagination. Having looked round, I made sure once more that I was safe. By the park bench there was a large tree with many branches. Right in front of me lay a large beautiful clearing. It was summertime and a light breeze was blowing gently. As well, the birds chirped in the branches, so I didn't feel like leaving. What kind of danger could have awaited me if there was a freeway only 300-450 feet away?

Absorbed in my needlework I shuddered frightfully when I heard a muffled growl close by. As I lifted my eyes, I noticed a huge bulldog within three feet from me. Fear paralyzed me. I could not move or scream. In Germany usually all dogs are on leash, especially the ones like German shepherds and bulldogs. Far off at the edge of the clearing two women walked out of the woods and one of them was apparently the owner of the dog. Seeing the situation that was developing in front of her eyes, she yelled something to her bulldog in horror, but it did not pay any attention to her. Baring its fangs the dog stood right in front of me and maliciously growled.

"O, Lord!" The words swept through my head. "Have mercy on me!" In that instance, something extraordinary happened. By some unknown and powerful blow the canine was thrown back, fell on the ground, then got on its feet, and fleeing behind the tree standing in close proximity, remained there miserably whimpering and not daring to come close any more.

Then the owner came.

"What did you do? What did you say to him?" she asked me anxiously, while she tried to put a collar over her dog who was now frightened no less than I was and was hardly able to drag him from his spot. Naturally, I was not able to answer her or explain anything and silently shrugged my shoulders, for I too did not understand what had happened.

While quickly running up the path leading to the road, I was still in a state of shock.

"Lord," I whispered, "Lord, thank You for protecting me once more! Please, forgive my disobedience to Your voice! I praise You for Your protection and Your great mercy!"

In addition to this, there have been many other cases where I have obviously experienced God's grace. His guardianship had really been like a protecting wall surrounding me, when I uttered those insane words, "You can take Your protection off me." It was that wall that collapsed, and let the devil, who had been hunting for my soul, have direct access to it. Now, many years later, when I think of it, the thought of it terrifies me. How mad can a person become in hardening his heart against God!

Indeed, we do not know ourselves. We cannot even imagine what we might be capable of, if we give place to the devil by embittering our hearts. Then, he can first use us as his tool, and later, destroy us, if not physically, then certainly spiritually. Although, it is difficult for me to remember how loathsome, disgusting and ungrateful I had been in God's sight, I nevertheless don't regret what I experienced. Otherwise, I would not have been able to understand my brothers and sisters in the faith, when in certain moments they become so unrecognizably different, unbearable and detestable by giving room to the devil; and when, humanly speaking, you wish to part with them forever or as they say, "to walk round them by the tenth road"[29]. Fortunately, such a condition usually passes away and when the Lord in His mercy opens their spiritual eyes, they come to their senses all surprised and stunned. Sin always makes a person blind and foolish.

But, I must get back to the events experienced in that awful night. Slowly coming back to my senses after the dreadful fight with the devil and absorbed in my memories I had not noticed it was morning. The alarm went off and awoke my husband who had been sleeping soundly. The hands of the clock indicated seven o'clock in the morning. The sun was struggling through the veil of morning fog. Saturday was promising to be an excellent day, but only one thought pulsed through my head – to get to counseling as soon as possible. I wasn't able to wait until evening.

During breakfast we were told that today there would be a trip to the worship service at Claridge, and all co-workers of the mission as well as the guests from Europe would be going there by buses. At the same time when everyone else rejoiced at the announcement, I just wanted to cry. I had planned to find Friedel Stegen immediately that morning to pour out my heart in the counseling conversation. But now it was impossible, because in an hour he was to ride together with all of us. My head ached so much that it seemed it would crack to pieces. I didn't want to move, much less to go for a two-hour trip in a stuffy bus under the scorching African sun! But to remain in the hut all by myself for the entire day I didn't dare. Therefore, I had no choice but to quickly change my clothes and find a seat inside a crowded bus.

"What's wrong with you?" my husband asked, looking at me attentively. "You look awful. Has something happened?"

"Oh . . . . It's nothing . . . ." I answered evasively. "I have a severe headache and in general, I am not feeling well." (I didn't want to tell him anything before I got to see the counselor).

I don't know how I survived the next several hours. My head burned as if in a fire, and caused an awful nausea that was difficult to keep down. When the bus finally stopped and we started going to the church building I was barely able to move my legs. I pled with God to give me strength at least to sit through the service. I simply couldn't perceive the words of the sermon. After the worship service was over, my husband, very concerned with my terrible appearance, took me into the shade of some trees.

As I leaned against one of the trunks I inwardly called upon the Lord, "Father! I beg You, have mercy on me and send Friedel Stegen

---

[29] A Russian idiom, meaning: to stay away from someone as far as possible.

here, otherwise I will collapse." The cry was still silently sounding within my heart when on the far end of the path the figure of Friedel showed up. He was apparently on the run and rapidly walked in the opposite from us direction.

"Lord!" I cried out inwardly in despair. "Stop him! Turn him around and bring him here, to us. Please, show me in this, that You have granted me Your mercy!"

In that instance, a miracle took place. Brother Friedel as if staggered, suddenly stopped, hesitantly looked back, then made a sharp turn around and started walking towards our side. It appeared that he himself did not realize exactly what he was doing. Seeing such a clear answer to my soul's cry, I whispered to my husband to stand aside and sheepishly stepped forward to face the approaching man.

"Brother Friedel!" I said with emotion, mixing German and Russian words. "Last night God commanded me to go to you for confession. If I don't do it, the devil will destroy me." I could not add anything else. My strength left me, and I began weeping. Apparently, my look of anguish said it more eloquently that my words, because Friedel glanced at my face and quickly answered,

"Very well. You will come to my room for counseling right after we return to Kwa Sizabantu."

And with these words, he turned around and disappeared in the direction from which he had come. After that, everything happened as in a fog. I believe we had dinner, but I did not feel like eating. The thought of going back into the overcrowded and airless bus was making me sick. Seeing my plight, they put me in a private car, but it began to break down on the way and finally stalled. Another car passed us by and stopped. To my surprise, Friedel Stegen climbed out of it and for a time worked on the car together with the driver. At last it started again. Getting back inside his car, he noticed and recognized me.

As he considered my sad state, he said anxiously, "We will meet right after arriving at the mission."

All the rest of the way I repeated in my mind, "Lord, please, give me strength to get there and accomplish what I have to do."

After we arrived, I got out of the car and plodded to barracks, swaying but thanking God that the bus had not pulled in yet, and that I would not need to wait in line. Brother Friedel came by in a few minutes, asked me to enter and suggested we sit down. Choking with tears and having difficulty finding the right German words, I told him how I had refused to go to him for counseling and what had happened to me last night.

As he handed me a glass of water he slowly announced, "For three years I prayed for you from when I saw you the first time after your arrival in Germany."

Hardly being able to compose myself with a feeling of gratitude I whispered, "Thank you," and pressed my parched lips against the glass.

A person that has never experienced a deep humiliation and a similar type of confession would hardly understand what I am about to recount. Never in my life had I felt such agonizing realization of my sinfulness, my insignificance and my worthlessness . . . . Never had my heart been so crushed and broken. Never had I cried so much, confessing my sins in a secret prayer to God, as I did that day. I don't really know what Friedel Stegen could possibly understand from my confusing and muddled confession, made in half-German, half-Russian words, but I have no doubt the Lord heard and understood everything. When I finally stopped and quieted down, the counselor knelt and uttered a brief prayer.

"Lord! You have heard all that Your child said and You have understood her. I am asking You in Your name to forgive her those sins and wash her in Your holy blood! Cleanse her, sanctify her and take away the burden from her soul. Thank You, that You have heard me. Amen."

Believe it or not, but it seemed to me that the heaven itself put a seal under this final "amen". At that instant, the burden of sins, which heavily lay upon my soul for many years, fell off my shoulders. A happy sigh of relief escaped from my lips. It seemed I was capable of flying. Astounded I did not know what to say, both certain and uncertain, that it was for real. How was it possible that such a simple and short prayer could contain so much power!

At this moment, at last I understood the meaning of words of the Holy Scripture, *"The effective, fervent prayer of a righteous man avails much"* (James 5:16). Involuntarily, a picture of the prophet Elijah, who had prayed to God at the altar on the Mount Carmel, came to my mind. "[. . .] *I am Your servant, and* [. . .] *I have done all these things at Your word. Hear me, O Lord, hear me* [. . .]" (1 Kings 18:36-37). In response, the fire of God fell from heaven to confirm that his prayer was heard.

In people's lives, there are moments when the answers they have sought for many years suddenly become evident in a few short fleeting minutes or even seconds. That was what happened to me. Still sobbing, yet not from despair but from happiness, I kept saying repeatedly, "Thank You, Lord, that You have revealed Yourself to me! I thank You for Your forgiveness and mercy!"

This was the day when my cleansing process began. During the following two weeks of our stay at Kwa Sizabantu the Lord almost constantly continued revealing my heart to me, pointing His finger at anything that defiled my soul and at things that I certainly thought had been "overgrown with grass"[30]. For example, He reminded me of a moment in my early childhood that I had completely forgotten. In my inner eye I saw a picture of our kitchen in Russia where I sat at a table with candies on top. My mother wanted to divide them among us six children. As she left the kitchen for a moment, I grabbed one candy and quickly hid it in my pocket.

"*You are a thief,*" the Lord told me in my heart. "*Do you understand you are a thief?*" Then, there was another incident and another one . . . . God showed me many instances in my life when I had taken something without asking or receiving permission. I would have never considered myself a thief and, more likely, would have been offended if anyone had dared to call me that. However, now, under God's definition of my behavior I could not resist. I remembered that as I worked at the clinic I took the bandages, cotton and alcohol that the nurses offered to me at the end of the month, since it was allowed to write off the remainders. To tell you the truth, in the former Soviet system, all of us, with rare exceptions, had been thieves. Everything belonged to the state then and was public property. Therefore, it was considered "ours". So, a person took everything that lay as a temptation in one's way without thinking that it had been stolen, or one invented the most pious excuses.

Next, I recalled a following scene: a locked room and I, still a little girl, looking through a keyhole in order to see what was going on inside. "*Do you remember this?*" The question resounded in my heart. Yes, I did remember. Oh, I wish I did not have to remember! Such things burn one with shame. Thus, step by step, the Lord walked me through my life beginning with my childhood. Only then did I realize how sinful a small child can be, although she may look like an angel from the outside. Time and time again, I was prompted to bring my sins into the light, and every time I felt ineffable relief after the confession. Finally, I was able to understand those I had seen on the post card and those who came out of the counseling rooms with faces enlightened with joy. Now I knew **what** was happening behind those doors. When it was difficult for me I comforted myself with a thought that yet a little longer and my cleansing would be finished. Silly me, I did not know that it was only the beginning.

The life at the mission station continued its course. Some guests were leaving and others arrived in their place. There were new encounters and acquaintances. What different kinds of people we saw there! And each of them had their own life with its difficulties and

---

[30] A Russian idiom, meaning that something has become completely forgotten and therefore, is taken care of and does not need any attention.

problems that eventually led one there on a quest for a solution. No one had asked anybody what congregation he or she was from and what denomination one belonged to. No one tried to convince anyone or force his personal opinion in faith matters on another. The same was preached to everyone and the main preaching theme was the problem of sin and the necessity of cleansing and sanctification. It must be said that you would rarely hear these topics discussed in traditional or nominal churches, where they are inclined to preach about God's mercy and love, forgiveness and salvation by grace. No doubt, it is just as correct, but there is also something, which makes us wretched and separates from God. This "something" is sin, which entered man's life almost from the beginning and made him a toy in Satan's hands. Perhaps, that is why the searching souls tend to be drawn towards sermons on sin and cleansing. They recognize their imperfection and impotence in the battle against sin. Who knows, but perhaps it was for the same reason that crowds of sinners went to the desert to listen to the fiery preaching of John the Baptist, who mercilessly exposed and detected sin?

All visitors at Kwa Sizabantu ate the same simple food that consisted of bread, maize cooked in water, beans or rice with green salad and some plain sauce. Once a week they cooked meat. In a long cue of people there stood judges, doctors, pastors, teachers, farmers, students, pupils, homemakers and workers. No consideration of national or social differences was made. From several hundreds to a thousand people were present at the station on any given day, and thousands arrived by cars, buses and trucks for Sunday services.

There, at Kwa Sizabantu, in that memorable 1986 we celebrated Christmas and the New Year 1987. For the first time in my life, I observed these holidays not in the midst of cold winter, but in the intense heat of summer. Right after the New Year, I was summoned to the office of Erlo Stegen. I had no clue what it meant, since we did not know each other personally until then. When at the appointed time my husband and I came to him, he said that I was the first Russian who had visited Kwa Sizabantu.

"We have already had Germans from Russia here more than once," he explained. But there had never been a real Russian. Zulu people would love to see what the true Russian looks like. Will you not agree to give them your testimony?"

Wow . . . ! This was like a bolt from the blue. I wondered when he was planning to do that and heard his reply, "You should be ready any time." It was amusing, but it seemed that at this mission station nobody knew how to plan anything. Everything happened spontaneously and indeed, it was necessary always to be prepared for anything. However, after a while, one got used to this and deemed such ordering of things as standard procedure.

A day after our conversation Erlo Stegen made an announcement from the pulpit that there was a Russian woman in the sanctuary who would give her testimony and everyone would hear how the Russian language sounded. It was good that I had forewarned my interpreter about it, so he got up without delay and came forward with me to the pulpit. I recall that I spoke not so much about myself as about Russia and the Russian people whom I loved and for whom I grieved that for more than seventy years they had lived in an atheistic political system deprived of God and the Good News of salvation. I also shared my dream of Kwa Sizabantu, which I had experienced seven years before in Estonia, about the postcard that came to life in my dream and about the voice from heaven that had replied to my wish to come here.

"It has been exactly seven years," I finished my speech, "and now, I am here at last." At these words, a woman from the back rows stood up abruptly and swiftly left the sanctuary. I did not pay attention to her at the time, but after the service, she approached and speaking in German, extended to me the same postcard with a question,

"Is this what you saw in a dream?"

"Yes, it is the same card."

"I must tell you, that exactly seven years ago my husband and I were here, at Kwa Sizabantu for the first time and he took this picture, which upon our return to Germany he published as a postcard. Today we arrived here for the second time and have only spent a few hours here," she continued with emotion. So you can probably understand why your story has touched me! We could not have even imagined that somewhere in a foreign country God would speak to a soul through this card we had published and then, miraculously, make it possible to come and meet each other! Today! It is exactly today! In the day of our arrival! You could have shared your testimony some other day earlier when we were not yet here, and we would not have known about it. I do not know what it means for you, but for my husband and me it is a real miracle . . . !"

The woman kept chatting on and on, but I wasn't listening anymore; and not that I did not share her joy. However, only a half an hour before I had experienced something tremendous, something that was meant to change my future life drastically. This is what happened.

As soon as I had finished giving my testimony and gone back to my seat, an unusual event took place. Suddenly there was a dead silence. I saw how the lips of the preacher were moving as he spoke the words of his sermon. I also observed the movement of my interpreter's mouth close by, but I couldn't hear a thing. All of the sounds in the sanctuary were somehow turned off and I was surrounded by a complete stillness.

But, out of the blue a clear voice spoke to me, *"Ludmila, you have just said that you love your people. Prove it to Me, that you really love them."*
"Prove it??!! To You . . . ?!" I asked again silently in my thoughts, having no doubts it was the voice of God. "But how would I do it?"

"Write a book."
"A book . . . ?! What book?!"
"Bring this sermon to your people in Russia."
"But, Lord! Surely, I am a doctor, not an author! I do not know how to write!"

"I will help you."
"But what kind of book will this be?"
"A book made up of the sermons and testimonies of Erlo Stegen."
"Yes, but I only speak Russian, and he preaches in other languages."

"Do not fear. I will help you . . . ."
The voice grew quiet just as unexpectedly as it had appeared, and I began hearing what was going on in the room yet again. My translator continued his work. Neither he, nor my husband or the people around us noticed anything or heard any kind of voice. Thus, I was given a task or rather a directive that I was expected to carry out.

I sat startled, trying to cope with the flood of thoughts. "How do I do this? How do the books get written? Why has the Lord chosen me for this task when I do not know German and there are so many Germans from Russia who speak perfect Russian? Why do I have to do this? Besides, I am simply unworthy of this charge! Now that my spiritual eyes have opened and I can see myself so sinful and pathetic – how can I ever begin to work on such a book?! No, I cannot! I have no right to! But wait, Ludmila. It was God, Who told you this! How can you disobey God if only a few days ago during that awful night of fighting the devil, you begged Him to give you a chance?! Only one chance . . . ! Can you really say 'no' to Him after all that?! It is good that there are sermons and testimonies of Erlo Stegen in German on audiotapes, which could be used for the book. Yes, but I do not know German. Until today, I always needed someone to interpret for me. How can I even undertake such work? Even if I use a reference book and a dictionary, I will not be able to do an exact translation and that means that an incorrect translation will go to Russia. No, that is impossible! It is too much of a responsibility! To give millions of people something that perhaps, was written incorrectly! No, I cannot do that! I just can't . . . !"

The picture of Kwa Sizabantu mission, which I saw in motion in my dream.

Exactly 7 years later I am standing at the same spot. My first trip to Republic of South Africa to Kwa Sizabantu. December 1986.

However, my heart clearly continued picking up the voice of God saying, *"Don't be afraid. I will help you."*

The next morning I came up to my translator and without going into details asked him to go to Erlo Stegen with me. Soon we saw him at the central building of the mission. As I approached him, I briefly stated that I wished for people in the Soviet Union to know about the revival in Africa, but did not say a word about my experience during the meeting yesterday. In reply, Erlo Stegen suggested translating a book *Gott unter den Zulus* (God among the Zulus) by a doctor of theology Kurt Koch. At that, our conversation ended and I returned to our hut with the sense that God had told me differently.

A month of our stay at Kwa Sizabantu drew to an end. Soon we boarded a large airliner taking us from a hot African summer to a cold European winter. After I returned home, I did not start working on the book right away because fear had gripped me once more that nothing would come of this. Humanly speaking, this project looked too unreal. If it was taking place in Russia or, at least, among Russian-speaking people, then it would be different. I could have asked, clarified, talked, inquired and so on about anything I needed. But here, the lack of a thorough knowledge of German language had kept my mouth shut. Moreover, I had not a slightest idea how to write a book and what rules and principles were involved in doing that. In general, the art of writing was all a dark forest[31] to me. I also had no one who could help or advise me in this. Moreover, thoughts of unworthiness bothered me. And so three months passed.

The spring drew closer and Erlo Stegen once more arrived in Germany with his coworkers. In one of the cities where I went with my husband for worship there was a black Zulu giving his testimony at the service. He said that all his life he had dreamt of becoming a medical doctor, but once asked at school by his teacher what he wanted to be, he suddenly for himself blurted out, "A preacher of the Gospel," even though he was a heathen at the time. Several years later when he studied in the medical faculty at a university, the Lord reminded him of his words, said in his childhood, and made him aware that this was his calling.

As the black brother was relating his story a forgotten picture from my own childhood came to surface, a school hallway and a question posed by two women teachers about what I wanted to be when I grew up. Then my semi-humorous answer, "An actress!"

And then the unknown voice that followed and said, *"An actress? No, **you will write books**."* It might seem strange, but in the past years I had not remembered it even once. It did not come to my mind at

---

[31] In Russian, this idiom literally translates: "as in a dark forest".

Kwa Sizabantu, when God gave me the order to write a book, by this confirming the calling revealed in my childhood. But now, in the days of the agonizing battle with my Self, this forgotten scene of the early years came back so vividly before my eyes during the service, that I almost shouted.

To my embarrassment I must admit, that in my head a thought darted, "So, I must write not only about someone else but also for someone else, all the time remaining in the shadow of the other name?"

Momentarily, I heard a question in my heart, *"And do you want to stand in the light of your own glory?"*

I was ashamed and could only ask, "Forgive me, Lord! Please, forgive me! Oh, I am really unworthy of undertaking the work."

Although, it seemed that I received a clear affirmation of my calling through this reminder, my torments continued. Whether it was a foretaste of what was to come, I know not. Nevertheless, my soul was trembling before something unknown. Therefore, days, weeks, and months went by in this continuous inner struggle. The thought that I could lose my last chance begged of God on that horrifying night troubled me. In an attempt to quiet the inward pain I tried to apply myself to something else and decided to work in the kitchen of the church we then attended. Later, I started sewing for the needs of the mission.

However, no matter what I did, the voice inside my heart kept repeating over and over again, *"This is not your calling. You are doing something different from what you are supposed to do. You flee from the face of the Lord like Jonah did."* It was very difficult, but I shared my experiences with no one.

Four months later, during one of the church services the Lord had said the following words in a wonderful way, *"Ludmila! You can do much for Me, but without Me during your entire life you would not accomplish the only important thing I have called you for."*

These words ended all my hesitation. Two days later as I was walking with my husband I told him what had lain on my heart as a stone for several months. There was no doubt that if I started working on the book it would mean that the load of our financial needs would rest on him, and not just for a couple of years, but possibly for the rest of our lives.

My husband received the news in an amazingly calm way. After a moment of quiet, he said, "If you are absolutely sure it is the will of God then, do what the Lord tells you to do." Since that time many years had flown by, but never did he take his words back – no matter how hard it has been for us at times – and I am grateful to him beyond measure for it.

In the book of Isaiah the prophet (8:11), the following words are written, *"For the Lord spoke thus to me with a strong hand."* When God speaks, you cannot escape. If once the voice of God reaches you, you cannot mistake the intensity with which it sounds in the language understandable to you. God's calling touches our heart by means of hearing or by way of circumstances, or in some other way. From the time of the calling, God comes claiming His right on you entirely, and from that point on your future life will be submitted to your calling.

The vision the Apostle Paul had on his way to Damascus wasn't some temporary fleeting emotional experience. It was something that gave him clear and certain direction. When He met with Saul on the road he was traveling, God said, *"For I have appeared unto thee for this purpose, to make thee a minister and a witness both of these things which thou hast seen, and of those things in which I will appear unto thee [. . .]"* (Acts 26:16 KJV). In other words, the Lord let him know the following, "All your life will be submitted unto Me, and you have no other goals, no other ambitions and desires besides Me, because you are My chosen vessel."

The response to this calling and choosing for service was his determined step to commitment and full obedience, *"I was not disobedient unto the heavenly vision [. . .]"* (Acts 26:19, KJV). I had to do the same thing and, in spite of all, have never regretted that decision.

I think everyone of us must find his or her place in life. In a spiritual sense, one discovers it only when one accepts the ministry given by the Lord. Joy comes from fulfillment of that for which one was created and born from above. The joy of our Lord Jesus Christ was grounded in the fact that He was carrying out the work for which He was sent to earth by His Father. If one receives a ministry from God, then one should be faithful to Him and value one's own life only as much as it helps to accomplish that ministry. And how rewarding it would be in eternity to hear these words, "Well done, My good and faithful servant!" and find out that you have completed all for which you were sent.

Oswald Chambers says this about the calling, "Our Lord never lays down the conditions of discipleship as the conditions of salvation. We are condemned to salvation through the Cross of Jesus Christ. Discipleship has an option with it - *"IF any man* [. . .]" Paul's words have to do with being made a servant of Jesus Christ, and our permission is never asked as to what we will do or where we will go. God makes us broken bread and poured-out wine to please Himself. To be "separated unto the gospel" means to hear the call of God; and when a man begins to overhear that call, then begins agony that is worthy of the name. Every ambition is nipped in the bud, every desire of life quenched, every outlook completely extinguished and blotted out, saving one thing only - *"separated unto the gospel."* Woe be to the soul who tries to put his foot in any other direction when once that call has come to him".[32]

Dear Reader! If God chooses you for a specific task by clearly revealing His will, then cast off all the other attractions and wholeheartedly devote yourself to this one calling.

---

[32] http://www.myutmost.org/02/0202.html. Taken from *My Utmost for His Highest* by Oswald Chambers. February 2nd . (c) 1935 by Dodd Mead & Co., renewed (c) 1963 by the Oswald Chambers Publications Assn., Ltd., and is used by permission of Discovery House Publishers, Box 3566, Grand Rapids MI 49501. All rights reserved.

Chapter 8

The Work On the Book

Revival Begins with Me

The name for the first book, *Revival Begins with Me,* had been on my heart even during our stay at Kwa Sizabantu. It had reflected in the best way not only what was told by Erlo Stegen from the pages of the book but also what was happening inside my own soul at the time of working on it. Several audiotapes in German language, which we brought back from Kwa Sizabantu, had served as a base material for the book. There Erlo Stegen related a story about his own quest for God during the first twelve years of his missionary service among the Zulu tribe and about the beginning of revival at Mapomulu. Then a few dozens of other tapes with his sermons were added to the first batch. Those tapes got into my hands by some wonderful ways from different people we have come to know through Kwa Sizabantu. Altogether, I listened to approximately one hundred and eighty tapes, recorded within the first twenty years since the revival had started. From this group I picked twenty major recordings, joining them with numerous clips and quotes from the rest of one hundred and sixty tapes. And no matter what housework I was doing – cooking, laundry, ironing, washing or cleaning – the small player had always hung on my chest containing the next audiotape. Once and again I had to stop and run for a dictionary to find an unfamiliar word. Simultaneously, this was the way I was learning German. After spending several months of listening to audiotapes, all the necessary material was selected, and equipping myself with dictionaries and reference books I began a written translation. But the work was moving extremely slow, so much so, that I took to despair. Exhausted, one day I fell on my knees and bitterly wept. "Lord!" I said, "with my pathetic knowledge of German it is quite impossible for me to accomplish this work. However, You have promised to aid me. Then, please, do help me, because I feel absolutely helpless . . . ." Soon after the words were spoken, the phone rang. I got up from my knees and lifted the receiver. There was a voice of a young brother who had translated for me at worship services and was with us at Kwa Sizabantu. "Ludmila," he said. "I felt prompted to call you and ask if you needed any of my help." Astonished I almost lost the ability to speak. Just a minute ago I cried out to the Lord for His help and His answer came right away, without any delay! Devoid of getting into details I related a story about the beginning of my work, about difficulties in connection with translation and my fears that due to the lack of language knowledge I could translate something incorrectly. I asked him not to tell anyone about it yet, because I wanted to keep it in secret until the book was completed. When he listened to all I had to say, he readily concurred to assist me, and we agreed that I would copy all the necessary material to new tapes and give them to him for translation. Then he would translate it vocally word to word and record it on another tape and after that, hand it to me so I could make a grammatically correct Russian translation. Our experiment did work out perfectly, and since that time, the work went a lot faster and smoother. By listening to German sentences with the following Russian interpretation I began not only getting a hang of the language, but at the same time started learning how to translate. My joy was endless, because I was truly seeing the hand of God in this work. As I listened to 180 audiotapes, I intuitively guessed the sequence of events, of which Erlo Stegen spoke, since he rarely mentioned any dates when things had occurred. It appeared not an easy task to combine and link together separate quotations and excerpts to create a consecutive account and convert a lively verbal speech into a precise shape of a book. I had to rewrite the whole book by hand three times! It took me over two years. When the manuscript was ready, the question arose about typing the text on a typewriter, an occupation which I had never learned before. It had no sense asking someone to do that for me, because not many could have made out my fine hand-writing. I needed to learn typing in a shortest time possible. It would be practically unreal to find a self-paced training book for touch-typing in Russian language during those years in Germany. So I began to pray, asking God to help me with this problem. Two weeks later I held in my hands the necessary manual for getting the skills on touch-typing, meant for a year of self-paced study. A whole year sounded incredibly long; therefore, I had to get back on my knees pleading with God to enable me to master this technique in a quickest time feasible. The Heavenly Father heard my prayer, and in two weeks I began typing my book in a "blind" manner. After two or three months I realized that it wouldn't work very well without a computer. We had to buy a used computer and my husband got absorbed into learning of its functions, after which he also started to teach me how to use it. I must admit, I have absolutely no clue in a way of equipment, and it wasn't easy to teach such a dim-witted student the details of computer typing. However, finally, it worked and I was able to transfer from a type-writer to a computer.

Months followed after months and it seemed there would be no end to this book typing. When, at last, it was finished, the question arose about having it grammatically checked. Having no funds whatsoever to pay someone for such a service, I buried myself under the volumes of textbooks and basically returned to a school course of

Russian grammar, beginning with the seventh grade. Five times I read and re-read the book, constantly finding grammar mistakes as far as syntax was concerned. When hopelessness again crouched upon me, the Lord sent a man who used to work as a teacher in Russia and after reading the book he made the final corrections.

The third year of work was coming towards the end, but we still had no means of publishing it. During all this time I often asked the Lord in prayer, where we would get the money for printing the book at a publishing company, and every time there came a reply in my heart, *"This is not of your concern. Do what you must and leave the rest up to Me."*

Besides, there was another problem in regards to transporting thousands of books to the Soviet Union, which at the time still remained a country "behind the iron curtain". Humanly speaking, it was practically impossible and therefore, we had no other way but to entrust it also into the hands of the Lord. God remained faithful to His word and continually granted His help. When the book was ready to be published, a widow of Kurt Koch, the Doctor in Theology, approached me during one of the church services, where she came from another town. Ten years ago her late husband wrote the first book about this revival in German language, called *Gott Unter Den Zulus.* "I accidentally found out", she said, "That you too have written a book about the revival. The fact is that my husband really wanted to visit the Soviet Union in his lifetime, but had never had an opportunity. He wished to finance the publishing of such a book in Russian, if it would ever have been accomplished. Therefore, after his death I want to fulfill his desire and pay for the publishing of the book you had worked on, through the means of the Bible-printing mission he founded."

I became flabbergasted with joy and amazement. God surely does not haste, but is never late. And there is nothing impossible for Him! When you think, you have come to the end of your wits; He had already prepared for you a way out.

Right at this time, Friedel Stegen was in Germany on his missionary trip. He was my counselor and the only one who knew the details about my work on this book. Many times I told him that I wanted to record Erlo Stegen's name as the author of the book, but every time he reacted negatively. "But, why?" I couldn't understand, "This book was made exclusively out of his testimonies and sermons. I added nothing on my own. Even though I did the work of putting things together, but all the contents are his!" Nevertheless, in spite of all of my arguments, the leadership of Kwa Sizabantu insisted on listing my name as the author of the book. I continued my fight, not wanting any future blame on misappropriating things that somebody else had said or done. "Please, finally, try to understand me," I struggled to persuade brother Friedel. "This book carries the name *Revival Begins with Me* for a reason. Revival begins with the one who tells about it. So, it starts with Erlo Stegen, not with Ludmila Plett! Why can't you recognize this?" Without answer, Friedel Stegen sharply got up, pointed at me with his finger and declared, "Revival begins **with you!**" Then, he turned around and left. I remained sitting there, tormented by conflicting thoughts.

After the conversation, I began earnestly praying, asking the Lord to reveal His will and to my surprise I was convinced to use my name. This was the end of my resistance. Erlo Stegen did not know about this work until the book was prepared for publishing.

It must be mentioned, that during all time this work went on, the Lord labored on me non-stop. Therefore, those years became a spiritual windmill for me, which mills slowly but fine. When my hand was writing the lines, telling how God cleansed the lives of different people from their sins, a question inevitably would pop up, *"And how does it look like in your life, Ludmila? Are you free from that sin? How is everything in this matter or in the other?"* The pictures of the past floated in my memory, showing that one or the other certain sin I had also committed and if it was not for real, then certainly, in my thoughts. At such moment, I stopped the work and would start writing a letter, bringing to light that, which was hidden in the dark until now. If I did not do that, all labor would come to a halt. It displayed in a way that all the right thought process ceased or I wrote pages after pages and subsequently tore them in pieces and threw away after reading. Day after day would pass like that. I worked, but the book did not increase by a single page. And only after I opened in confession things that the Lord's finger pointed at, the work would move forward.

I felt as if squeezed in the clamps from which I could not release myself. Never in my life were the sins of the past presented to me in such an astounding clearness as during those hard but blessed years. Never had I imagined myself such a repulsive sinner in need of forgiveness. Thus, for the first time in my life, being a Christian from birth, I deeply and sincerely repented my sins at the age of forty. Then I realized that there are no big and small sins before God. For Him, sin is sin. Therefore, things I considered insignificant in former times, arose before me like a mountain weighing heavily and oppressing my soul. I wept and wept in repentance and brokenness. There were instances when I wanted to cry out, "Save me, Lord, for I am perishing!" Perhaps, some may think of this as strange, obscure and even suspicious. But for me, undeniably, those were the most blessed years of all my life, during which I intimately deeply recognized my sinfulness. It will not be an exaggeration to say that the book *Revival Begins with Me* was literally bathed in my tears. Therefore, when people later asked me, why they could not read the book without tears, I usually replied, that possibly it was because of me first weeping over it.

During the cleansing process, God was so strict with me that at times I thought I would not last long. "Lord!" I would say in a prayer. "You are so demanding towards me that I cannot withstand it any longer." His reply did not linger, *"Can't you?"* I heard in my heart. *"But didn't you ask me for a revival? And now, when I am doing it, you say, you can't? Don't you know that I love the sinner but hate sin? Without cleansing there could be no revival."* That made me tremble and I was only able to answer, "Lord, forgive me! Please, go on. Do what You like. Don't stop . . . ." After going through such a spiritual windmill, I am absolutely and positively sure that it is impossible to carry on the way of your calling without deep repentance. In fact, it gives the beginning to our calling.

In that uneasy period I, as never before, understood the words said to Peter by his Lord, *"Most assuredly, I say to you, when you were younger, you girded yourself and walked where you wished; but when you are old, you will stretch out your hands, and another will gird you and carry you where you do not wish"* (John 21:18). Oh, if only we knew, how often we walk in our own ways, setting off to where we want! How few are the people who walk in the way where God leads them to places they do not want to go. In my youth, I recall a question that bothered me often: how many people get saved? Why is it written that: "[. . .] *narrow is the gate and difficult is the way which leads to life, and there are **few** who find it"* (Matt. 7:14)? What does the "few" mean? How many are there? Why did the disciples while listening to the warnings being given to them by Jesus once exclaimed in astonishment, *"Who then can be saved?"* (Matt. 19:25). But we, in contrast, do everything to make our paths easier and meticulously simplify them! And it is only because we do not want to walk the narrow way, for it is too narrow and thorny for us.

In the process of working on the first book, the Lord once showed me how the narrow way looked in His eyes. It was a wonderful dream, where I saw myself romping on a beautiful clearing. I picked flowers and braided wreaths, putting them on my head. Then, at the edge of the clearing I noticed a girl who told me, "Come here and I will show you where you should walk." When I approached her, she pointed at the spot where I needed to go down a slope. Then the girl disappeared, and I began descending at the appointed place, until I felt a firm support under my feet. It was a mountain path: on one side of it there was a vertical cliff, and on the other – precipice, leading down to a terrifying abyss. The path was so narrow, that you could only walk there by tightly leaning against the rock, while clenching to it with both hands. At a certain moment I slipped and turning back, looked down. There was a deep, bottomless chasm. At this sight I screamed with fear, "Lord, I knew that the path was narrow and dangerous, but I couldn't have even imagined that is was so narrow and so dangerous!" My body trembling and afraid to make another step, I stopped and suddenly heard a voice, "Don't be afraid!" Turning around I saw a man a few steps away from me, who said in comforting tone, "Don't be afraid. Keep going. We have passed through and, so will you." With these words he disappeared, but a thought crossed my mind, "What if I return . . . ?" I felt an urge to turn around and look at the place where I started descending to this path. As I did, I saw there was now a seething waterfall. Huge mass of water was falling down as a solid avalanche. There was no way back. My heart sank, and the words escaped my lips, "Lord, I won't make it!" At that instance a voice sounded, "Look upward!" As I lifted my eyes, far at a distance I saw a shining city on the top of a mountain. The same voice said, "This is your goal and you must get there."

When I awoke, I couldn't forget that dream and prayerfully asked, "Lord! Is it really a path leading to You, which is so narrow?! Is it true that You showed it to me the way it actually is?" In response to my questions, the Lord gave me a desire to visit one brother in faith. I had a feeling that I would get a confirmation of what I had seen. When my husband and I came to his house one evening, that brother greeted us at the doors. As he saw me, he exclaimed with gladness, "Ludmila! Let me you show you something. Somebody gave me some amazing pictures by an artist who only draws animals, but in such a way that it surpasses photographical images!" Entering a room, he picked up a large album from a table and flipping it randomly offered me the first opened page with a picture. As I looked at it, I gasped. There was an image of what I had seen in my dream that night. It was the exact vertical slope and that same narrow mountain trail. At the spot where I stood with the young man there were depicted two white mountain goats flattened against the rock, and to the left of them there was a rapid frothing torrent. The picture repeated what I had seen with such accuracy that I was speechless. Without going into any explanations, I asked to borrow the album with illustrations for a short time; then I went to a friend living nearby and asked him to make a photo, which I have kept now for many years. Looking at the mountain trail depicted there, one can imagine how dangerous and difficult the narrow path is.

Unfortunately, we live in such a time when very little is spoken about narrowness and difficulty of a Christian way. Widely spread theories of "Christianity of prosperity" and "guaranteed salvation", along with others that teach an easy approach to Christianity, insistently convince people how easy the way leading to salvation is. The wide way is defined as the way to destruction, which is followed by people of this world, but all believers will get saved in one manner or another. Equipped with such theories and doctrines, children of

God are not afraid to sin. The narrow path to eternal life is widened, simplified and lightened to such extent that Christians become no different than secular people. Anything goes and is allowed; only believe, become a member of a Christian congregation and attend worship services on a regular basis. The narrow way, of which the Word of God tells us, has become too narrow for us to understand it literally. This definition developed into more of an allegory rather than a reality of a Christian life. Freedom in Christ is replaced with universal "you-may-do-it-all" motto, and Christians easily allow themselves things that are unspeakable in the Holy Scriptures. One Russian Christian song says it amazingly true: "Straight are the gates and narrow is the way that lead to heaven, And there are only few who understand those words, and there are only few who follow it."

As you ponder about these words, it involuntarily reminds you about Christians of the Apostolic times, whose life, faith and love of God strike with their wholeheartedness. With readiness, they suffered hardships, accepted sorrows and sufferings up to the horrible deaths in fires, on crosses and in jaws of hungry lions, - all for the glory of the great Name of the Lord. They were despised, hated, persecuted, falsely accused, thrown into prisons, stoned and brutally murdered. In spite of all, they were prepared to pay any price to remain the light and the salt to the world around them that was decaying in its lusts. Those folks differed from others in all aspects: relationship between each other, their speech, behavior, manners in society and clothing. They weren't afraid to get belittled and ridiculed by atheists. In contrary, it was a great honor for them to suffer for their faith in Jesus Christ. How different they were from us, modern Christians, who try to imitate the life of this world out of fear to look old-fashioned and foolish! Many are ashamed to pray for food at a table out of fear to be mocked by others. We often speak about God's love towards us; however, we do not display mutual love and faithfulness towards Him. In common human hardships and difficulties we moan and groan, and grumble at God, filled with indignation as to why we, in particular, must endure this trial. Sufferings and death for Christ sound nonetheless as the echoes of the long gone past. And if we hear about something similar happening in the countries of the third world, we sigh with relief that, fortunately, we do not live there. Increasingly the definition of a "narrow way" is becoming to us some godly, but not completely understood and not really acceptable expression.

Guiding me through the cleansing process, the Lord has shown me His holiness several times. I will not forget one instance when I worked on composition of the eleventh chapter at the computer. With my lack of typing speed I spent on it almost two weeks. One time, when there were only two or three paragraphs left to the end of the chapter, my husband came home from work. "Ludmila!" he said briefly, walking into the room, "Enough of typing. We must quickly go to take care of a certain matter." I do not know why, but all of the sudden I exploded. Whatever you may say, but I am doing God's work and here is such impudence! "Can't you wait ten minutes?! " I exclaimed and sharply turned around to him. "I have only several lines left, and the chapter will be finished!" My voice sounded with obvious irritation. My husband was looking at me, not saying a word. I got uneasy feeling. When I turned back to computer screen, I gasped. For whatever reason the typed text of the whole chapter has vanished right in front of my eyes. The fruit of the two weeks of labor was destroyed in matter of seconds. In despair, I hid my face in my hands, repeating, "I have understood it, Lord . . . ! I have understood it all," and in reply, in my heart I heard the words, *Remember that no unclean thing can enter into **My** work.*

That was how God revealed His absolute holiness to me. The experience had become a bitter but a very important lesson, and whenever I forgot it, I unavoidably had to pay for it. It makes one wonder: how much activity goes on for God in our day and age in full certainty that this or that is really God's work. However, if what God had showed me was true and anything unclean cannot enter His work, then, whom do we mean to do it for, if it's done with irritation, revolt, wrath, disagreements, falsehood, contrivances and all kinds of lies? Aren't we guilty in labeling things as "God's work", where there is not even a trace of honesty, purity and holiness?

The work on the book *Revival Begins with Me* continued for three years, but the Lord does everything in His good time. He is not in a hurry and is never late. Whether it was a fortunate coincidence or God's plan – I know not. Nevertheless, when the book was brought to a publisher, radical changes took place in the former Soviet Union, and the huge state, which lived behind the iron curtain, ceased to exist, being split into separate, sovereign countries. This way all the doors flung open, and in December of 1989, first copies of the book were sent in parcels to Russia, Belarus, Moldova, Kazakhstan, Ukraine, Estonia, Lithuania, and Latvia, and so on. A year later, a large batch of eleven thousand books was transported there by truck. Later, the books were published again in the Russian city of Volgograd.

In as little as three-four weeks after sending out the first books we began receiving letters from readers, whose number constantly grew. At times, two hundred letters came in one day. Readers' reaction succeeded all expectations. Then, for the first time I received a spiritual insight of the tired and weary of searching for truth Christians. Not only believers wrote letters, but also the secular people, who didn't know God, including those, who were inveterate ardent atheists. After reading the book, some of them addressed the Lord with the words: "God, if You are like **this**, and if there is **such** Christianity, then I also want to be a Christian. Anything else does not satisfy me." In the archives of our mission, we keep many letters ranging from the most unnoticed church members to the pastors, missionaries and bishops, who shared how their hearts were touched through that, which was written in the book. They noted how they wept and repented in their sins; how they put things in order in their lives and changed the way they treated their relatives; how they returned what was stolen from the workplaces; how wives asked forgiveness from their husbands and how children humbled before their parents; how those who contemplated suicide, forfeit their fatal decision and found a new meaning of life with the Lord. To back up some of my statements here, I will quote from several letters:

Alexander from town of Zaporozhe: "I have just finished reading a book *Revival Begins with Me*. I am 55 years old. I am a journalist by trade. In my life I have read hundreds if not thousands of books and those were mostly of philosophical context. In the past I had been an fervent atheist, but fifteen years ago turned to God This book gave me spiritually a lot more than all of what I have read so far collectively. I thank God that this book got into my hands. While reading it, for the first time I realized how great my sins are. Please, pray for me, a sinner".

A father of Sh. family from Lithuania: "Dear friends! Our family thanks you from the bottom of our hearts for the book *Revival Begins with Me* you sent to us. Through this book I had come to faith in God, repented in my sins and accepted the Lord as my Savior. The same happened with my wife and our three children. We are so thankful to everyone who wrote the book, prepared it for printing and distributed it. Because of it, we awoke, asked forgiveness and found peace and comfort in the Lord. I have read it several times in a row and every time found something new for me. This book helps people to grow spiritually".

A pastor of a Russian-Ukrainian congregation from the state of Minnesota, USA: "I am positive that all the numerous readers of this book are grateful to you that you had it in your heart to write and publish it. We would be extremely happy to meet you personally, here, on American land, where there is so much labor among Russian and Ukrainian immigrants".

A brother B. from city of Karaganda: "I thank God that He fulfilled my dream and I was able to receive and attentively read the book *Revival Begins with Me*. Not only has its context touched my heart but all the useful examples, as well. I have been a Christian for fourteen years and all this time have been asking me a question: why are there so much resentment, arguments, quarrels and divisions, why does love go with hatred hand in hand? Instead of humility one finds pride and instead of bold preaching – cowardice and fear. Shouldn't we be the courageous followers or Christ with hearts entirely given up to Him?! Unfortunately, in our congregation there is always battle going on. A lot of things in our worship services are nominal and only render the established order. We faithfully get together at a certain time; listen to the Word of God for two hours; sing and pray, then just as promptly conclude the service and leave. Outwardly, we sometimes are joyous, but more often we go home with an empty and sad heart, which didn't receive healthy spiritual food, of which we all are in such a dire need. The book about revival supplied answers to many of my tormenting questions. Unfortunately, having now all the freedom one becomes spiritually lazy, falls into a spiritual slumber and self-consolation. But we must be watchful and sober! Oh, how much we do need a revival"!

Sister D. from city of Vladivostok: "I heartily thank you for the book *Revival Begins with Me*. The Holy Spirit performs an amazing work because of it, working wonderfully in the hearts of believers. One sister from our congregation read the book and being overwhelmed by deep conviction, urged other members to repentance and cleansing. Quoting paragraphs from the book in front of all, she cried, realizing her sinfulness, and the whole gathering wept with her. After the joint reading of this book during services, many members were spiritually nourished and became filled with desire to change their life. Our women were especially thankful. Advices given to us in the book, if you put them into practice, perform true miracles. The light of God's love entered into our families! May the Lord bless you in a special way for publishing this book".

Young 16-year old Christian from Armenia: "I serve the Lord in one small evangelical church in Armenia. After I read the book *Revival Begins with Me*, I want to say, this book was written under guidance and a power of the Holy Spirit. While reading God repeatedly deeply touched my heart, showing to me many things, of which I have not even thought before. Never have I imagined that there is so much dirtiness and filth in my life. At the same time, my pride began to speak and hardened me to the limit. I wanted to tear this book to thousands of pieces. However, later I had to admit to myself that in the past year I had not even thought of being a pure God's vessel and had not tried to be a genuine Christian. I started calling upon the Lord, and He, by His grace, broke through my "Ego", and created something new out of me. Oh, how thankful I am to Him for doing that!"

Sister M. from Ukraine: "The book *Revival Begins with Me* I read not with my eyes, but with my heart. I was literally shaken by its every page, and I cried. In this book, I recognized myself. It became a mirror of my faith and my walk before God. I comprehended what pity of a person I had been with my pride, arrogance, and haughtiness. I cannot even describe it all. You have to live through it. Now, I have no doubt that spiritual filth must be brought to light. I felt as if the Day of Judgment had already begun for me. I had no rest. I lost my sleep. But I am grateful to the Lord that I could experience it yet here, on earth, and feel God's presence and His holiness".

Brother G. from city of Kharkov: "I only want to praise and thank God for such a necessary book. As I received it from you and read it, I passed it on to the members of our congregation. It seemed as if a bomb had exploded! While reading, many started seeing their lives with different eyes. That way, the whole congregation awoke, which we, the preachers, had not been able to achieve for several years".

Brother D. from Zaporozhe: "We need your book *Revival Begins with Me* as air for breathing. It is like a mirror for us, Christians, where you can see if you are still in faith and if you know God or not. When I was reading it, I could not remain indifferent to my life. The same was happening to other people whom I gave the book to read. All of them have decided to correct and change their lives. There has not been a similar book and, perhaps, there will be none like it, which would be able to wake sleeping Christians up. We deeply humble ourselves and thank you for truly good news, which this book had brought us".

Brother B. from Ural area: "Brothers and I have seriously studied the book *Revival Begins with Me* that you sent us, and have concluded that it is not only useful, but rather necessary. Therefore, we kindly ask you to send us several more books for our missionary courses. It will be of great help for our future missionaries. We look forward to your future publications of similar books".

Sister N. from town of Aktyubinsk: "After reading the book about revival, I just cannot refrain from writing to you. For us, Christians, who had grieved the Lord and quenched the work of the Holy Spirit, this book is like a balm. Every believer should read it, and not just read it, but also digest it in our spiritual stomachs, so that those treasures stay with us for the rest of our lives. While we are spiritually asleep, we are not able to bring fruits. Speaking this way, I, first of all, mean myself, but there are a lot of those like me".

Brother from city of Kostopol: "Here, there are many believers belonging to most different confessions, but majority of them are Christians only by name, because their actions tell otherwise. They are more of an obstacle, than a blessing to others. We evangelize in various places. People come to listen, agree, but only few turn to the Lord. God cannot use us, because we, who carry the Good News to others, are unclean vessels. In short, we are in need of revival: first and foremost – in our Christian churches and later, - among unbelievers. That is why the book *Revival Begins with Me* is so important and appropriate in our time".

Brother G. from town of Sumy: "Your book about revival causes great interest among believers just as well as among non-believers. Many wish to read it. They talk about it, discuss it, and ask about it everywhere. In order to borrow it for reading, there are long waiting lists that usually go on for months. And no one who reads it remains indifferent. Nowadays, Christianity needs a revival, needs a victory over "Self" and over sins, and over devil's power. It needs what is written in the book of Acts".

A letter from city of Lviv: "The one who is writing to you is a sinful atheist and a spiteful enemy of God. Not paying attention to my unwillingness and rejection, one Baptist preacher gave me the book *Revival Begins with Me* to read. Today I have finished my reading and rush to write this letter to you. In the beginning the book touched me, but later, I was reading it with cold indifference and unbelief. However, as I was getting to an end of my reading, my heart suddenly began to tremble. Now I have no other desire as to repent, cleanse, be sanctified and wholly belong to the Lord".

From the town of Divnogorsk in Eastern Siberia we received the following: "In some churches of our town, including the one I belong to, pastors along with other elders have determined to get on a way of cleansing, and the results of it are obvious. Those brothers do not tell anyone about their decision, but the church members go to them for counseling without any kind of urging, which had never happened before".

Sister L. from Tashkent: "After reading the book *Revival Begins with Me* I immediately turned to my unbelieving ex-husband, asking him for forgiveness. And even though, he chose not to forgive me, I forgave him. Unfortunately, he is a staunch atheist. This book helped me to realize my own guilt before God and my ex-husband. It helped me overcome hatred; become a better person; learn how to love and better understand the Lord and His teaching".

I remember well a letter from a non-Christian mailwoman. She wrote that feeling absolutely despondent, she made her mind to commit suicide. Hardly being able to think clearly any longer, she was automatically putting mail into mailboxes for the last time, when suddenly her foot stepped on something. She looked down and saw a yellow book on a floor of the building entrance. Picking it up she returned home with all intensions to carry out her decision. But somehow, not really knowing why, she opened that book and could not close it until finished reading the last page. It was a sunrise, when

Christ entered into a shattered life of this woman. That's how another human life was saved, and one more soul has found her Savior. On the yellow cover of the book there were the words: *Revival Begins with Me . . . .*

Another girl informed us that once she was walking towards a river with the firm resolution to take her life by drowning. Unexpectedly, her foot tripped at something. As she looked on the road, the girl noticed a small book with yellow cover right in front of her. The name drew her attention. *Revival Begins with Me* — she read and with a bitter smile thought to herself, that revival will never be able to begin with her. Although, moved by curiosity, she still bent down and picked up the book. Flipping through several pages she suddenly stumbled at words addressing those who nurture thoughts about suicide in their hearts. Not being able to stop, she spent many hours reading by the river. Then, the girl got up and decisively went home. And so yet another life was saved.

I cannot forget the contents of one more letter, where the elders' committee of a large congregation in Russia expressed their gratitude for books about revival. After reading them, all young people who rebelled against the church authorities, came back acknowledging their fault and asking for forgiveness in organizing a spiritual mutiny. The brothers wrote with emotion, that where all their efforts to make youth listen to reason kept failing, God was able to use the books in a most incredible way.

Such letters were countless; therefore, I will limit myself to several more brief quotes:

"[. . .] I read this book on one breath. It is really astounding".

"[. . .] There are many doctrines in Christianity and a lot of confessions, but for me personally and for the hearts of other people, this book has become a stream of living waters and the source, which is our Lord Jesus Christ".

"[. . .] I have no doubts whatsoever, that God Himself put it on Ludmila Plett's heart to compose this wonderful book and give it to Russian Christianity. As I was reading it, I understood for the first time that I really needed such "chewed over food" as a little toothless child".

"[. . .] I am sure, God saw a spiritual hunger of our Russian nation, and therefore, He found such people abroad, through whom He was able to help us".

"[. . .] If only every Christian had read this book, he would see himself as in a mirror and be ashamed of many of his thoughts and actions".

"[. . .] Our Russian nation is like a parched, dried out soil, that hasn't been irrigated with living water for a long time".

"[. . .] My greatest desire is that our Russian people received millions of copies of these books".

"[. . .] This book about revival is a balm for our sick souls. It is like a current of fresh air for us".

"[. . .] This book completely revolutionized my life, although I have only had it for 24 hours. Now I know how I must live".

"[. . .] I have read a lot of spiritual literature, but this book, as no other, changes people radically, making them absolutely new".

'[. . .] This precious, honest and unsophisticated book penetrates to the depth of heart. It helps all seeking souls. But it won't help those, who are content and don't search for anything".

As I was reading letters, I was becoming more and more convinced that it was the voice of God who urged me to take up a pen. These lines filled with joy and gratitude gave me strength and prepared for what I would be experiencing much later and what I will tell you in a short while.

Only a few months passed since the book *Revival Begins with Me* was published, when we started receiving invitations from churches and congregations of various towns of the former Soviet Union, asking us to come together with Erlo Stegen to lead the evangelizing services. In early nineties it was not an easy task, since the entry of foreign evangelists and missionaries was extremely limited and strictly controlled by the Department of Internal Affairs. However, nothing is impossible for the Lord, and in the summer of 1991 we received permission for our mission team to enter Moscow and Kiev. Till the end of my days I will not forget this first missionary trip to my Motherland. The worship services were being held not just in various churches but in the parks, at the stadiums, in private apartments packed with people, and even in a forest in the outer edge of Moscow, where believers came from all different places of our immense country. There I even met my countrymen from Far East.

This trip concluded with the conference of presiding brothers of different congregations and churches of Moscow and its suburbs. They asked Erlo Stegen to tell about the beginnings and the future development of the revival in South Africa. Due to having no knowledge of the Russian language, he wasn't aware of what was recorded in the book and, therefore, he basically repeated its context almost word for word, so that the attendees started to be indignant, wishing to hear something new, which wasn't written in the book. As for me, it gave me a great joy, since during the trip I had already heard some people say that perhaps, the book was partly fancied by me for the sake of the work of art's beauty. Erlo Stegen's story that was told in Moscow, his testimony, and answers to the questions of those present, all proved that there were no "add-ons" and fantasies on my part.

After that trip, the other ones followed. In a course of ten years we visited many cities in Russia and Ukraine, in particular: Volgograd, different towns in Northern Caucasus, Novosibirsk, Kemerovo, Ryazanskaya region, Tolyatti, Samara, Sumy, Berdichev, Simferopol, Sevastopol, Yalta, etc. Later we were invited to a Russian community of immigrants in USA, where we have gone to see congregations of a range of cities and states. I was also fortunate to make a trip to Israel, being invited there by some Jewish people who emigrated from the Soviet Union earlier. Everywhere we appeared, we met up with the ecstatic readers, whose lives underwent great changes performed by God after the book reading.

During the mission trip to the Siberia towns in 1993 (from left to right: Erlo Stegen, Ludmila Plett, translator Benno Neufeld, Lidia Dube, Friedel Stegen)

Meetings and contacts with hundreds and thousands of believers from various churches and confessions confirmed time and again, how many Christians were not satisfied with their superficial, formal and, alas, often Pharisee-like Christianity, which all came down to outward appearance of worship. People were thirsty to understand the reason behind their stagnation and lack of spiritual growth. I think, the book *Revival Begins with Me* had become something like a "discovery of America" for many of them, because it made it clear to them what hindrance the sins, which were not put in order, created in a spiritual development of a person.

There was an opinion expressed in many of the letters from readers that the book literally became a "bomb" in sin matters, which caused a real spiritual revolution in minds of Christians. Unfortunately, it is too rare, when they speak about sins from the pulpits, or otherwise it is too softly spoken, usually in a common vague form of a sentence, without calling things their true names. Therefore, God's people are not afraid to sin. The product of it all is a superficial Christianity, loss of first love towards God, spiritual apathy and laziness, moral degradation of Church and absence of spiritual growth among its members. A lot of Christians couldn't care less about it. They are pretty much content with their regular attendance of the church services; with membership in congregations; with carrying out a certain ministry within and participation in different church activities. However, there are such people who understand that being a child of God means a lot more and goes beyond the bounds of external worship. They seek to be close to God, His guidance and personal contact with Him, and in their quest they rarely find someone to identify with. They are told that they should not worry because they have all they need and therefore, must be happy and thank the Lord, being fully convinced in their salvation. Although they don't always easily get convinced and their souls continue to be tormented, trying to comprehend what is missing and becoming discouraged and totally despaired.

All the time I had been thinking that such believers were a singular kind and therefore, was utterly amazed, as I ran into hundreds and thousands of those souls. They wrote to me that when they had read the book, they finally found answers to many disquieting questions and asked for explanation of something that wasn't clear to them. Thus, the idea of writing the next two books was born, both of which, in a similar fashion to the first one, were based on sermons, testimonies and stories told by Erlo Stegen. They have also included the answers to the questions and issues brought up by readers of the first book.

᪣᪣

Chapter 9

Through Gloom of Temptations and Problems.

And again, there were tapes, tapes and more tapes to sort through . . . . And again, the sheets of paper covered with a small writing of translated text one by one laid on my desk. Now there was no need in having the interpreter's help, and the work progressed quicker. The chapters followed the chapters. Readers of the first book without knowing it, actively helped me to sort out the right material by asking numerous questions in their letters, sharing their sorrows and grief they met while searching for truth. They told about the problems in their congregations and churches, being indignant about the man-made rules existed there and describing all kinds of unfairness and lawlessness concealed under the mask of piety. While reading these letters, not once my heart bled. I wanted to cry out of pity, sympathy and pain. Reluctantly, Chapter 8 from the book of Ezekiel came to my mind and the terror that the prophet experienced when the Lord showed him the abominations committed in the house of God and even before the sanctuary of the Lord.

I am writing about it now only to make clear why the second book was written the way it was written, and why it was called *Time for a Judgment to Begin with the House of God*. It mirrored cry for help, tears, sorrow, despair and discouragement of hundreds and thousands of believers longing to serve the Lord, but every time pushing against a sharp picket fence, stakes and thorns of "unchristian" Christianity.

The work on the second book took half as much time as the first book – only one and a half years, during which the fierce devil's attacks never slowed down, as well as the continuous resistance from different people. In fact, they were mostly the ones I had never expected it from. It was a harsh time, and not once I had thought of those three years, when I worked on the first book, when hardly anybody knew anything and, therefore, did not interfere. Then, the battle went on mostly with my own ego, as the Lord led me through process of cleansing. And He does not operate like a man, *"For He bruises, but He binds up; He wounds, but His hands make whole"*[33]. Even in the very difficult moments, when He was especially strict with me, time and again I was being convinced that His "[. . .] *mercy triumphs over judgment"*[34]. You will not find such quality among humans. Far from being perfect, they, nevertheless, mercilessly judged my words and deeds in all that did not fit their understanding of a "right" ministry. If

---

[33] Job 5:18, NKJV
[34] James 2:13, NKJV

one experiences something of a sort, it is easy to understand King David in his trial, when he committed sin by counting people of Israel and had to choose one out of three plagues, offered to him by God – seven years of famine, three months of being chased by his enemy, or three days of the wrath of God. David chose the last plague, saying, "[. . .] *I am in a great strait: let us fall now into the hand of the Lord; for his mercies are great: and let me not fall into the hand of man*" (2 Sam.24:14). How many times I have attested these words to be very true, experiencing severity of people's judgments, after I "fell into the hands of men"!

Just as in the case with the first and later, the third book, the second book was used by the Lord to continue the work He began in me. Nothing of what was written there passed my heart by. Again and again He posed questions to me, "*Ludmila, how are you doing here? And how does it look with this or that?*" During those years I didn't understand many things, and therefore what was happening to me seemed like a torture of my soul. However, now, so many years later, reaping the fruits of His labor I can only thank God for what He had done then.

And in the meantime, letters from the readers of the first book kept coming, forcing me to work almost without stopping for rest, because of the heart-rending groans and cries for help expressed in them. For many months I spent eight to ten hours per day without getting up from my chair, entering all my notes into the computer and following up with correction. As a result, when the book was given to a publisher I experienced a nervous breakdown with a dynamic disorder of blood circulation to my brain. Once when I got up in a morning, I lost my balance and fell down. I began intense vomiting. Doctors couldn't determine what was wrong with me and suspected a brain tumor. But none of the physical and x-ray check-ups proved it. Weeks after weeks didn't bring any changes. Walking with great efforts, I mostly kept to my bed so that one Christian sister from a distance took a vacation and came over to take care of me. Due to experiencing much of hostility from some of my formerly close friends while working on the second book, I felt a heavy burden on my soul that caused me to despair. "Lord, what did I not do right? Why did this happen? Was it that You didn't will for me to work on the second book?" I called quietly, staying in bed. This last thought had especially bothered me. Is it really that the second book is only a fruit of my human zeal, where the name of God isn't glorified?! Have I really made a mistake? And if so, then what? What will this be in the eyes of the Lord and in the light of eternity? Wouldn't this be a living judgment for me?

No one knew about my inner struggle. I did not share it with anyone, not even my husband or counselor. Just the Lord knew everything and only He was able to answer my questions in an amazing manner. One time, when the sister who took care of me was cooking dinner, a woman, also from our congregation, visited us. When they both peacefully carried a conversation, something extraordinary, which I had never had felt, happened to me. Lying on my bed with eyes closed, I suddenly sensed an inner push. It seemed as if something inside of me separated from the rest. It was as if I disengaged from by body and started quickly ascending upward. In some unusual way I saw myself still in bed and the two sisters sitting next to me who, without noticing anything, went on with their serene talking. Was it my soul or my spirit, but it kept its swift rising amid some grayish fog, when a thought pierced my mind, "Now I will stand before the Lord and will stand before Him empty-handed!" All that I have achieved during over forty years of my life dimmed in the blink of an eye and lost its meaning. All blessings I experienced along with gifts and talents had no more value to them. Everything turned into nothing. A terror gripped me. I was sure that in a short time I would stand before God "empty-handed". The definition "empty-handed" suddenly gained such unbelievably deep sense that I screamed with fear. In this moment I heard a voice, *Do not fear. You will not stand with "empty hands". Look there.* As I looked in a pointed direction I saw two shining dots in a distance that quickly moved towards me and soon stopped right in front of my eyes. Those were the two books: *Revival Begins with Me* and *Time for a Judgment to Begin with the House of God*. By means understandable only in eternity, it became clear that they were the only precious things in my life that will allow me to stand before the Lord not "empty-handed". Joy, peace and quiet welled up in my heart. In the same instance my moving upward stopped, and I began descending. Again, in my body I felt inner push, and found myself lying in bed. The words of sisters' conversation reached my ears. They chitchatted about things, dress fashions, - simply about worldly matters. The first thought that carried through my mind was: "How could they talk about it?!" That which they busied themselves with seemed so pathetic, shallow and meaningless on the background of eternity I had just encountered, that I could hardly keep myself from crying out to them, "How can you. . . ?? Oh, how can you . . . ??" With an effort I opened my eyes. "Oh, we thought you were sleeping!" they immediately turned to face me, "You were resting so quietly, it seemed you were in a deep slumber."

I did not answer. There was no desire to talk or to speak about my current experience. I softly shut my eyes, trying to recollect in my memory the sights I have just seen. It was hard and almost impossible to describe them with human words. One thing that deeply etched in my mind and became completely apparent was that in all matters the eternity had a totally different system of measurements and evaluation of values.

Such a wonderful Lord's response for agonizing questions of my soul absolutely shattered my doubts and gave strength to endure all rebukes, reproaches, sarcasm and numerous accusations, which poured from all sides in connection with the publishing of the next book. Even its name, *Time for a Judgment to Begin with the House of God*, had become a stumbling block, causing fear and rejection in many Christians.

"How can you even write such a thing?!" indignantly exclaimed some of them. "It is clearly said in the Word of God, that believers do not *"come into judgment"*[35]"!

"You destroy faith in people with your books!" echoed others. "God forbid, they get into the hands of the world! Can't you understand that with your book you shame our good name in front of all worldly people!"

"Why did you make known all the negative sides of our Christian churches?" scolded the third group, "Now the unbelievers will not even want to hear anything about God!"

I tried not to justify myself and not to explain anything. These souls could not have known that heavens looked at it completely different. Plus, the letters from readers testified the opposite reaction. Just to confirm it, I will quote the excerpts from some of them:

A Pastor from Rostovskaya region wrote: "Dear brothers and sisters! Thank you for the books *Time for a Judgment to Begin with the House of God* you sent to me. Now I read this book during our services before the whole congregation. It shocks and deeply touches my heart personally, as well as the hearts of other church members. Thank you for doing so much for our suffering, spiritually starving people".

A preacher from Poland: "I am so thankful to the Lord and to you for the book *Time for a Judgment to Begin with the House of God*. For me personally, as well as for many other ministers of God this book had been a great blessing. I finished reading it, but have a desire to read it again. It is very enlightening and provokes deep thinking. I thank God that by means of this book, He can so clearly and frankly speak to our hearts. Even though I too preach the Word of God, while reading, I had come to a lot deeper and better understanding of many things. When I share something from what I had read, people desire to read it for themselves".

A sister E. from Ukraine: "In the book *Time for a Judgment to Begin with the House of God* one can find not only shocking and condemning facts for us Christians, but also precious teachings, which

---

[35] John 5:24, NKJV

we really need. As you read it, it frightens you, for it seems that the day of judgment is already here for you. However, such fear generates the desire to bring your life in order without delay. The words of Apostle Peter, which became the name of the book, taken from his first epistle to Christians scattered to various places on the globe, express the context of the writing in the best way. They are like a shout, which warns about danger us, the spiritually sleeping lukewarm Christians of the last times".

A letter from Moldova: "I cannot find worthy words to express my thanks to you for sending the book *Time for a Judgment to Begin with the House of God*. It passes through many hands, and if you could only see how brethren completely change after reading it, and become a blessing for others."

In response to my accusations about non-believers who will not want to hear anything about God after reading about shortcomings and negative sides of Christianity, I can say that strangely enough, most of those who turned to God were particularly among the readers of the second book. Maybe it is hard to understand for us, Christians, but it is true. I cannot copy here all the letters of the new believers, but will provide at least one to confirm it. I received this letter while writing this chapter. It came from a sister living in Finland: "For the glory of God I want to tell you how I turned to God and became a Christian through the book *Time for a Judgment to Begin with the House of God*. It happened when I still lived in Russia. I read this book aloud to my grandmother who was a believer. That which I read affected me so much that I simply could not live the same way as before any longer. Of course, it was the Lord. I do not remember that any other ministers influenced my repentance, but unmistakably the Lord called me through that book. By His grace, I responded to His call . . . ."

As you see, God looks at things quite differently than we, human beings. Indeed, this is true as it is written, "[. . .] *My thoughts are not your thoughts, nor are your ways My ways," says the Lord. For as the heavens are higher than the earth, so are My ways higher than your ways, and My thoughts than your thoughts*" (Isa. 55:8-9). One more letter endorses the truth of these words: "Just a year ago I held in my hands a wonderful book *Revival Begins with Me*, which deeply touched our hearts, opened our spiritual eyes on shocking reality of our lukewarm, nominal Christianity and became a really vital and necessary help for our souls. This book we read during our church services and discussed a lot. Nobody was left unmoved. And now we read its sequel – the book *Time for a Judgment to Begin with the House of God*, which we receive with broken hearts. No doubt, that both of these books were written under God's blessing".

After an amazing revelation that God gave me about the books my health began improving, and in two weeks, although feeble, I was still able to go on the next missionary trip to Russia – to Northern Caucasus and city of Volgograd.

As time went by, Satan increased his attacks. He obviously was retaliating for all the given blessings, and, in fact, more often used Christians and even my closest friends for that purpose. That, in particular, cut into my inner strength causing distress. By the way, long time ago I understood that if devil wants to destroy someone spiritually, he exploits people dearest to your heart, even those whom you especially trust and usually rely on. Here he acts unmistakably, striking at you with the heavy and crushing blows. Same thing happened to me. At the time, when after a short break I started working on the third book, Satan went forward into a vicious assault. Those were the most distressing moments of crisis, when he wheeled out all of his heavy artillery. It seemed that the sky clouded, the earth trembled and there was not even a single ray of hope. In one of such minutes of despair, having no strength, I inwardly screamed, "Lord! I cannot do that anymore! I will stop working on this book, and will never write again!" Suddenly I heard a calm reply in my heart, "*Very well. Quit. Only know, that the blood of all these souls I will require from your hands*". Instantly, by some mysterious spiritual vision I saw the following picture: hundreds of thousands, if not millions of people stood in front of me, filling up the vast space and forming a living human stream, hiding behind the horizon. I was terrified. If God requires the blood of only one soul of my hands, I will perish. But what will happen, if the blood of all who stood before me falls on my head?! No . . . ! No . . . ! A thousand times no! This should never happen!

This shock brought me out of despair and spiritual crisis. Now I knew that I must write no matter what, paying attention to no one, including the devil himself. So the work on the third book continued, though Satan in every possible way attempted to stop it. There were times when while sitting at my desk and still holding a pencil I virtually felt disengaged and fell asleep. Often, having no strength to fight against an overcoming sleepiness, I got up from my chair and moved toward a near standing sofa to lie down. However, as soon as I did that, I immediately heard the authoritative voice, "*Get up! Get up immediately and write again! Be a conqueror in this temptation and the enemy will flee*". I jumped up from the sofa as if bitten by a snake and almost swaying walked to my desk, and as soon as I took a pen, the sleepiness was gone. And I optimistically wrote on, marveling about a sudden change of my conditions and forgetting about sleep and fatigue.

The Lord had continuously been giving me His assistance in this work sending my way, in the most amazing manner, the necessary and the best fitted to the subject of the book sermons of Erlo Stegen. I would still be finishing one chapter when there had already been gathered enough material for the next one. Therefore, on one hand the devil did everything possible to stop the work or at least to hinder it, but on the other, I constantly felt God's presence and His help. The months were flying by.

The stream of readers' letters with orders for the first and second books was increasingly growing, so that we were barely able to satisfy all of them. Certainly, it gave us much joy and inspired confidence that the Lord was behind all this work. Nevertheless, my heart wrung with foreboding of something that was slowly but inevitably coming on. It's great that I didn't know a thing of what exactly was waiting for me; otherwise, I would not have finished the third book. You can't stop wondering how the Lord measures everything up, allowing only so much in full accordance to what you are capable of enduring. Day by day, giving us strength to overcome the difficulties of today, He tempers and thus, prepares for the approaching new sorrows.

During that period, God had more often spoken to my soul by means of His Word. At times, when I was engulfed by a feeling of incomprehensible trouble and disturbing anticipation of something awful, I got up from the table, went down on my knees and prayerfully opened the Bible, reading a passage to where my gaze fell. Once, with a trembling heart I read the following words, *"Then the word of the LORD came to me, saying: "Before I formed you in the womb I knew you; Before you were born I sanctified you; I ordained you a prophet to the nations." Then said I: "Ah, Lord GOD! Behold, I cannot speak, for I am a youth." But the LORD said to me: "Do not say, 'I am a youth,' For you shall go to all to whom I send you, And whatever I command you, you shall speak. Do not be afraid of their faces, For I am with you to deliver you," says the LORD"* (Jer. 1:4-8). When I was reading this passage of Holy Scripture, an image of an old granny, a friend of my youth, floated up in my memory, of which I had written before, and her words that stuck in my soul, "The Lord revealed to me during one prayer that He had chosen you from your mother's womb for a special ministry." At that time it perplexed me, but now it made me reflect on in. I could not have said as Jeremiah that I was still very young, since I was already in my forties. However, I had another obstacle – I was a female, and therefore, must be silent. Furthermore, speaking to Jeremiah, the Lord said, *"See, I have this day set you over the nations and over the kingdoms, To root out and to pull down, To destroy and to throw down, To build and to plan."* (Jer. 1:10). Amazingly, four times it says here about destruction and only twice, about building up. I wonder how Jeremiah felt when God firmly continued, *"Therefore prepare yourself and arise, And speak to them all that I command you. Do not be dismayed before their faces, Lest I dismay you before them. For behold, I have made you this day A fortified city and an iron pillar, And bronze walls against the whole land— Against the kings of Judah, Against its princes, Against its priests, And against the people of the land. They will fight against you, But they shall not prevail against you. For I am with you," says the LORD, "to deliver you"* (Jer. 1:17-19). It sure was an amazing calling and a striking promise! From henceforth Jeremiah did not belong to himself. His life was placed on God's altar and as a result he forgot what it was like to have peace and calm. There were only a few, who, while longing to help their people, suffered so much humiliation, insults, torments and disdain, as Jeremiah did. This was the man, who undividedly loved his people; suffered with them; mourned over their bitter fate, which they bore for their infidelity and apostasy from God. As I was thinking about it, my own tribulation, suffering and reviling seemed petty in comparison with those experienced by Jeremiah, and the great herald of God was becoming much more precious and dear to me.

Some other time, when it got very difficult because of uncontrollable reproaches and accusations, I knelt again before God and opened my Bible. Right in front of me was the words, as if etched, *"Indeed they shall surely assemble, but not because of Me. Whoever assembles against you shall fall for your sake. Behold, I have created the blacksmith Who blows the coals in the fire, Who brings forth an instrument for his work; And I have created the spoiler to destroy. No weapon formed against you shall prosper, And every tongue which rises against you in judgment You shall condemn. This is the heritage of the servants of the LORD, And their righteousness is from Me," Says the LORD"* (Isa. 54:15-17).

I froze, as if blow-stricken. Was it really the Lord speaking to me personally? But who am I that He would stand up for me like that?! I wanted to drop before Him face down and keep crying and crying. Tears welled in my eyes as I was reading chapter 54 of the book of Isaiah from the beginning. Every word spoke to my heart, becoming alive and pouring a precious balm on its wounds. It seemed as if everything was written for me and about me, *"Fear not; for thou shalt not be ashamed: neither be thou confounded; for thou shalt not be put to shame [. . .] For the mountains shall depart, and the hills be removed; but my kindness shall not depart from thee, neither shall the covenant of my peace be removed, saith the LORD that hath mercy on thee. O thou afflicted, tossed with tempest, and not comforted, behold, I will lay thy stones with fair colors, and lay thy foundations with sapphires [. . .] In righteousness shalt thou be established: thou shalt be far from oppression; for thou shalt not fear: and from terror; for it shall not come near thee."*[36]

---

[36] King James Version.

No one, not even the most tender and loving mother could have comforted me as much as God did. It was His grace that I had not deserved; and it was pity, understanding and compassion of the One, Who Himself suffered greatly. My heart melted from the intimacy and love of God. During such moments one especially treasures and understands the psalmist, who recorded his glorious phrases on the pages of the Holy Scripture, "*Unless the LORD had been my help, my soul had almost dwelt in silence. When I said, My foot slippeth; thy mercy, O LORD, held me up. In the multitude of my thoughts within me thy comforts delight my soul*" (Psalm 94:17-19). There isn't anything comparable to the sweetness of comfort, which is received in the close communion with the Lord. Once you experience it, you will seek that closeness again and again, not being satisfied with something less.

The more I worked on the third book, the more refined and furious were getting the enemy's attacks. "Who do you think you are? He whispered in my mind. Who do you imagine yourself? What are you making yourself a hero of our time?! Imagine – such a master writer! You are just an imposter, who covers up her desire to show off behind the fancy words of supposedly fulfilling God's will". Those whisperings instigating doubts had so much exhausted me that I once pleaded God not being able to tolerate it any longer, "Lord! Give me affirmation that this, what I do, is really Your will. Please, answer me, so that devil does not have an opportunity to torment my soul. If possible, use Your Word for it". Then, I picked up the Bible and prayerfully opened it. I almost gasped with amazement as I read the following words, "*Calling a ravenous bird from the east, the man that executeth my counsel from a far country: yea, I have spoken it, I will also bring it to pass; I have purposed it, I will also do it*" (Isa. 46:11). I do not know how this passage of the Holy Scriptures is interpreted by the theologians, but for me it sounded as a personal address; as the Lord's reply to my request; as a confirmation to what tormented me and what devil had used as his weapon to assault. "***Calling a ravenous bird from the east, the man that executeth my counsel from a far country***". Literally word by word, it could have been applied to me also. For many years my life was similar to a migrant bird, since due to different circumstances I had lived in various places. However, I considered Far **East** to be my motherland, where I spent my childhood and youth. There, in Vladivostok, I graduated from school and the medical institute. There my spiritual quest had started. There, as I was leaving, my decision slowly matured to seek the living God and once found, to consecrate my whole life to Him. I moved to Siberia from the Far **East**, then to Leningrad and again to Siberia. Later, I came to Estonia, where I left for Germany. Now almost twelve thousand kilometers separated me from the place where my way of searching had first begun. The Far

East of Russia had really turned into **a far country** for me. God answered me remarkably precise using the words of the Holy Scripture, written thousands of years ago. I read and re-read those lines that suddenly had become living and so precious to me. Besides, the words *"**the man that executeth my counsel**"* validated the will of God in the clearest possible approach.

I did not listen to anyone anymore and went on with the started work, without realizing what it would eventually bring. One and a half years later after the book *Time for a Judgment to Begin with the House of God* was published, in summer of 1994 the final part of trilogy, *Voice of the One Crying in the Desert*, became available. I don't know why, but I have already had it in my heart – there would only be three books about the revival. Even though readers had asked me to write the next sequel, all of my attempts to do that had no success.

After finishing the work on the third book I was finally able to take a deep breath and put down my pen with the feeling of the accomplished mission. Joy filled my heart. Looking back at the seven years spent doing this whole work, I could only marvel and thank the Lord for His revealed grace, His help and strength He had given me. No doubt, without all of it, I would not have been able to write any of that. During the seven years God remained faithful to His promise, given to me that unforgettable evening at Kwa Sizabantu, when my frightened words "To write a book?? No, Lord, I cannot do that!" were met with His response, *"Do not be afraid. **I will help you.**"* That, which seemed to me absolutely unthinkable and practically unfeasible, was made real because of God's help. That's why I wholeheartedly agree with the famous theologian and a man of God William McDonald who wrote, that "[. . .] *We must always remember that whenever the Lord tells us to do something, He gives us the needed power. All His commands include His enablement, even when His commands are in the realm of the impossible.*

Jethro said to Moses, "If thou shalt do this thing, and God command thee so, then thou shalt be able to endure" (Ex. 18:23)." The principle is that God assumes full responsibility for enabling His man to fulfil every task to which He has appointed him" (J.O. Sanders).

In His ministry the Lord Jesus met at least two men who were paralyzed (Matt. 9:6, John 5:9). On both occasions He told them to get up and carry their pad. As they exercised the will to obey, power flowed into their helpless limbs.

Peter sensed that if the Lord Jesus called him to come on the water, then he could walk on water. As soon as Jesus said "Come," Peter went down out of the ship and walked on the water.

It is doubtful that the man with the withered hand could stretch it out; yet when our Lord told him to do it, he did and the hand was restored.

The idea of feeding 5000 with a few loaves and fishes is out of question. But whenever Jesus said to the disciples, "Give them to eat," the impossibility vanished.

Lazarus had lain in the grave for four days when Jesus called, "Lazarus, come forth." The command was accompanied by the necessary power. Lazarus came forth.

We should appropriate this truth. When God leads us, we should never cop out with the plea that we can't do it. If He tells us to do something, He will supply the power. It has been said, "The will of God will never lead you where the grace of God will not sustain you."

It is equally true that when God orders something, He pays for what He orders. If we are sure of His leading, we need not worry about the finances. He will provide.

The God who opened the Red Sea and the Jordan so that His people could pass over is the same today. He is still in the business of removing impossibilities when His people obey His will. He still supplies all needed grace to do whatever He commands. He still works in us both to will and to do of His good pleasure."[37] How definitely true it is written, *"But to each one of us grace was given according to the measure of Christ's gift* (Eph. 4:7)."

Publishing of the second and third books caused a new tide of letters from the readers, where our spiritually bankrupt, poor and weak Christianity of our times was exposed even more. Unsatisfied with superficiality, formalism and ritualism of traditionally followed forms of worship, people searched for truth, crying for help. Unfortunately, most of those who call themselves Christian and among those even born-again believers, do not know how to live the true life of victory. Many of them are like unbelievers, filled with fears and worries, cares and anxieties and even, despair, with which they are not able to cope. How many Christians there are that in contrary to their faith creed, exist without loving their neighbor, packed with criticism toward others, torn apart internally by grudges, bitterness, envy and malice. Unwittingly, the words of Apostle Paul come to mind, that amazingly precise describe the Christians of the last days, "[. . .] *having a form of godliness, but denying its power"* (2 Tim. 3:5). To confirm it, I will quote here from just a few letters, which display anxiety and heartache of many a Christian.

One sister believer from Leningrad wrote the following: "I have read the books about revival. Never in my life had I experienced a similar blessing while reading a book. They hold everything that we,

---

[37] permission granted by Gospel Folio Press to use this quote from: One Day at a Time, by William MacDonald. "March 24", page 88. Copyright ©1985 William MacDonald.

as Christians, need. They reflect the current truthful condition of the Church of Jesus Christ today, as if in a mirror. And if one can compare it with the apostolic church, then, you cannot really find a better definition but to call it "playing the church". It is hard to believe that the life of faith could actually be like this. We are being preached on: "You have repented. You have been baptized and you do not have any apparent, open sins. Try to keep the Lord's commandments and you can be absolutely sure of your salvation. Because of that, there is no need to concern yourselves with anything else, since it may bring harm to your spiritual state". However, the Spirit of God says that all of the above is not it. This is only the first step of the way of faith. That, in particular, was the agonizing question and the fret of my heart. That is why I was so happy to find the answer and the affirmation of my concern in these books. Every Christian needs the truth that these books contain and to aspire for what it says there. Only then, we will be able to do the will of God here, on this earth, on which we live".

Brother B. from Estonia: "We have just finished reading the books about the revival by Ludmila Plett with the whole family. They have made a great influence on us. Personally, they basically turned me upside down. Some chapters I was reading with tears - the Spirit of God worked so strong. This was the best I had ever read in my entire life with the exception of the Bible. Therefore, I want to thank everyone from the bottom of my heart who has contributed to the cause of distributing these books so that they made it into our hands. Oh, how precious and how essential it is for our forgotten, slumbering country! These books are practically being read by believers from all confessions of faith: Baptists, Adventists, Pentecostals, Lutherans, Catholics and Orthodox alike. All of them could see themselves in there as if in a mirror. In their light I could also see my own mistakes, sins and appalling traits of my character. While reading many a time I fell on my knees with repentance of my sins before the Lord. And the more I read, the better I realized something that hadn't crossed my mind before. Please, do not stop to publish such books, because they penetrate to the depth of human soul; illuminate our life with the light of God's Word, causing to walk in obedience to the Lord Jesus Christ. They are like a powerful ray of light, which breaks through the dark curtain of sin, destroying it. These books make no room for a false, hypocritical, Pharisee-like Christianity which flourishes in our day and age, carrying a sinister imprint of the last times".

Brother P. from Ukraine: "Dear brothers and sisters! You are being troubled by the people who were deeply touched by the books about revival. Truly, the power of the Spirit of God shook our souls and hearts, opened our eyes to concealed things of our lives, and we realized that for many years only wore the mask of Christianity. We have been self-assured hypocrites. Oh, how incredible the grace of God is that He does not wish for us to perish and therefore, awakes, convicts, admonishes and warns us! Please, send us these books for the sake of our salvation and those, who want to be real Christians, faithful to the Bible and desiring to be counted among His Church".

Chapter 10

Criticism, Hostility, Accusations

As I have shared the background of writing the trilogy and quoted some paragraphs from readers' letters with the positive reaction to the books, I would also like to touch on the opposite subject in order to explain why I had to call upon the Lord time and again, asking Him to give me strength to endure that, which had become a direct consequence to my ministry.

Approximately six months after the book *Revival Begins with Me* was published, among the stream of appreciative letters I came across the first few ones full of critique and negative statements in connection with my writings. In the beginning, it was done in a cautious, polite format, for instance: "Excuse me, but this book is being advertised like a folk remedy volume of a wide profile. This is highly inappropriate. With regards, sister R".

However, in time I started receiving increasingly ill-intentioned remarks, blames, as well as some grave charges of an unknown origin and without any foundation to them. I was scolded for spreading a dangerous heretical teaching; blamed for exaggerations and twisting of facts; for adding fantasies when retelling events and for making up things, as well as for using the demonic powers, which influenced people's souls, and many more. It didn't really stop at written statements, but became a subject of discussions in open letters, at brethren meetings and conventions; on pages of Christian publishing volumes and behind the pulpits of congregations and churches. Interestingly enough, those accusations were pouring out only against me. Erlo Stegen, whose sermons, testimonies and stories all three books consisted of, was regarded with indisputable authority, whereas Ludmila Plett was to be blamed for everything. So that there are no unsubstantiated statements, I will cite several quotations from a large article called "Ludmila Plett and Her Books", which was written by a pastor from town of Saransk and published in a Christian magazine "Mission news" No. 5 under the heading "To Missionaries about Religions and Cults". There the author was sharing that after reading the book *Revival Begins with Me*, he turned away from the right path because in the cleansing process he got under the influence of a deceiving spirit. Here are some excerpts from that article.

"[. . .] I wrote a letter to Ludmila Plett and told her what was happening with me. Six months later I received a reply from Ludmila Plett. She wrote that she didn't know what was going on and couldn't give me an answer, but informed me that Erlo Stegen was coming to a town of Cherkassy, where I would be able to meet with him and share my problems. Due to an illness, I was unable to get to Cherkassy, but some time later I saw a picture of Erlo Stegen at my friend's house. His mother-in-law had just returned from there and I immediately asked her to tell me about Erlo Stegen's speech. She said that he was a blessed preacher. Many people turned their lives to God at the stadium. When a note was sent to him asking, "Erlo, will you heal the people as we have read about it in your book?" He replied, "I have come not to heal your bodies and show miracles, but to preach the gospel of the Kingdom of God". The woman continued, "Also, Ludmila Plett asked to forgive her for the book she wrote". I asked her, "What for?" – "She apologized and admitted that when she was writing the book, she added some of her own fantasies to embellish her work of literature." For me it became a cardinal and a decisive answer why the book created so many problems in churches. Where there is even a little bit of lies, it is being used by Satan, since he is the father of lies. Therefore, the good which occurred at Kwa Sizabantu mission, the devil turned into temptation and deceit. . . . I thought that this spiritual decease went away in the beginning of nineties and believers had sorted out the devil's lies, but it goes on even today. Recently, I was invited to town of Lipetsk. There, the influence of this book seized the churches; young brothers and sisters got together and went to Ludmila Plett in Germany to confess their sins. . . . We can create our own philosophies, which come not from God, but from "spiritual *hosts* of wickedness in the heavenly *places*"[38], and such theories are not based on calling to sin but, seemingly, to purity and holiness. However, this is a spirit of despondency, which afflicts soul and leads a man to suicide or to heresy. Unfortunately, Ludmila Plett did not pay attention to those letters and stories which were sent to her from all the ends of the former Soviet Union and persisted in her activity by writing two more books. She receives her admirers, who come to Germany from all over the former Soviet Union for confession, because perhaps, in Russia God doesn't yet hear the prayers of believers as well as in the presence of Ludmila Plett [. . .]"

Quoting these excerpts from the rather long article, I have done it not to humiliate its author in some way, but to help his searching soul to sort through things and understand where the apparently false information had led him, because it was received from the mouth of people who took upon themselves the responsibility to tell others things which did not exist. It makes one wonder how some Christians can lie, forgetting that they will have to give an account for every wrong word.

---

[38] Ephesians 6:12 (NKJV)

I could certainly go over each line of this article to disprove the facts and charges, stated there by citing from letters and documents, which I have more than enough. Nevertheless, I will not do such a thing, but will give it over into the hands of the Lord. I can only say, that during our visit to the town of Cherkassy, as well as during any other mission trips to the towns and republics of the former Soviet Union, I had never apologized before anybody for seemingly made additions of my own fantasies and fabrications to the books for the sake of beautifying my work of literature and it is for the simple reason: having no need to apologize for something you had never done. I wrote only the facts which were said and preached by Erlo Stegen, as he also endorsed it in his interview given to a magazine "The Immigrant" during his mission trip to Minneapolis, USA. While answering questions posed by P. Ozerkov holding an interview, Erlo Stegen not only called all three books about the revival **his own**, but also affirmed that they reflected only things of which he once spoke or preached about. Here is a brief quote from the dialogue:

P. Ozerkov: I recently went to Russia. In the office of one Christian organization I saw a list called "Dangerous books". Among others there were named **your** three books: *Revival Begins with Me, Time for a Judgment to Begin with the House of God* and *Voice of the One Crying in the Desert*. Why do you think **your** books got on a black roll?

E. Stegen: I know that **my books** are loved in many parts of the world and read with great interest. They are translated into many languages. But why they got on the black list I can't even begin to tell you. Can you, perhaps, tell me, why . . . ?

P. Ozerkov: These books were written by your coworker Ludmila Plett, and you could not have been able to read them originally, since they were written in Russian language. Could she have warped any facts?

E. Stegen: I have read the books in English language. **All that was written there was true.** Of course, I cannot read them in Russian, but I trust her one hundred percent. She is a good Christian and genuinely loves the Lord. (The magazine "Immigrant", February 2000, page 7). *Author's remark: Unfortunately, Erlo Stegen slipped in saying that. He read the first book in Dutch language, not English, of which he had told me personally. There is no English translation of these books.*

In the course of some other mission trips to the former Soviet Union and USA the same question whether I have perverted the facts and blew them out of proportion or added to them in the books have been asked several times in my presence and invariably Erlo Stegen replied that all which was written corresponded to the truth. Therefore, the contents of the above-mentioned critical essay "Ludmila Plett and her books" as well as the expression of a preacher from Russia who

145

said: "Ludmila Plett is a female, and females have a tendency to beautify things, presenting that what they wish for as facts", were, to put it mildly, tactless. The best proof that I have not added anything to the books are the actual audiotapes with recordings of Erlo Stegen's sermons and testimonies, which were used for the purpose of writing the three books and which I have kept until now. They are the indisputable proof of my being not privy to additions and exaggerations. I repeat that only what was shared by Erlo Stegen had made into the books, and if there really was something misleading, it would not be my fault.

In connection with the statement that I receive admirers at my home who come to Germany to see me from all over the former Soviet Union and from town of Lipetsk, in particular, I leave it up to the conscience of those who were spreading such deliberately fabricated information. By the way, it was not the only lie that reached throughout the former USSR after our mission trip to Ukraine in **1992**. Soon after my return, in the fall of that same year, I received a letter, containing a "prophecy", which supposedly was uttered by Erlo Stegen in **Russian language** in Kiev. I had to reply and say that the account about him prophesying was a pure fiction, since I had accompanied Erlo Stegen along with other coworkers of the mission during that trip and could testify that there wasn't any kind of prophecy, especially in Russian, spoken by him. After that letter, in a course of several years I had gotten several letters with the similar content from different places with "the prophecy" attached, which to my amusement, began to expand, growing with new add-ons. It started with a header: "Revelation of Jesus Christ". The second line had the words, "Declare now – maybe they will receive that which is spoken by the Holy Spirit, for it is announced from heaven." Then, the actual prophecy followed, "Heavens are above the heads, heavens are above which bless My people! Why all the sacrifices, many confessions of My Name, coming to a house of prayer, if there is no humility, no blessing, no obedience to the Holy Spirit [. . .]", and so on and so forth. It was a big sheet of paper completely covered with fine writing – a pathetic imitation of Erlo Stegen's speech so familiar by the three books about revival. At the end of this so-called "heavenly message-prophecy" later a footnote appeared: "This is a revelation from God, which was sent through brother Erlo Stegen, when he was at the conference in Kiev in May 1998. The revelation was presented in Russian, although he did not know the language".

When you read the "prophecy", you don't know if you should laugh or cry, because there are these kinds of "children of God" who have not a slightest fear before the Lord to create and spread such an obvious lie, calling it a revelation of Jesus Christ in the meantime.

During our scheduled mission trip to Russia in August 1997, at a Christian convention which was held in Ryazanskaya region, somebody directly from the audience asked Erlo Stegen a question in regards to this revelation. He shrugged his shoulders in perplexity and said that he knew nothing about it. By the way, in 1998 (the year, the latest and greatest version of the circulated "prophecy" was dated), neither Erlo Stegen, nor anyone from his coworkers were in Ukraine or any other republic of the former USSR, because that year he was invited by Russian immigrants to visit USA for the first time.

As you can see, pursuing a definite goal some Christians are even capable of all sorts of falsifications, presenting them to be the truth. May God be their Judge! The sad part is that, seemingly, those who should teach truth to the people of God, become the transmitters of lies instead. To confirm it I will quote from letters received from our readers:

One brother in Russia, for example, writes: "It is interesting how in the hearts of some people these books kindle a flame, whereas, in others – resentment and wild hatred. When I once mentioned about what I had read in my sermon, I was strictly stopped and forbidden to preach. However, it is nothing new. Pharisees also hated Jesus. So it is now: not the outside world but our spiritual elders and deacons take it upon themselves to play a role of "firemen" and extinguish the fire of revival".

Another brother in the Lord shared with us the following: "For many years I have been a member of one Christian congregation. A year ago I read a book *Revival Begins with Me* and sincerely repented in my sins in a presence of a minister and in front of the congregation. For doing this I was excluded from my church. Now I am not a church member any longer, but I am free from sins that have been torturing me. When I revealed my offenses before the congregation, a preacher said that it was forbidden to read such books. My family and friends tell me that I am out of my mind. It hurts me to hear that, but I rejoice that the Lord had taken away my burden of sin".

Someone wrote from Odessa[39]: "Some brothers visited our congregation. They looked very honest and righteous, but tried really hard to set people against these books, speaking only negative about them. In the beginning their speech brought me to a complete confusion, but when I prayed, the Lord shed His light for me in this matter, and poured peace, serenity and sense of liberty into my heart. Alas, our situation in the church is very pathetic. We are in the middle of a bog of lies and subtly netted web of hypocrisy, which only God can penetrate with His light".

---

[39] A city on the shore of the Black Sea, in Ukraine.

From city of Kursk came this information: "Unfortunately, these books meet opposition and resistance. For many they don't fall into the category of a "usual Christianity". If God reveals Himself other than what these people imagine, they declare a war against it. As a rule, these are lifeless Christians, spiritually heavy stones, Pharisees, and there are enough of them, sorry to say. But those, who are weary and tired in searching for the true way; those, who are pleasing to God, they understand and receive with gladness that which was written".

A sister from Ukraine shared her pain with sadness: "On the day of my water baptism God made me a gift. By pure "accident" He gave me a book "Time for judgment to begin at the house of God" from the hands of some people I wasn't acquainted with. This gift of God I put into hands of our local preacher, who after reading it, said, "I would have torn it apart! Where did you get this?!" I knew that the book condemned him. I also know that I cannot speak about sins of others, because I am still a spiritual babe. I am writing to you because I feel burdened. Nobody needs me. My church split into three groups and became ridicule for the outside world. One pastor calls the other one "an adulterer", while the latter dubs him "a murderer" in return. So many people come to our congregation, repent in their sins and, afterwards, go back into the world. But I don't want to go back, because I cannot live without God anymore. Oh, how I long to find a true church of Christ and meet the living God"!

Another brother from Russia in his letter noticed as a matter of fact: "Certainly, there are some enemies of these books. But there are only a few of them". Yes, it's true. At least, if you judge by the amount of letters we have received. For more than ten years there were maximum ten-fifteen disapproving or highly negative letters among thousands and thousands of correspondence with positive replies. Several Christians in their letters informed us that their leaders advised them to throw the books about revival in the fire. I want to remark that among such letters there was a communication from an occult-dependent woman, who was most likely a witch, possessed by evil spirits. Showering me with curses, she wrote that when she received the book *Revival Begins with Me* from someone and began to read, evil spirits and creepy demons started appearing to her for real, and torturing her body, demanded from her to immediately burn that book. The horrendous torments went on until their miserable victim threw the book in the fire, after which demons calmed down and bothered her no longer. Unintentionally, a question comes up: how do you explain this very similar reaction of ardent hatred by servants of devil with that of some Christian leaders, persuading believers to throw these books into the fire due to being especially dangerous. . . ? Personally, it remained an unfathomable mystery to me.

In one of the letters that came from a rather renowned theological college in the countries of the former USSR, I was charged with averting people from church, making myself a mediator between God and people, destroying Christian congregations, spreading of extremely erroneous and heretical ideas in matters of sin, purification and holiness, depriving Christians of peace and quiet, and driving them to the point of losing assurance of their salvation. I would say these are very serious and some pretty grave accusations. But God is my witness, this was not my aim. Having myself once disillusioned by weakness, spiritual coldness, and deadness of a nominal, superficial Christianity, I only desired to show a way out of stagnation and deadlock. Surely, it is no secret that the spiritual condition of a prevailing number of Christian congregations and churches remains much to be seen. It is being recognized and openly written and spoken about by many serious theologians of our times. This is the fact which reflects our reality, and nothing changes if we only try to diminish it or mellow it down. We must have enough courage to look into face of a bitter reality and together search for a way out of this heartrending state of affairs, instead of arming ourselves up to war against those, whom God uses to tell His people the truth about their spiritual state. Why should we impersonate those, who in the Old Testament times persecuted and killed the prophets sent by God to reprove, admonish and convince God's people that had wandered away from the truth? Why should we, like hypocritical Pharisees, in our jealousy and envy compel those who have the courage to speak today, to be quiet?!

However, history repeats itself. At all times, the devil succeeded in finding a target for his fiery darts, which he shot by the hands of the so-called "pious", who had made it their highest objective to keep the external peace, which only mimicked spiritual welfare. Such zealots were ready to pay any price in order to achieve their goal, including the crucifixion of the Son of God, Whom they saw not as their Savior but as a major disturber of peace. Being corrupted themselves, they accused of corruption those of God's people whom the Lord sent to them for instruction and rectification. And if such "arms of the law" could have said about Jesus that, "*We found this fellow perverting the nation*"[40], then, is it any wonder that those who dare to raise their voice against hypocrisy and break the set "order" today are called rebels and debauchers? But what do we guard? Do we guard orders established by us or do we guard the keeping of God's commandments? Usually, those who, so to say, spoke against the opinion of the world, were the ones who brought a fresh winnowing into a stagnant, nominal worship. And the greatest revolutionary in a whole history had been

---

[40] Luke 23:2, NKJV

our Savior Jesus Christ, Who cut through the customary, established beliefs and traditions, gaining numerous enemies among "the pious". He was considered a breaker of the Law, given to people by God, whereas at the same time He said about Himself, *"Do not think that I came to destroy the Law or the Prophets. I did not come to destroy but to fulfill"* (Matt. 5:17). On the other hand, the way Jesus did it could not accommodate teachers of the law so much, that they preferred to do away with this perpetrator as soon as possible.

Certainly, by saying this, I am far from asserting that we should accept everything new without grounds or discernment; however, rushing into conclusion and rejecting without a thorough examination of a proposed subject simply because it does not fit into our accustomed notions is just as unreasonable. In connection with this, believers from town of Berea could be a fine example for us, of whom the Holy Scripture says, *"These were more fair-minded than those in Thessalonica, in that they received the word with all readiness, and searched the Scriptures daily to find out whether these things were so. Therefore many of them believed [. . .]"* (Acts 17:11-12). By the way, the apostle Paul was also a disturber of "peace" in those days, often preaching the "indigestible" things, although, he was nevertheless a messenger of God and a herald of truth. That is why it is so important to always remain sound, not scurrying to draw a hasty supposition and make thoughtless decisions.

As to the accusations of destroying faith in people and depriving them of assurance in their salvation through my books, I would love to respond by asking: what kind of **faith** and what sort of **assurance of salvation** are these, if they can be destroyed in Christians by some books with a single blow?? Most likely, they had never had **a real faith** and **a true assurance of salvation** to begin with. For the ones that they did have, were only a counterfeit and the sooner people realize it, the better it will be for them. Then, they will quicker ask themselves a question: "What kind of faith and assurance of salvation do I have, if they can crumple so easily? Maybe, I have been erecting my spiritual building not on a rock, which is Christ Himself, but on sand, which were my own humanistic ideas and convictions!" If only by reading these books, we cannot withstand the judgment they and our own conscience cause, then how are we going to stand before the Lord's judgment? The Word of God states it rather clear, that *"we shall all stand before the judgment seat of Christ"* (Rom.14:10).

The next allegation has to do with the idea that after "having read a lot" of these books, people start viewing their quiet, peaceful congregation with suspicion and come to conclusion that both, the church and the pastor are not what they're supposed to be. Some of them become disappointed even in Christianity in general and fall away from the Church. Unfortunately, I must say, that based on the readers' letters, I am aware of a few similar reactions in response to reading of the books about revival. Alas, it usually happens when a man trying to break free from spiritual stagnation, does not begin with his own life, but with the lives of others. Then, all kinds of charges get thrown into the face of ministers, pastors, leadership and surrounding folks, but not in one's own face, in spite of the fact that the name of the first book, all by itself underlines the main thought – the revival and all spiritual changes in connection with it, must begin with the one who desires it and searches it out. Those who understand this idea properly do have the right reaction. The problem is that many a Christian has developed a strong spirit of censure and criticism. They brilliantly see the deficiencies, mistakes, vices and sins in whomever they please, except in themselves.

Involuntarily, a famous Russian tale about a monkey written by Ivan Krylov[41] comes to mind. A monkey was looking at her own image in a mirror and chatting about gossip bearers who had such an unsightly and repulsive appearance, like the one she was now seeing in the mirror. The monkey used the occasion to tittle-tattle about others, pointing at their flaws. She got so carried away criticizing and giving a good scolding to her acquaintances that did not pay attention to a wise counsel from a bear: "Instead of counting the flaws of your good friends, you, gossipmonger, better turn and look now at yourself! – The bear noticed. Though, the bear's advice was uttered all in vain".[42]

With all outward naivety, this fable describes the most widely spread problem among Christians with an amazing accuracy – judging and criticizing others for things they tend to do themselves. The Scripture reaffirms it with the following passage, *"Therefore you are inexcusable, O man, whoever you are who judge, for in whatever you judge another you condemn yourself; for you who judge practice the same things. But we know that the judgment of God is according to truth against those who practice such things. And do you think this, O man, you who judge those practicing such things, and doing the same, that you will escape the judgment of God?"* (Romans 2:1-3). The advice of the bear made to the monkey was truly uttered in vain, but should we, Christians, be like a silly marmoset, ignoring the warning that comes from the Word of God?

Another accusation was charged to me having to do with sowing doubts in people as far as their justification and salvation was

---

41 Ivan Andreyevich Krylov is Russian best known fabulist who wrote series of animal tales. By the time he died in 1844, 77,000 copies of his fables had been sold in Russia, and his unique brand of wisdom and humor gained popularity. His fables were often rooted in historic events, and are easily recognizable by their style of language and engaging story. (From Wikipedia, the free encyclopedia)

42English translation rendered by the translator of this book..

concerned where, because of my books, a person starts looking to himself, instead of to Christ, and cycles his mind around the idea of purifying himself until he stops sinning altogether. The author of that letter challenging me to a discussion stated that "a Christian sins until he dies, even though he has no desire to do that, but by God's grace he, nevertheless, does not lose his salvation." This earlier mentioned **theory of eternal election**, presumably established by a theologian John Calvin, in the past few decades have really found a wide recognition and acceptance not only in USA but in many other countries of the world, including the former Soviet Union. While visiting different churches of Russian immigrants in the US and making mission trips within the countries of the former Soviet block, I could see first-hand what horrifying consequences it caused in the hearts and lives of those who formerly knew very well what it meant to walk in the fear of God. Personally, this theory reminds me of the times of Martin Luther, when in the Catholic Church people could obtain a "peace of mind" for money in a form of indulgencies relieving them from sin, and then went on sinning with a quieted conscience, since the document purchased from the priests guaranteed their forgiveness and salvation. In the book of Ezekiel 18:24 it is written, *"But when a righteous man turns away from his righteousness and commits iniquity, and does according to all the abominations that the wicked man does, shall he live? All the righteousness which he has done shall not be remembered; because of the unfaithfulness of which he is guilty and the sin which he has committed, because of them he shall die"*. A little more down, in verse 26 we also read, *"When a righteous man turns away from his righteousness, commits iniquity, and dies in it, it is because of the iniquity which he has done that he dies"*. We read about the same thing in Ezekiel 3:20 and 18:31. Perhaps, one may say that it was in the Old Testament and we live in time of grace and mercy now. That is correct. But do you know what the Lord says in the New Testament through the one, whom we like to call the Apostle of love? Here what it says, *"He who sins is of the devil, for the devil has sinned from the beginning.* **For this purpose the Son of God was manifested, that He might destroy the works of the devil. Whoever has been born of God does not sin**, *for His seed remains in him; and* **he cannot sin, because he has been born of God**" (1 John 3:8-10).

Of course, many may object to it by saying that in that same epistle of John 1:8 it is written, *"If we say that we have no sin, we deceive ourselves, and the truth is not in us"*. I think, these two seemingly contradicting each other verses can be reconciled if one approaches sin not as something inevitable, to which one must willingly or unwillingly subdue, but as a disaster, a tragedy or unforeseeable crash, which one tries to avoid and prevent at all costs. Otherwise, such an eased up attitude towards sin makes the thoughts, the heart, and the life of a

Christian a backyard with a through-passage for the devil. And here I mean not a gross type of sins, such as adultery, fornication and drinking problem, but things to which we are pretty much accustomed to and used to, not considering it as anything serious, like irritation, for instance, or resentment, blame and backbiting. After many years of counseling ministry, I can say with confidence that the main reason why a Christian cannot leave his sin behind is his love towards it, which is something that is hard to admit. And the excuse, such as, "I don't want to sin, but I simply cannot stop sinning" – is just a sly trick and an attempt to justify oneself. It is impossible to stop sinning until you start hating sin, and I have been convinced about the truth of it in numerous times.

One can only be in awe how refined Christians can be in seeking and finding the alleviated ways of approaching an issue of sin. For sermons they carefully choose those verses that can explain and justify spiritual weakness. A world-wide renowned preacher had once said in this connection that the Bible is the most blessed and at the same time, the most dangerous book of all, depending on who is holding it. This expression may have been hard to understand, until you think of how many sects and dangerous false doctrines have spread their views, while having the Bible in their hands, and then, you feel compelled to agree to that saying. And it would be only half the trouble if merely sects and obvious false teachings were doing that. The real trouble is that from many pulpits of traditional churches of various confessions lulling and comforting words are spoken to reaffirm Christians that everything is all right and they need not to worry; that once they've received the Lord as their Savior, they should just thank Him and continue to trust Him. Therefore, it makes an impression that salvation and eternal life with God are guaranteed to them after their repentance despite the way they are going to live later. As a result of such teaching and consolation, people have no fear of sin. Freedom, which Christ has granted to us, is replaced by anything-is-permitted attitude, and Christians do as they think fit, being confident that God will forgive them nevertheless. In other words, the principle of such faith is laid out as follows: "once saved is forever saved".

In one letter I was asked a question, "Do you think that cleansing after repentance is necessary for every Christian or does it only pertain to you?" Frankly, it surprised me a lot, because it came from a person responsible for theological training of preachers, missionaries, pastors and other ministers of God.

In my opinion, the definitions of "cleansing" and "sanctification" are inseparably linked and, according to the Bible, both of them are God's will for us, Christians. Therefore, I don't imagine they become obsolete after repentance. It is a process which lasts our entire life, and

153

if it goes in a right direction, it will definitely show progress. A good example of such a life could be the process of cleansing and sanctification of the Apostle Paul. After his first encounter with Jesus, he cries out in horror, *"For the good that I will to do, I do not do; but the evil I will not to do, that I practice. Now if I do what I will not to do, it is no longer I who do it, but sin that dwells in me [. . .] O wretched man that I am! Who will deliver me from this body of death?"* (Rom. 7:19-20, 24).

Such was his beginning. Then, the next step occurs – wrestling against sin and dying of his "Self", as he speaks of it, *"Therefore I run thus: not with uncertainty. Thus I fight: not as one who beats the air. But I discipline my body and bring it into subjection, lest, when I have preached to others, I myself should become disqualified."* (1 Cor. 9:26-27).

We do not know how long Paul's battle continued; it is known, however, that this "wretched man", who groaned under his weakness, could say with his own lips later, *"**I can do all things** through Christ who strengthens me"* (Phillip. 4:13).

Is it any wonder that progressing through all three stages of cleansing process, the Apostle Paul was approaching eternity with full confidence in his salvation, awaiting to receive a crown. No one and nothing can shake such assurance, unlike us for whom the reading of a book or reminding of a verse from Proverbs 14:12 *"There is a way that seems right to a man, but its end is the way of death"* happens to be enough to lose our assurance of salvation. So-called "assurance" is a false one and therefore, the sooner it is destroyed, the better it is for a person.

The Apostle Paul said that the grace of God towards him was not in vain. The grace of God is absolute, and salvation achieved by Christ is perfect and eternal: but we must now carry out in our lives that which had already been done by God. In Philippians 2:12, the same apostle Paul says, *"work out your own salvation with fear and trembling"*, which really means to realize; to carry out; to put into practice. Oswald Chambers had once said that every believer can keep himself and his body under complete control for God's sake. God made us capable of ruling over our own temple, where the Holy Spirit lives; capable of controlling our thoughts and intentions. We are responsible for them and, therefore, in no way should give room to those thoughts and desires that are not pleasing to God.

I wholeheartedly agree with this man of God and have no doubt, whatsoever, that without redeeming sacrifice of our Lord Jesus Christ, all of our efforts and endeavors would have been pointless vain attempts unable to lead us to salvation. However, it does not grant us any rights to remain inert and sluggish. In Holy Scriptures there are many passages that point out **what** exactly we, as Christians, must do so that salvation finished on the cross of Calvary would become our lot, too. It is not written for nothing, *"And from the days of John the Baptist* *until the present time, the kingdom of heaven has endured violent assault, and violent men seize it by force* [as a precious prize--a share in the heavenly kingdom is sought with most ardent zeal and intense exertion]" (Matt. 11:12)[43]. Other verses of the Bible speak to us about the same idea, for example: Matthew 5:20 and 7:21; Isaiah 59:1-2, Colossians 3:5-15.

Wouldn't you agree that these and many other passages of the Bible, figuratively speaking, pull the ground from under the feet of **our lethargy towards the matter of salvation?** In order to explain what I mean when using the word "lethargy", I will make a very simple, childlike example, which in my opinion serves as a very good illustration to the above-mentioned subject. Let's pretend that I want to drink and literally feel like dying from thirst. Turning to you, I ask you to give me a glass of water. In response to my call you bring the glass of water and place it in front of me. I look at it but without making a single move, keep asking for a drink. You look at me bewildered, not getting why I don't drink water sitting in front of me. My thirst increases and I continue pleading, in spite of the fact that the very thing I require is right before me eyes.

Do you understand what I mean? In order for me not to die from thirst next to water, I must do something in person, namely: reach out my hand, take the glass, bring it to my lips, make a first sip, swallow all water down and if necessary, ask for more.

Similar to this is the situation with our salvation. It has been achieved by the death of Jesus Christ on the cross of Calvary and is offered to each and every man. We only need to accept it and apply it to our lives. In the letter to Colossians it says amazingly clear and simple, *"If then you were raised with Christ, **seek those things which are above**, where Christ is, sitting at the right hand of God. **Set your mind on things above**, not on things on the earth. For you died, and your life is hidden with Christ in God. When Christ who is our life appears, then you also will appear with Him in glory. Therefore **put to death** your members which are on the earth: fornication, uncleanness, passion, evil desire, and covetousness, which is idolatry. Because of these things the wrath of God is coming upon the sons of disobedience [. . .] But now **you yourselves are to put off** all these: anger, wrath, malice, blasphemy, filthy language out of your mouth. **Do not lie** to one another, since you have put off the old man with his deeds, and have put on the new man who is renewed in knowledge according to the image of Him who created him [. . .] Therefore, as the elect of God, holy and beloved, **put on** tender mercies, kindness, humility, meekness, longsuffering; **bearing** with one another, and **forgiving** one another, if anyone has a complaint against another; even as Christ forgave you, so*

---

[43] Text is taken from the Amplified Bible (AMP) as having the closest interpretation of the meaning according to the Russian Synodal Version. Also by Joseph Thayer, a Greek-English Lexicon.

you also must do. But above all these things **put on** *love, which is the bond of perfection. And* **let the peace of God rule in your hearts**, *to which also you were called in one body; and* **be thankful**' (Colossians 3:1-2, 4-6, 8-10, 12-15).

As you can see, it doesn't even mention a passive sitting around with hands folded. There is not a word about God doing everything for us so that we could have all we need for a new life with Christ. It just as well doesn't say that we should wait until the Lord mortifies all the above-listed sins in us and transforms us from a former old and sinful man into a new creature. Instead, in this passage of Scripture the Lord commands us to do what is necessary for our own renewal, sanctification and inheritance of life hidden with Christ in God. Thus, the call to action: put to death..., put off..., do not lie..., put on..., bear with one another..., forgive..., love..., be thankful and so on. Based on that, we can understand why the Apostle Paul wrote about himself, "*[. . .] I die daily..., I discipline my body and bring it into subjection..., Therefore I run thus: not with uncertainty. Thus I fight: not as* one who *beats the air [. . .]*" (1 Cor. 9:26-27, 5:31).

Christ died for him then, just as He died for us who live today, and therefore, granted us salvation. Although, unlike many of us, the Apostle Paul was way more active at implementing the gift of salvation in his life and this is why he says, while addressing us, "*work out your own salvation*"[44].

In the course of my life I have met many believers, who have indignantly said, "For so many years I have been asking the Lord to cleanse my heart and set me free from all grudges, envy, irritation, impure sexual thoughts and lust of the flesh, but years go by, and He doesn't do anything, so I remain in the same state!" And thus it looks like it is God's fault that once becoming a believer I remained the same old-natured person with all of my sinful dispositions.

After the struggle with his former sinful "Self" the Apostle Paul was finally able to say "***I can do all things*** *through Christ who strengthens me*"[45]. But we, modern Christians, very often cannot say that, as if we don't have that same strengthening Jesus Christ. Isn't it so because we do not do what we must do? We are enslaved by indifference, passivity and spiritual laziness in all things, including the matter of our personal salvation. Somebody else, God including, should do it for us. And in such spiritual demands and insolence we keep forgetting that He had already done everything for us, - everything! Up to a torturing death on the cross, where He shed His last drop of blood for us.

---

[44] Philip. 2:12 NKJV
[45] Philip. 4:13 NKJV
156

And the last thing I wanted to pause on here. I have been rebuked and accused that after reading my books about revival and choosing the road of cleansing, people began to be guided by a false spirit, which depressed souls by condemning their sins, tormenting and keeping them in constant fear. Well, judging by certain letters, these things have taken place, indeed. Usually, it is stipulated by the incorrect understanding by such person about what happens in his own soul when the Holy Spirit starts His work by opening his eyes to the sins, to the righteousness of God and to His judgment. Unfortunately, in Christian churches and fellowships the question of counseling is either too weak or completely ignored. Consequently, often there is no one capable to admonish and help a soul with a much needed advice in such an important and responsible moment for him or for her. Being condemned in their conscience, believers did not know what to do. Somebody went to an elder of his congregation asking to listen to his confession, but was met with a rejection, being explained that everything must be confessed directly to God. If such people tried to clarify that it didn't bring any relief and that's why they have asked to give them an opportunity to speak out, they were being told that there was no such need in doing that. Some folks were able to come to agreement with the ministers but more than once they experienced disappointment, because they did not receive any relief or the secrecy of their confession was revealed, which led to more problems and even to the expulsion from the church. The bravest of all ventured to get up during the service and reveal their sins in front of everybody, asking for forgiveness, which also usually ended quite sadly, since not many people were able to bear this and responded with judgment and isolation, which instead of helping those repenting, only intensified their peculiar situation. There were cases similar to those mentioned by the author of the article "Ludmila Plett and her books", when devil contrived to the cleansing process and began to torture person, imposing on him thoughts about things he had never done or sinned by. It is nothing extraordinary, because Satan is able to assume an air of an angel of light. He does not care what tool to use in order to conceal the acts of darkness. Therefore, the good which could have served as an invaluable assistance to many, was turned into a ground for reviling. But, praise God, that those who have been blessed by the books are hundreds and thousands times more. Of course, it would be proper to talk about counseling now and about the positive and dangerous sides of this difficult but such a precious and looked-for ministry, except this topic is so extensive and resourceful that it would require an additional book. Therefore, if it is pleasing to God, perhaps, it shall also be written some day.

∽ॐ

Chapter 11

Calling to a Counseling Ministry

Now I will have to go back in my story to the time when the work over a manuscript for the book *Revival Begins with Me* was drawing to a conclusion. It was in April of 1989. Only a few days passed since I had turned forty. In my perception that age associated with a concept of maturity. In Germany, in Schwab republic where we live, there is an aphorism among the local residents which says that a Schwab becomes smart only at forty. It's a joke, of course, although, number "forty" is also mentioned in the Bible as a number of completion. During the Flood it had rained for forty days and forty nights. Moses had spent forty years at the Pharaoh's house. His wanderings in Midian desert amounted to forty years and became a vital school for him. Harsh life conditions in the desert tempered Moses and prepared him for a future service; gave him something he couldn't gain at the Pharaoh's palace. Having lived for forty years in the wilderness, Moses got well acquainted with the topography of the area, where he consequently led the people of Israel. Forty years flew by after Moses left the house of Pharaoh, when he heard the Voice from the burning bush that told him to go back to Egypt and free God's people. Now Moses wasn't as ambitious as he once felt in his younger years, and accepted appointment with great reluctance. Only after receiving God's assurance of His help and being equipped with the power from above and a miracle-working gift, did he go to Pharaoh. Finally, our Lord Jesus Christ had been in a desert for forty days, being tempted by the devil.

Time and again I returned to this fact in my thoughts as I celebrated my forty years mark. "What will this age bring me?" I pondered, "Does the Lord have a definite plan for me as well?" Involuntarily, I recalled the words of my friend, the old Granny, who said to me twenty years ago, "The Lord had revealed to me that He allotted a special ministry for you, only not now, but when you come of age". Was it true? Will it really come to pass? Was it a revelation from the Lord?

My birthday had passed. One week went by and the second one began. I stopped thinking about it, when again, and as always unexpectedly, I heard God's voice speaking to me. That day, my husband and I went to a worship service at a neighboring town, where Erlo Stegen was preaching as he toured Germany during his regular mission trip. We delayed on our way and, therefore, entered a sanctuary no more than ten minutes before the opening. We had barely settled in the few seats that were still available, when an authoritative

159

voice said inside my heart, *"Get up! Go to Friedel Stegen and tell him that I am calling you to a counseling ministry"*. Suddenly, I felt lost from this surprise. What did that mean? Was it a voice of God or was Satan tempting me? But the beginning of worship service was only minutes away! Can God really demand this of me? How can I get up in front of the whole congregation and come up to the first pew where Friedel Stegen is sitting to strike a conversation with him? What will they think of me?? This would be bad manners all right! A courteous person would never do such a thing. It can very well be done after the service without drawing anybody's attention. And what kind of counseling are we talking about if I am still in such a need of a counselor myself??

While I meditated about it in disarray, the remaining minutes expired, and the service began. I was troubled at heart. What if it really was God's voice and I acted in disobedience? But can the Lord demand to do something that goes against common sense? Fully occupied with such thoughts I was hardly able to listen to the singing of a choir and the opening address of a local pastor, forcing me to concentrate only when Erlo Stegen got behind the pulpit. "Dear friends!" he addressed the audience, "I want to notify you so you are not surprised when my brother Friedel will have to leave the sanctuary right after the service. The thing is that we received an urgent message from South Africa that requires his immediate return."

These words resonated like a thunder. I hardly controlled myself from crying out. That's why the Lord wanted me to approach Friedel before the worship service. He knew what was hidden from me. And I had gotten into reasoning instead of being obedient from the start!

I can't recall what Erlo Stegen was preaching about that evening. Torturing myself with remorse for my stubbornness and disobedience, I pleaded the Lord to forgive me and begged Him to detain Friedel Stegen in the auditorium yet for a couple of minutes, so that I would be able to approach him and tell him what I needed. The choir hadn't finished its closing song when I darted towards Friedel Stegen who was about to leave, without paying attention to anyone around me. "Uncle Friedel," I whispered catching my breath in agitation, "Before the service God told me that He was calling me to a ministry of counseling. Not knowing about your leave I was disobedient and hadn't come right away. Please, tell me, what must I do now?"

Being accustomed to all sorts of surprises, Friedel Stegen quickly glanced at me and without saying another word, bowed his head and prayed: "Lord Jesus! You know where this voice came from. If this ministry is really Your will, confirm it to Your child. Amen." After these words he got up and hurriedly strolled out of the hall, and I slowly walked back to my seat, trying not to notice my husband's questioning look.

Some time later, after one of the services, an unfamiliar woman came up to me and said, "You are Ludmila, aren't you? I wanted to tell you that over the past few days I felt a desire to bring my sins to light in confession. When I prayed about it to the Lord, I was impelled to go to you. Do you agree to listen to me?"

Caught by surprise I felt lost. I hadn't told anyone, except Friedel Stegen, about the voice which had called me to a counseling ministry. Nobody had made an announcement and not a single person introduced me to others as a counselor. Therefore, the Lord must have prompted this soul to come up to me with her request in order to confirm His will. Yes, but I had absolutely no idea how to do it! I wasn't prepared to this kind of ministry.

"Perhaps, you would prefer to go to one of the brothers, who are ministers?" I offered hesitantly, "Especially, since you definitely have some pretty good German language skills.

"Yes, I do speak German," she replied, "But it is totally clear to me that I should turn with my need to you particularly."

"But, I am not an official counselor, you see," I was trying to stop her, "And truthfully, I don't know exactly how to do it.

"Oh, it doesn't matter to me," I heard her answer. "What's important to me is to be faithful to God's will. And the Lord has sent me to you."

After those words I had no choice but to find a secluded place and shyly listened to what she had on her heart. My prayer for that penitent soul was very timid and lacked confidence, however by God's grace, it was heard, and help had been granted. Two days later that sister came again, then once more and yet again. For several years we had had counseling association together, until that woman became a vessel of God herself, ready for His use and capable of helping other souls.

Upon becoming a counselor that way, I continued to keep silent, telling no one about the ministry I was entrusted. Yet people found me on their own. They called me on the phone or wrote letters, affirming that in prayer they received a clear understanding from the Lord to turn to me with their problems.

This was the beginning of my ministry which as of now has been carrying on non-stop for fourteen years[46]. If I had lost sight of some people, others came in their place. During all this time hundreds and thousands of lives have journeyed through my heart. Thousands of tear-stricken faces and souls suffering from sin flashed before my eyes.

---

[46] By the time of publishing the English version of this book, the author had been in counseling ministry for over twenty years.

This way, the Lord confirmed that it was truly His calling, which had begun without me asking for it or even desiring for such a ministry.

It took many years before I understood what it meant to be a "physician for soul". Oh, how many of God's children tortured by sin fill up houses of prayer, fellowship halls and churches today! An unseen realm, candid and real, unwraps "as is" for those who carry on the counseling ministry. Everything else is only a religious spectacle, which we all play one in front of each other, often times without recognizing it. We get together for worship and prayer, listen to the Word of God, make decisions about church matters, smile and greet each other, but at the same time behind the scenes live out another life concealed from others, which is in direct contrast to what we say and do. The difference between a seeming outward picture and the reality can be so great that it makes it hard to believe that this is one and the same person. At the meetings, a man may pose as a very pious and devout Christian: preach, recite poems, play an instrument or sing in a choir. Yet in his own family, he brings his relatives to despair by his irritability, quarrelsome disposition, grumpiness, spitefulness, criticism and ever-swinging moodiness. It is possible to show yourself friendly, well meaning and courteous when associating with other people, yet in reality be wicked, demanding, fussy and always dissatisfied. During evangelizing campaigns you can witness, telling others how the Lord saved you and gave you a new life, but in fact, remain just the way you used to be: with your anger, indignity, inability to forgive, covetousness, envy, adultery and the most loathing thoughts. All of that makes an impression of a double life, which we live daily, trying to somehow reconcile between who we are in reality and who we present ourselves to be to the others. How truthfully, though, the Word of God describes this condition, *"These people draw near to Me with their mouth, and honor Me with their lips, but their heart is far from Me"* (Matt.15:8).

About the perversity of human heart, it says in the Gospel of Matthew 15:19, *"For out of the heart proceed evil thoughts, murders, adulteries, fornications, thefts, false witness, blasphemies"*. I think this list could be extended to no end. Moreover, all this filth we craftily conceal, confident that people cannot see our heart as well as unable to read our minds. Therefore, we have an opportunity to smokescreen, presenting ourselves in a quite different light, far from who we really are. Consequently, we not only become hypocrites ourselves, but also make hypocrites of those whom we try to bring to Christ. As the time goes by, one gets used to the role so much that he truly begins to believe being the one he tries to pass for. Only when the light of God deeply penetrates our heart and lights up that which was hidden in darkness, our eyes begin to see the veiled spiritual realm the way it is. Namely, this previously unknown spiritual realm of Christians literally shocked me and forced to ponder and reevaluate much. At that time I understood **the main reason** for absence of a close relationship between God and His child, which creates an isolating wall between them. And then, it finally dawned on me why my prayers sometimes came back unheard, as if bounced off a lead ceiling. The answer for it we find in Chapter 59 of the prophet Isaiah, *"Behold, the Lord's hand is not shortened, that it cannot save; nor His ear heavy, that it cannot hear. But your iniquities have separated you from your God; and your sins have hidden His face from you, so that He will not hear"* (Isa. 59:1-2).

The counseling ministry became a new landmark on my course of life, drawing a line under my ignorance, naivety and spiritual immaturity. Instead, my spiritual education have then begun, which perhaps would end only with my crossing over to eternity. Since then, I do not stop learning, perceiving the mysteries of human soul and standing amazed in its depths and intricate labyrinths. The more you know the people, the more you wonder at their ignorance of themselves. Man's behavior, his deeds and actions can be so unpredictable that you are unable to foresee it. In counseling, I often meet folks who admit that as they understand more of their own heart, they fret themselves. A Russian proverb says, "The human heart is a dark mystery", and I agree with its truth more and more. It is amazing, how quickly a person can change. I don't think it happens as an unforeseen, suddenly occurring phenomenon. Most likely, something which had already been present inside that the man was unaware of, reveals itself under certain conditions and in some situations and circumstances. For example, a betrayer does not all of the sudden becomes one. Some specific circumstances, which are favorable for such trait, occurring in an unexpected moment, show what was hidden inside the man and what neither he nor others around him could have suspected. No, we do not know ourselves. This is why King David, made wise by his life experience, exclaims, *"Search me, O God, and know my heart; try me, and know my anxieties; and see if there is any wicked way in me, and lead me in the way everlasting"* (Psalm 139:23-24). Perhaps, the incident with Bathsheba did open his eyes as well to something he did not know about himself, but what, alas, he was capable of doing. Possibly, he hadn't conceived that for the sake of achieving his own goal he would be prepared to commit an insidious crime of murdering his loyal subject. The Bible tells us, *"The heart is deceitful above all things, And desperately wicked; who can know it?"* (Jer. 17:9). And how unfortunate, indeed, that among God's people there are just a few of those who like David, ask the Lord to search and try their hearts revealing hidden sins and secret thoughts. The main segment of Christians prefers to dwell in self-delusion, comforting themselves that they are no worse than others and therefore, their salvation is secured.

I have no doubt that if Christians had wanted to see themselves the way God saw them, many things in Christianity would look completely different.

That is why it gives such a joy to encounter souls who pursue a closer walk with God discontented with an all-too-common carefree calm, and in His light they begin to know their heart, finding out things they haven't seen there before. In the beginning of my ministry it seemed to me that there was just a handful of this kind of people. But to my delight, through counseling I got persuaded that there were hundreds and thousands of unsatisfied seeking souls. Long time ago, in the Old Testament era, the prophet Elijah spoke in despair, *"[. . .] the children of Israel have forsaken Your covenant... I alone am left; and they seek to take my life." In response he heard: "Yet I have reserved seven thousand in Israel, all whose knees have not bowed to Baal [. . .]"* (1 Kings 19:10, 18). Seven thousand people remained faithful to the living God during those terrifying, troubled times! Yet Israel wasn't that big of a nation. The same holds true for our days. In the midst of universal quenching and apostasy, God preserves tens of thousands or perhaps, hundreds of thousands of people not wanting to compromise with sin and bow to secular Christianity. They are the ones who usually come for counseling.

As I studied medicine, I could not stop wondering about the variety of diseases that assault human body. Thus, there are so many kinds of medical specialists. They are surgeons, general practitioners, pediatricians, orthopedists, ophthalmologists, otolaryngologists, cardiologists, pulmonologists, hematologists, urologists, gynecologists, traumatologists, dermatologists, oncologists, etc. The list can go on and in fact, each one of them deals with tens and hundreds of different sicknesses, which human organism is exposed to. It may be hard to believe but there are no less diseases that attack human soul. If you arm yourself with a pencil and walk through the pages of the Bible, writing down these ailments, the abundant quantity of them will shock you. The following books of the Scripture catalog a multitude of spiritual sicknesses, combined under one word, so familiar to us all, "sin": Exodus and Deuteronomy, all books of Old Testament prophets, four Gospels of the New Testament, Acts and the Epistles, especially, in Epistles of the Apostle Paul to Romans, Corinthians, Thessalonians, Galatians, Ephesians, Philippians, Colossians, Hebrews and also in letters to Timothy, Titus and Philemon. These are: hatred of God, idolatry, fortune-telling, sorcery, worship of Satan and evil spirits, hatred, gluttony, tightfistedness, avidity, greed, adultery, theft, fraud, ill-intentions, ill-will, envy, jealousy, uncleanness, evil lusts, fornication, infidelity, homosexuality, sexual relationship with an animal (bestiality), apostasy, false witness, lies, unfaithfulness, betrayal, inability to forgive, revenge, grumble, irritation, indignation, anger, spite, self-interest, insolence, shamelessness, drunkenness, impiety, malicious talk, swearing, judging, hypocrisy, Pharisee-like disposition, laziness, violence, hostility, sly suspicions, self-love, pride, arrogance, love of money, recklessness, ingratitude, unfriendliness, lack of self-control, cruelty, pomposity, partiality, stubbornness, insubordination, disobedience, rebelliousness, inventiveness for evil, treachery, insidiousness, murder, etc. Alas, this is a much uncompleted register of diseases which can strike man's soul and transform it from a crown of creation into a ferocious beast, whose image may be hard to describe in human words. When reading chapter 59 of Isaiah the prophet, chapter 9 of the prophet Jeremiah; the Epistle to Colossians 3:5-9; the Epistle to Romans 3:1-7; 2 Timothy 3:1-7 and many other passages of the Holy Scripture, one can come to conclusion that the Bible depicts a very gloomy picture of a carnal man. And if we are honest with ourselves, we must admit that the image is accurate and truthful.

I think it may be appropriate to cite an excerpt from a tiny booklet "The Grace of God" by William MacDonald. One of its chapters called "The Sinfulness of Man" relates the following,

"Man is an ungodly sinner. It is a condition that dates from birth. He is "estranged from the womb." He goes astray as soon as he is born, speaking lies (Psalm 58:3). In his infancy, he does not have to be taught to do wrong; he does that naturally. But he does have to be taught to do right as long as he lives (Proverbs 22:15).

He is a sinner by nature and by practice (Romans 3:23). What he is in himself and what he has done are alike sinful. And what he is in himself is a lot worse than anything he has ever done. Within him lies a pit of corruption, a hell of iniquity, a cesspool of sin.

His thought-life would not bear exposure (Matthew 15:19). He could not publish a book containing the record of his innermost thoughts; it would be against the law to print it. He would not want to walk around for one hour with a poster announcing the most evil thought he has had during the last week.

Down through the centuries, men have been writing their vile thoughts on the walls of public buildings — revealing the depravity of their hearts.

There is a vast difference in every man between what he is and what he wants people to think he is. He does not want people to know him as he actually is, and so he puts on a false front. His person is what he actually is; his personality is what he wants people to think about him. Thus man is a hypocrite.

Someone has said that man is what he is in the dark. God says, "Men loved darkness rather than light, because their deeds were evil" (John 3:19).

When man sees fault, failure or sin in others, it appears very revolting and repulsive to him. But when he commits the same sin himself, it does not seem nearly so bad. "And thinkest thou this, O man, that judgest them which do such things, and doest the same, that thou shalt escape the judgment of God?" (Romans 2:3)

This guilt of sin applies to all mankind, to all who are born of human father and mother. "There is none righteous, no, not one: there is none that understandeth, there is none that seeketh after God. They are all gone out of the way, they are together become unprofitable; there is none that doeth good, no, not one" (Romans 3:10-13).

No only has sin affected all mankind; it has also affected every part of man's being – his throat, tongue, lips, mouth, feet, and eyes. "Their throat is an open sepulcher; with their tongues they have used deceit; the poison of asps is under their lips: whose mouth is full of cursing and bitterness: their feet are swift to shed blood: destruction and misery are in their ways: and the way of peace have they not known: there is no fear of God before their eyes" (Romans 3: 13-18).

Man sins against his God, against his neighbor, and against himself.

Instead of worshipping his God, he insults Him by making idols and bowing down to them. His gods are images of man, of birds, of four-footed beasts, and of creeping things (Romans 1:23). Instead of being thankful to God for life, food, clothing, and shelter, man curses God. He does not swear by popes, presidents, or princes, but he takes the Name of the Lord, his God, in vain (Exodus 20:7). He has feelings of settled enmity against God instead of love for Him. He is only happy when he can forget God, and only sad when he remembers Him.

Not only does man sin against God; he sins against his fellow men. He not only engages in vile pleasures himself, but encourages others to do the same. "Who knowing the judgment of God, that they which commit such things are worthy of death, not only do the same, but have pleasure in them that do them" (Romans 1:32). "For they sleep not, except they have done mischief; and their sleep is taken away, unless they cause some to fall" (Proverbs 4:16).

Man is selfish. He must come first. He must have his own way. In order to satisfy his bodily passions, he corrupts others through adultery, fornication, and other forms of vile sexual behavior.

He tells lies in order to further his own ends. He cannot be trusted. "Cease ye from man, whose breath is in his nostrils: for wherein is he to be accounted of?" (Isaiah 2:22). Whoever trusts him is cursed (Jeremiah 17:5).

He rejoices when calamity comes to others – rejoices that it does not affect him.

He vents his anger and malice on his neighbor. He envies those who have more than he and plots to steal what does not belong to him.

And if he finds a man who is more righteous than he, what does he do? Does he seek to bring his own life up to the higher standard? On the contrary, he seeks to destroy the one whose virtuous life exposes him (John 3:19, 20)!

He not only sins against his God and his neighbor; he sins against himself. He abuses his body through drunkenness, immorality, and dissipation. He wastes his talents and squanders his possessions. He refuses wise counsel and rejects his truest Friend. If he only knew it, he is his own worst enemy.

Man does not like to think of God showing grace. "Grace – which means the full and free forgiveness of every sin, without God demanding or expecting anything from the one so forgiven – is a principle so opposed to all man's thought and ways, *so far above man, that he dislikes it. His own heart often secretly calls it injustice. He does not deal in this way and he does not like to think of God doing so."* – *J.N. Darby.*

Various illustrations are used in the Bible to describe man's sinful state. For instance, he is likened to a leper (Matthew 8:2), speaking of his vile, and incurable, contaminating condition. He is paralyzed (John 5:5), deaf (Mark 7:32), dumb (Mark 9:17), blind (John 9:1), and dead in trespasses and in sins (Ephesians 2:1). He is fallen, polluted, helpless and hell-deserving.

The climax of man's sin came [more than[47]] nineteen hundred years ago. When God came to this world in the Person of Jesus Christ, men looked at the only perfect Man Who ever lived; yet they could not tolerate Him. He did not come to steal, kill, or destroy, but to give life and to give it more abundantly (John 10:10); yet the creatures whom His hands had made cried, "This is the heir: come, let us kill him" (Luke 20:14)" (End of quote)[48].

I admit that I haven't met with a better well-aimed, exact and truthful definition of man's sinfulness than this. Now, with over two decades of the counseling ministry behind me, I can only confirm the above said with "yea" and "amen". No doubt, such accurate characteristic can only by given by someone who is a counselor himself, because only a soul's physician is so knowledgeable about soul's sicknesses. And really, only when people come to counseling, all masks abate. Then, each and every thing gets called its proper name, and a man stands before the light of God as is. We, humans, are not just corrupted, but unbelievably, horribly, indescribably corrupted; and only in acknowledging this fact can we truly understand it for the first time how undeserving we are of this mercy and grace bestowed upon us by God through His Son Jesus Christ. There is only one explanation, why in spite of all the corruption the Lord still loves us, and it is the holy blood of the Lamb of God shed on the cross of Golgotha. And the price of Christ's blood namely is what transfers us from being unworthy to becoming precious in the eyes of God. Therefore, I don't know how to express my gratitude to God for being entrusted with His most valuable possession of all – human soul. With passing years there were many things I needed to realize and had much to learn in this ministry. One of them, for example, was to love people not because they were to my liking, but because Jesus loved them; to suffer and bear a lot of harsh things from them, not because I was so patient by nature, but because Christ had long-suffered for them; to wait and hope they would change only because the Lord has been waiting for them and "not writing anybody off". He taught me to

---

[47] Time reference is added by the translator.
[48] Used by permission from ECS Ministries at www.ecsministries.org where the book is still available.

forgive and to forget unfaithfulness and betrayal of people, while turning it over to God's justice, because He showed me how disloyal I had been toward Him.

I won't forget one event which has become a good spiritual lesson for the rest of my life. The Lord placed it on a woman's heart to go to me for counseling. She was almost 10 years older than I and had had quite a few counselors so far. Therefore, she did not want to accept the motive as a will of God and resisted it for many months. However, the Lord surmounted her resistance, and one time she came to speak with me. For many months and even years we continued our joint struggle with sin which tormented her for decades, until, finally her soul with God's help, found freedom. But time went on, and after a series of certain events a wall rose up between us. Her soul completely shut up. Silence became reticence, which in time grew to hostility. I felt very heavy for I couldn't understand the reason for this. Once, when I was feeling sad about this soul, my husband and I were getting back home after a church service. It got very late. It was pouring outside, and while listening to the rain's scathing beats on our car's windows, I began silently crying, swallowing up my tears and discreetly brushing them off my face, so that my husband wouldn't see it. Fortunately, he was deep in his own thoughts and wasn't noticing anything anyway, so I could safely give myself over to my grief. "Lord!" I was calling heavens in my thoughts. "Please, take her away from me. She causes me so much pain! You know, I haven't done her anything wrong. Neither have I sought her friendship. You Yourself brought her to me and told me to pray. Oh, how many sleepless nights I have spent because of her…! How much struggle I have gone through! Ah, how hard and ungrateful a human heart can be!"

Thus I have pitied myself and mourned when suddenly a voice in my heart said, "*Are you crying, Ludmila?? Stop, and consider Me. Do you remember how being crucified on a cross, spat upon, mocked and beaten by those for whom I suffered, tortured by spiritual torment and physical pain, I prayed: 'Father, forgive them, for they know not what they do!'? That's how you should pray: 'Forgive this soul, because she does not know what she does'*". The voice grew silent. My tears immediately dried up, and the ache breaking my own soul apart, was gone. Peace descended into my heart. Some wonderful heavenly calm filled and overfilled my whole being. It felt like a miracle! I quieted down, listening to my soul and being amazed at the sudden inner change. There was no more sadness nor hurt, nor self-mourning. There was only compassion and love towards that person, as well as a desire to pray for her even more than before. That's how I met again with the Lord Who while endlessly loving a man's soul teaches His child to love in the same manner. After a while the woman restored her connection with me and has been assistance and a blessing to me for many years.

That episode taught me a lot. And when later other people who had formerly come for counseling, for different reasons turned away and in their rebellion said spiteful things about me or even at times treacherously "stabbed in the back", time and again I have recalled these words, "Father, forgive them, for they know not what they do".

Counseling is a peculiar ministry and, in my opinion, only a person called by God is able to carry it out, otherwise, one will not endure it and break down spiritually. But if the Lord determined it for you, He then will undoubtedly give you the necessary strength to perform it. Devil does not remain passive when someone prayerfully stands up for an enslaved soul. He takes vengeance in all fierceness of his satanic nature, and in fact, uses those for his purpose, who call themselves children of God. With their "aid" he especially quickly reaches his goal – to bring a counselor to despair, break his spiritual strength and force him to quit his ministry.

There are so many Christians who need counseling help and advocated prayer and there are only a handful of those, who forgetting themselves, are capable of helping these people! It seems to me that the ratio may be even as much as 98% to 2%; however, those 2% typically have no break at all. Although I must say there is nothing unusual about it. It was similar to that in the past, and it is now, and it will always be. Just recall the prophets of the Old Testament and their cries to heaven, when while interceding for His people before God they were banished, tortured, trampled and persecuted. Therefore, the prophet Elijah, being driven to despair and asking that he might die, said, *"It is enough! Now, Lord, take my life, for I am no better than my fathers! [. . .] For the children of Israel have forsaken Your covenant, torn down Your altars, and killed Your prophets with the sword. I alone am left; and they seek to take my life"* (1Kings 19:4, 10). The prophet Jeremiah, worn out by persecution and tortures, complains to the Lord and repeats after Elijah, saying, *"Cursed be the day in which I was born! [. . .]Why did I come forth from the womb to see labor and sorrow, that my days should be consumed with shame?"* (Jerem. 20:14, 18) or *"I have become the ridicule of all my people – Their taunting song all the day [. . .] My enemies without cause hunted me down like a bird. They silenced my life in the pit and threw stones at me. The waters flowed over my head; I said, "I am cut off!"[. . .] You have seen all their vengeance, all their schemes against me. You have heard their reproach, O Lord, all their schemes against me, the lips of my enemies and their whispering against me all the day"* (Lam. 3:14, 52-54, 60-62). The Lord Himself spoke about scornful treatment the prophet was getting from God's people, *"So my people come pretending to be sincere and sit before you.* **They listen to your words, but they have no intention of doing what you say**. *Their mouths are full of lustful*

169

words, and their hearts seek only after money. You are very entertaining to them, like someone who sings love songs with a beautiful voice or plays fine music on an instrument. **They hear what you say, but they don't act on it!'** (Ezek.33:31-32). The reading of these words involuntarily makes one think about many a church service where God's people go to nowadays. Won't you agree there is a remarkable parallel to the description of the meetings God was telling Ezekiel about?

In New Testament times the Apostle Paul might be a striking example of a suffering minister of God, who gave himself completely over to serve people. And how did it go? What was his "reward" for such undivided selfless giving? Here is what the apostle Paul says about it, *"Are they ministers of Christ?—I speak as a fool—I* am *more: in labors more abundant, in stripes above measure, in prisons more frequently, in deaths often. From the Jews five times I received forty* stripes *minus one. Three times I was beaten with rods; once I was stoned; three times I was shipwrecked; a night and a day I have been in the deep; in journeys often, in perils of waters, in perils of robbers, in perils of my own countrymen, in perils of the Gentiles, in perils in the city, in perils in the wilderness, in perils in the sea, in perils among false brethren; in weariness and toil, in sleeplessness often, in hunger and thirst, in fastings often, in cold and nakedness— besides the other things, what comes upon me daily: my deep concern for all the churches. Who is weak, and I am not weak? Who is made to stumble, and I do not burn with indignation?"* (2 Cor.11:23-29).

What a glorious minister of the Gospel! What a counselor! What a model for imitation of following the Lord! And at the same time, what a symbol of a man misunderstood by others, forsaken and hated by many!

This is only a short list taken from pages of the Holy Scripture; the list which was later added to by next generation of the faithful bearers of God's truth, many of whom became martyrs for Christ in their life and death. In the Epistle to Hebrews, Chapter 11, verses 36-38 there recorded the most amazing words, *"Still others had trial of mockings and scourgings, yes, and of chains and imprisonment. They were stoned, they were sawn in two, were tempted, were slain with the sword. They wandered about in sheepskins and goatskins, being destitute, afflicted, tormented—* **of whom the world was not worthy.** *They wandered in deserts and mountains, in dens and caves of the earth".*

Well, as they say, the history repeats itself, confirming that humanity has not changed in its core. Just as in ancient times 'the born of the flesh' persecuted 'the born of the spirit', so it is now: those living by the flesh persecute the ones living by the spirit, being genuinely sure that by doing it they serve God.

Praise the Lord that the Holy Scriptures contain examples, through which one can learn a lot. It rejuvenates and builds up in hope, and gives a new strength to press on. Very often, when I lost heart, when I was exhausted and wanted to quit everything, my memory recalled the wonderful passages from the Word of God, which during such times as these spoke with amazing clarity and became priceless spiritual help. For instance, when one person hardened her heart, lacking understanding of my motives and began to say spiteful things, the Lord reminded me these words, *"For there is not a just man on earth who does good and does not sin. Also do not take to heart everything people say, lest you hear your servant cursing you. For many times, also, your own heart has known that even you have cursed others"* (Eccl. *7:20-22*). When dark clouds thickened above my soul and it seemed there was no breakthrough, the words of comfort sounded in my heart, *"Nevertheless the gloom will not be upon her who is distressed"*[49] (Isa. 9:1). When plunged into disappointment, tiredness and despair I wished to forget everything and take a break, leaving the ministry, a thought drilled my mind, *"[. . .]not lagging in diligence, fervent in spirit, serving the Lord; rejoicing in hope, patient in tribulation, continuing steadfastly in prayer[. . .]"*[50] (Rom.12:11-12). When I thought I had found a person who would understand and share my burden, a verse from the Scripture would float up in my memory, *"You are trusting in the staff of this broken reed, Egypt, on which if a man leans, it will go into his hand and pierce it"* (2 Kings 18:21). However, being a trusting person by nature and capable of quick affections, I disregarded that warning, and therefore, always paid dearly for it. As I went to the Lord with my belated remorse, again I found an exhortation in His Word, *"Confidence in an unfaithful* man *in time of trouble* is like *a bad tooth and a foot out of joint"* (Prov. 25:19). When I wanted to cry in pain, experiencing treachery of those whom I considered my confidants, and craved to pay back with the same, words of warning would come to my heart, *"Beloved, do not avenge yourselves, but* rather *give place to wrath; for it is written, "Vengeance is Mine, I will repay," says the Lord"* (Rom. 12:19). But the words God told the prophet Jeremiah, whom I love so much, helped me more often in those difficult times, *"If you return, then I will bring you back; you shall stand before Me; if you take out the precious from the vile, you shall be as My mouth. Let them return to you, but you must not return to them. And I will make you to this people a fortified bronze wall; and they will fight against you, but they shall not prevail against you; for I am with you to save you and deliver you," says the Lord. I will deliver you from the hand of the wicked, and I will redeem you from the grip of the terrible"* (Jerem. 15:19-21). Ah, how wonderful that we have the

---

[49] Russian Synodal text of Isaiah is recorded in chapter 8, verse 22 and says: "For darkness will not always be where it has now thickened."

[50] Again, Russian translation is emphasized in a following way: "Do not lag in diligence; be fervent in spirit; serve the Lord! Have comfort in hope, be patient in sorrow, be constant in prayer…"

Time flies…Fifty years of my life have already past.

Narrow Path

Word of God, but it is even better when it becomes alive and starts speaking, comforting, exhorting and convincing us!

That's how I am constantly learning. And the Lord, being faithful to His Word, turns my errors into good, continuing to work within my soul, prompting me to realize something, to repent in certain things, to leave some things behind, to reject other things completely and begin to see and understand things anew. Therefore, I am deeply thankful to the Heavenly Father that in my life the amazingly true words may also be fulfilled, "[. . .] *that all things work together for good to those who love God, to those who are the called according to* His *purpose"* (Romans 8:28).

Especially, I thank Him for the ministry of caring for souls He entrusted me with; souls, for whom He shed His blood and who continue to come, replacing one another. Many of them I don't get to meet for years.

I know them only by their correspondence and phone calls, because they live in different cities of Germany and other countries: USA, Israel, Australia, Finland, Great Britain, Spain, Russia, Ukraine, Belarus, Moldova, Latvia, Lithuania, Estonia and other territories of the former Soviet Union.

I do not have any kind of theological education and have never completed any classes for counselors; therefore, people who need help are my main "university" and the best spiritual school I get. Unwittingly, they become a help and a blessing to me, inadvertently teaching me the precious lessons that widen my horizon and enhance my own spiritual improvement and growth.

Nothing else but, namely, the ministry of counseling opened my heart to Christians of all denominations, notwithstanding their position in some or the other spiritual doctrines. I have not the slightest doubt that the body of Christ as a whole – the Church of Jesus Christ – will consist of people representing very different Christian confessions. Because in essence, there are only two kinds of Christians, namely, those **who truly are the children of God** and those **who only call themselves as such**; and besides, one can find both kinds in any Christian congregation. It is not the name of a denomination we belong to that characterizes our fundamental nature, but the fact whether we really are God's children living according to the Holy Scripture. Our Savior had not said these sobering words in vain, *"Not everyone* **who says** *to Me, 'Lord, Lord,' shall enter the kingdom of heaven, but he* **who does** *the will of My Father in heaven"* (Matt.7:21).

Counseling helped me to look at the believers through different eyes. During many years of my ministry I have had opportunities to meet with some wonderful, sincere, seeking souls among those whose company one is usually told to shun, as well as with cold in their

173

Pharisee-like piety, stiff in their unshakably "right" conceptions representatives of traditional "thriving" churches. Eternity only will reveal who will be considered a true child of God and a sheep of Jesus Christ, since up there, as I have said earlier, they have got quite different dimensions. I am afraid that a sizable portion of Christians will experience the greatest shock of their life as they cross its finish line, and realize how much off mark their ideas, opinions and assumptions had been. How shameful we'll feel one day because of the fact that while being on earth we have impudently dared to assume a role which by all rights belonged **only to God**.

Counseling or soul-caring[51] opens the eyes of the ministers to the true spiritual condition of the members of their congregations and churches. And in every respect I agree with many missionaries, evangelists and preachers, who visited the former Soviet Union, that absence of such necessary and very valuable ministry or the obvious limitation of it, is one of the weakest sides of Christianity in Russia, Ukraine, Moldova, Kazakhstan and other countries.

---

[51] It describes the meaning of the word "counseling" in Russian language the best (Translator's note).

Chapter 12

Parting with Kwa Sizabantu

Dear Reader! I have now come to the hardest moment of my narrative and to the most difficult of all experiences I had gone through in more than fifty years of my life. I would have given much to keep this pain from resurrecting in my heart's memory but, alas, can do nothing about it. Reality remains a reality, however harsh it might have been.

Seventeen years which I had spent in Kwa Sizabantu circle of friends and advocates included seven years of work on the trilogy and ten years of mission trips to the former Soviet Union and other countries along with Erlo Stegen and his other coworkers. All of that plus numerous meetings and conferences, where I participated as a coworker of Kwa Sizabantu and many years of counseling ministry have created tight bonds, which I could not have imagined to ever be broken.

It all started when the first book of the trilogy had been published and we began receiving invitations to hold evangelistic campaigns in Russia, Ukraine, Caucasus, and other republics of the former Soviet Union. In conjunction with that, the work of organizing and setting up those mission trips significantly increased. The trips usually lasted for ten to twelve days and took place in various cities and villages, churches and congregations of different denominations. During such trips one spends all his time together with others and, therefore, gets to have more contact and know each other a lot better. Under these circumstances while getting into different situations you can see, hear and observe many things which are impossible to notice when you are a simple listener in a sanctuary, attentively concentrating on what is being said from a pulpit. However you look at it, but our behavior and reactions, the incidentally dropped remarks and commentaries, our facial expressions, deeds and actions under certain clauses can definitely cross off everything we say, witness and preach; even if it be the absolute truth. And this is exactly what happened to me.

Right at the time of our second mission trip to Russia, in April 1992, some things which became evident to me really disturbed and confused me, also causing anxiety and my first alarming questions, "How could this be? Can you really do that? How can you combine it with what was written in the books about revival, and what brothers had preached about?" Being a coworker I had an opportunity to attend special meetings arranged by the leadership of Kwa Sizabantu for their preachers, pastors, counselors and other spiritual ministers, which also allowed me from time to time to see things happening behind the scenes.

It was one thing – to sit in an auditorium and listen to what is preached from the pulpit, and quite another – to see and experience it, which is limited to only a few. Besides, as I did counseling, I heard many facts from other people which matched to my own observations, forcing me to think, verify and compare the occurrences with the Holy Scripture that teaches us to examine all things. However, the idea was too intimidating to think that something wrong had penetrated the revival. I saw the fruits of our ministry, observed the blessings brought by the three books about the revival, leading hundreds and thousands of souls to acknowledging their sins, repentance and changeover. For that reason I refused all critical thoughts, especially because we had continuously been told that suspicions and judgment were horrendous sins destroying man's soul and God's work. Fearing to sin against the leaders by means of wrong assumptions had shackled, paralyzed and blocked my normal ability to think and assess in a healthy manner.

Counseling ministry and contact with Christians of different views, concepts and world views forced me to look for serious literature more frequently, where I could obtain necessary information and find answers to the questions raised by those who came to me. This way by reading quotations of the men of God from different eras and by drawing upon their rich spiritual experience, I came across things that shed light to what was going on with us, the group of followers of Kwa Sizabantu. The Word of God says it plainly that there is nothing new under heaven and in many a circumstance of our days, one can find the echoes of the past events. For instance, in all spiritual revivals, however dissimilar they may have seemed, there have always been a common ground, including mistakes, miscalculations and all sorts of deviations, which sooner or later lead to smothering and bringing to a complete halt something which was once a work of God.

While reading the books, pondering and comparing events, I had to admit that many things which guided one or the other revivals of the past to digression from the truth and destruction had already been present in Kwa Sizabantu movement for a while. But the heaviest blow I got when after counseling sessions with some former members of various sects, whose stories awakened a keen interest in me, I got a hold of a literature, explaining the essence of delusions in sects, cults, false doctrines and different spiritual misuses. To my horror, there were at least 70% to 80% of typical characteristics and features of sects listed, which described Kwa Sizabantu, and which I due to my ignorance simply did not pay attention to. Thus, little by little my eyes opened to the core of things that for me went without saying. Time and again the words of the Holy Scripture came to mind, "*Who is blind but My servant, or deaf as My messenger whom I send? Who is blind as he who is perfect, and blind as the Lord's servant? Seeing many things, but you do not observe; opening the ears, but he does not hear*" (Isaiah 42:19-20).

The same could have been said about me. Being a coworker I had an opportunity to see a lot, but as an active adherent of this work, I tried simply not to notice anything, thinking there were others who carried a responsibility to sort things out, whereas my business was only to pray, not criticize.

However, the time went on, and events developed in such a way that it was impossible not to see the apparently undesirable facts. More often than before the news reached our ears that one or the other involved member and devotee of Kwa Sizabantu in South Africa left the mission. Among those who left were first of all the close relatives of Erlo Stegen: his mother, two of his brothers and a sister with all their families. Almost all admirers of Kwa Sizabantu in Europe, including myself, considered those "poor souls" to be confused and departed from the truth, not troubling ourselves to investigate it deeper, or perhaps out of fear to displease and cause suspicion of our leaders. They didn't talk about those who left and tried not to remember them, as if they never existed (by the way, such fate was appointed to all who left Kwa Sizabantu). After a while the number of departed began to increase. For example, Friedel Stegen's son-in-law Koos, who had carried a rather important ministry at the mission, left the station. In 1995, a black coworker Muzi Kunene, in whom they had great hopes, had departed from Kwa Sizabantu. Behind him, he left a trail of rather scandalous stories which were carefully hidden by the leadership. Next year, in 1996, all members of European branches KSB in Germany, Switzerland, France, Holland and Belgium were shocked when they heard the news that Erlo Stegen's wife's own brother, Trevor Dahl, said farewell to the mission. He had been Erlo's right hand, a counselor, a great preacher and a blessed minister of the Gospel, valued and respected by the entire mission. Yet he left without explanation, declaring that God had shown him a different way.

The departure of this man of God hit a shattering blow to my confidence in the correctness of the revival teaching. Trevor Dahl knew this movement basically from its beginning, that is to say, for about thirty years, twenty-five of which he had lived directly at the mission station, where he led a colossal work and knew the structure of every Kwa Sizabantu activity as a few did. And such a man broke loose and said good-bye to something he had been devoted to for a major part of his life. His brief words that God had shown him a different way were a mystery to me. What was behind those words? What did really make him to leave behind his responsibilities, his numerous friends, well-established house at the mission and step into a complete obscurity? It had no sense to ask Kwa Sizabantu leaders about it, because everything was being done to make his name be forgotten as soon as possible.

In a fairly short time a seemingly serene world of calm and unshakable unity of European branches of Kwa Sizabantu shattered. Some unbelievable events started taking place and in spite of all precautionary measures of keeping them under a carpet they leaked out, reaching the ears of regular members. One by one our leading brothers started disappearing from the scene, and within a year one-third of leaders of Kwa Sizabantu Germany left the mission, including the pastor of our subdivision in a town of Schwäbisch Gmünd (Lindach). Then the ordinary members of the congregations could hardly understand what was truly going on. One thing was clear: primarily those **who were better informed** were leaving Kwa Sizabantu.

During that stage some people started coming to me for counseling. From them I learned about many scandalous stories that had to do with the mission. They asked for advice and sought help. Because of that, I turned to main leaders with some of the questions, which I have bitterly regretted later, having experienced the reaction I would have never expected. By that time I was already under suspicion. Time and again I faced the same question – what must I do: to please men or to do what the Word of God teaches? For the most part I could no longer reconcile my conscience to what was happening around.

When in October of 1999 we had our next mission trip with Erlo Stegen to USA, I realized it would be my last one. At the end of the trip I became very sick and could not participate in the worship services, a fact that made me very happy. As I got back to Germany, I called Erlo Stegen in South Africa and said that due to my poor health condition I must temporarily leave the ministry. My physical and emotional strength was undermined. I literally felt myself in ruins.

Day and night my soul called upon the Lord for guidance. I had a choice. I could either, continue my ministry, remain true to Kwa Sizabantu and compromise my conscience or leave the movement altogether and lose everything I gained there: hundreds of friends, their love and approval, popularity and, perhaps, even my ministry. The inner struggle went on for months. Memories of past blessings, of what was revealed and received through Kwa Sizabantu, of precious hours and days spent together, of all that had undeniably enriched me spiritually alternated with sadness, pain, doubts and countless disappointments in people, which had been an example for imitation and, as it seemed to me, of altruistic service to God.

I had a feeling that ground was slipping away from under my feet. There was nothing to stand on or to grab onto. Had all that I had experienced in the past seventeen years really been only a delusion?? Had that, which was written in the books about the revival, not reflected the reality?? Yes, but I had not made anything up! They only contained that which was told by Erlo Stegen! I was only a tool of Russian language for him! It would be inconceivable to think that he lied or grossly exaggerated! But if so, then I was the one who imparted it on my people, on all Russian-speaking population of many thousands or even millions of souls dispersed all over the globe! But I was so afraid to bring to others something which was not the truth and would have done harm to those for whom Christ had died! O, Lord, what was it?? Was it Your work and the truth or self-delusion, counterfeit revival, where there wasn't and isn't Your Spirit . . . ?? Then, all which had been done was done in vain and was a straw; a house built on sand; a work which would burn away and without any value in the light of eternity! But what do I do about the voice which spoke to me at Kwa Sizabantu and ordered to bring this preaching to Russia? How am I to interpret what I personally experienced in the moment of my own contact with eternity? How can I possibly compare it all? What should I accept? What must I refuse? How should I continue to live and what must I do anyway?? Will I ever be capable of trusting anyone anymore after all of this . . . ?

I was literally bent to the ground by bitter feelings of being deceived and being a deceiver of others against my will. The thoughts of it plunged me in such despair that all I wanted was to be a little mouse hiding in a tiny hole in order not to see anyone or say anything; not to know or hear anything. How many tears have I wept during those long restless nights! And how much spiritual strength and agonizing struggle it cost me – only God knows. I knew I was killing myself over it, but had no vigor to stop and pull myself together. It looked like a spiritual suicide, but I really did covet to die in those days. Like the disciples calling out to Jesus in the boat, "Master, Master, we are perishing!" I, too, shouted in the midst of the storm of my soul, "Lord, if You don't help me, I will perish!" And I also did not hear His answer. Although, perhaps, there was one, but in the roar of confusion it did not reach my spiritual ear. One time in an instance of a brief brightening up, as I, spiritually worn out, hoped and longed for nothing, the familiar calm voice clearly rang in my heart, asking me a simple question,

"Ludmila, is there anything permanent on earth?"

"No!" I answered without thinking and as always caught by a surprise, "Everything on earth is temporal."

179

"Then what are you weeping about and why are you tormenting yourself? How can you build on something that will end sooner or later?"

"Lord, but I believed the revival was true, and therefore I passed the news on to the others."

"Hadn't there been true spiritual revivals in the history of Christianity? But where are they now? Wasn't the Apostolic Church a sample of the first revival? But it does not exist anymore. Nevertheless, she gave birth to the Christianity of the generations to follow. Then why are you crying over something that is not permanent and sooner or later will pass away?"

My tears dried up instantly, and heavenly peace filled my aching heart. Really, why am I crying? Why am I trying to comprehend something that will, perhaps, be revealed only in eternity? How often in the history of God's people the Lord did something that was misunderstood by the masses. There are examples left on the pages of the Holy Scriptures that up until now are still unattainable for human brain. The Lord is Sovereign. He does what He wants, when He wants and the way He wants, being accountable to no one, without explanation and justification. Our mind is too small, narrow and limited to understand our boundless Creator. Perchance, only the afterlife will disclose things that were so unachievable and unapproachable for us here on this earth.

In any case I had to do only one thing – to ask the Lord to make known His will to me and carry it out at whatever the cost may be. I began to pray, asking Him to show me what Kwa Sizabantu is in His eyes at present time and whether I should remain there. Within several days I had three dreams, in which Kwa Sizabantu was presented to me in three ways:

1. As a powerful turbid stream, where many people drowned right before my eyes.

2. As a tall multifamily apartment building which had dangerous cracks and was shaking ready to tumble down, burying tenants under its ruins, where I was one of them. In the course of this dream I heard the words, "Flee from here! Flee and do not linger! Flee to the mountain!" When I fled with my husband away from this house, I yelled to the people in order for them to be saved but only a few followed us.

3. In my third dream I saw a jail surrounded by a high wall with a barbed wire. The amazing thing about it was that for those who were inside the wall it seemed to be a beautiful resort, rolled in lavish floral plants and greenery, which hid a prison wall from their view. Only the ones staying outside its boundaries noticed the wall and the jail.

These dreams shed light on the situation. I received the answer I sought.

It was June of 2000 when it was unexpectedly announced from the pulpit of our congregation in Lindach, that Lydia Dube (the one, who according to Erlo Stegen's words experienced death and miraculous resurrection) committed a grave sin and was no longer a co-worker at Kwa Sizabantu of South Africa. In addition, it was said that Barney Mabaso – a black pastor of the largest Christian fellowship of Zulu tribe in Tugela Ferry parted with Kwa Sizabantu and left the mission together with the eight hundred members of his church.

Such news for all who had gathered sounded like a thunder from the clear sky. I was sitting in a state of shock. Barney Mabaso, who was called "a fiery preacher" and who was characterized by Erlo Stegen himself as "a man of truth", broke off with Kwa Sizabantu movement . . . ?? How do you put this together . . . ?? If the truth is there, then why did "a man of truth" split off from this revival? Why did he, who came to the Lord through Erlo Stegen's preaching even before the revival started, leave his spiritual mentor, completely tearing off from him and all that was so dear and precious to him. . . ? O, how many "why's" have possibly cried out to heaven in the hearts and minds of those present in the sanctuary, but the people, trained not to ask unnecessary questions, kept silent.

That which I heard had finally confirmed the correctness of my decision. I stopped thinking about consequences, only waiting until the right time came for my exodus. In July, for the first time in those years I didn't go to the usual European conference lead by the Kwa Sizabantu mission in Switzerland. When it ended, on August 5, 2000 I sent out eight copies of my departure letter to the leaders of all European branches asking to read it in front of their congregations. I couldn't leave quietly and unnoticed, because for ten years I ministered as a counselor and co-worker, being responsible for all Russian-speaking believers who took this teaching to their hearts. Here are the contents of my letter:

To all churches, congregations, home groups and friends of Kwa Sizabantu for public reading.

Dear brothers and sisters!

I want to inform you all that following the long, disturbing contemplations and thorough scrutiny of occurring events; after extensive prayers and persistent petitions to the Lord asking for a clear guidance, I have come to an extremely difficult, literally heart-rending decision to severe my relations with Kwa Sizabantu mission.

A lot of things that have recently taken place in this revival movement do not agree with my conscience any longer. I cannot and have no right before God and His Church to further identify myself with it.

181

Our newly organized, just a year ago, Christian mission "Waters of Life" from now on shall work as a completely independent organization, having nothing to do with Kwa Sizabantu mission.

With heartfelt greetings,

Ludmila Plett.

Unfortunately, when this letter reached congregations, it was either ignored without mentioning it to anyone, or loosely quoted without actual reading but to the most extent in a similar word fashion as this, "Ludmila Plett broke her relations with Kwa Sizabantu because she had formed her own mission and wanted to work independently."

By the way, our mission "Waters of Life" was formed according to the advice of Kwa Sizabantu leaders themselves more than a year before my departure. The previously supposed name "Kwa Sizabantu of Russia" was replaced by "Waters of Life"[52] at Friedel Stegen's urgent request. Therefore, such oral interpretation did not correlate to the true contents of my letter and was in fact, a pure fiction.

After such an announcement several people phoned me, asking the same question, have I really become that proud that I did not want to work together with Kwa Sizabantu? Because of that I was then forced to send out copies of my letter to certain people, and later, publish it on the Internet, in order to explain the reason of my disappearance from the Kwa Sizabantu scene. The years went by. Since that time I have not written anything and haven't signed any papers or documents against this movement (as was alleged by many). I can only pity that Christians can lie so exquisitely. However, let it remain on their conscience.

After leaving Kwa Sizabantu I heard about various scandalous stories connected with the movement (of which much was said and written), but had no desire to spread them furthermore. God is the Judge of all and for all.

Subsequent to my departure almost all friends and acquaintances as well as individuals who had turned to me with counseling questions, - all from Kwa Sizabantu circles, - severed their contacts with me. Well, it was expected. I wasn't the first one and most certainly, not the last. Such is the fate of all who left the movement. Following my exit many Christians did the same and left Kwa Sizabantu. As far as I know, their number reached several hundred only in Germany.

I must admit that I had a difficult time after leaving Kwa Sizabantu. Seventeen years spent in its surroundings had made an impression on me, since I took in and absorbed everything we were

---

[52] The German name is "Wasser des Lebens mission".

taught and preached. Some of those things were good and right, others were extreme and obviously radical. After all I had experienced I felt tired, sick and literally, squeezed out. I needed time to spiritually regain strength and sort the whole thing out, as well as simply recover from shock that left a deep bleeding wound in my heart. As I met with people who also parted with Kwa Sizabantu, I saw how much they were soul-sick and spiritually disoriented, being unable to understand where the truth was. Among them there were some who getting completely disappointed in everything, went back into the world. Thus, I became convinced how dangerous it was to build ones faith on someone's great personality or a certain doctrine, because by getting disappointed in any of one's ideals, a man can come close to the intolerable – to become disappointed in God and turn away from Him. Also I have realized what a huge responsibility lays on those who lead God's people, because their mistakes, sins, deviations and failures can bring destruction to the weak souls, whose blood will be asked from their hands.

After leaving Kwa Sizabantu I had to choose my subsequent position towards the movement. The seemingly easiest way was to simply blame the leadership for everything, as many others had unfortunately done. But would it be the right way, especially considering that I did not know details of all events and only heard about those who left the mission as it was pictured by brethren from Kwa Sizabantu? What if I could meet with them and speak to them where they lived? It would surely be improper to make a decision without getting all the facts beforehand. Sadly, there is a widely spread disease among Christians – to come to conclusions and make judgment by listening to only one side of the party. Certainly, with such method of approach those decisions more often happen to be absolutely incorrect.

Therefore, several months later after departing from Kwa Sizabantu, in February 2001 I flew to South Africa for the sixth time, only not to the mission station but to the congregation of Barney Mabaso which separated from it, in Tugela Ferry.

In a course of two weeks I met with approximately twenty former coworkers of Kwa Sizabantu, who shared with me their cheerless stories. What I heard from them really shocked me; so much that I couldn't sleep at night. Slowly, step by step, **a tragedy that swept this revival movement has taken its form**. We, humans, are all so different and therefore, understand events and problems which we encounter in various ways. We see and evaluate them from different perspectives. As I was listening, I paid particular attention to the same facts, of which two or three witnesses spoke independently so that *"by the mouth of two or three witnesses every word may be established"* (Matt. 18:16).

This way the richest information which shed light on episodes taking place from the beginning of revival and during its development up until recent times was collected on audiotapes. People, who told me their accounts, knew about things first hand by experience and not from somebody else's words. Based on their stories, a true picture which stretched over a time of more than forty years, was shaping up like a puzzle, starting not from 1966, which signified the beginning of revival at Mapomulu, but many years before; and not with the name of Erlo Stegen, but a man named Anton Engelbrecht, by whose ministry Erlo Stegen came to the Lord at the age of fifteen. After I read two books by Pastor Anton Engelbrecht "Der Herr nahm von der Herde" and "Wie ein Adler", and put them side by side with what I have heard later, I was able to understand the revival a lot better. Unfortunately, the life of this formerly blessed man of God through whom the Lord had moved mightily, ended in complete devastation which, alas, often happened to famous ministers in God's service. The life story of this man really caught my attention, because it shed light to much of what was going on later in the revival.

While listening to numerous accounts and testimonies I kept asking myself question after question, "Was it really a revival? If yes, then when, at what precise moment did Satan join in, acting in parallel with God's workings? Was it all a reality or had it only appeared as such and was just a wishful thinking? If the statements of some people that there was no revival were true and if from the beginning forces of hell played a great part, then how would one explain its amazing fruits, which I saw in my own life and in lives of many others who found the way to Light because of it? Can the Lord move in the area where Satan works or is it totally out of question? Does the beginning made by God always go in the right direction? Of course, we all know that the end of the matter crowns it, not the beginning, but if the end is so wretched, does it really mean that it wasn't God who started this?"

Involuntarily, the story of King Saul came to memory. God Himself and nobody else selected him of all the people to anoint him a king over Israel. And no one, but God Himself rejected that same Saul, by giving him up to a terrible death. How does one comprehend it? Didn't God know that Saul would leave the way of obedience and choose his own way? Undoubtedly, He did. God is God because He knows everything about the future. Then, why did He start something out that was destined for failure . . . ?? Here again one faces the fact that human brain is incapable of understanding God's actions, and the more we try to figure them out, the quicker we hit the dead end. One thing is clear – the error lies not in God's plans but in our human disloyalty to carry them out.

Flying back from South Africa I felt literally crushed. In my hands I had a wealth of material, but what was I supposed to do with it? Should I write an exposing book — how some people really expected it from me? Should I get all the truth out in the light and unmask the real story of revival? But with this kind of "**truth**" and "**reality**" one can rather kill than heal the souls. I recalled an ancient medical motto: "**Do not harm!**" which meant if a doctor couldn't help his patient, he had to take care at least not to make it worse and aggravate his poor condition. This case was of a similar nature. How much would it really help if I inform people about one more tragedy, disclosing how Satan succeeded in bringing to nothing that which could have been a blessed work of God? It is apparent enough that devil benefits a lot if we allow him to act scot-free.

The words of a man of God who left Kwa Sizabantu and whom I held at a high esteem, being amazed by his patience, love and spiritual prudence came to mind. To my question, "Tell me, why you are silent — you, who knows so much like no one else?" He simply said, "Ludmila, every coin has two sides and the same is true in this matter. On one hand there is what has been claimed by leaders and followers of Kwa Sizabantu, on the other hand is what we know seeing things in a different light. However, both sides are very subjective and relative. The absolute truth is what lies between them and what only God knows. We must never forget that we will give account for every word we say on the Judgment Day. Do you realize the responsibility we have for things we say, affirm and write? If something in our "truth" doesn't correspond to God's truth in eternity, what then . . . ?"

Yes . . . . What, then . . . ? I recalled in my memory words spoken by my husband that stroke me with their profundity many years ago when fighting for justice I was ready to do hand-to-hand combat. "Ludmila," he said calmly and soberly, "There is no need to fight for truth. Truth fights for itself."

"Wow," I thought to myself, "He is right, indeed. God Himself is the Truth. So it looks like I am trying to defend Him in my own strength, being a nonentity in essence. He does not need my "help"; much less, my defense. Truth stands for itself and is invincible due to the fact that God is **the Truth**." How ridiculous and absurd can be our labors in futile attempt to affirm something that in reality needs no affirmation, and shield that, which doesn't need any protection! If God's truth is with us and in us, we have no need to prove it. The proof will come in time and in a way, which God will provide.

When I realized that, I stopped explaining, defending, attesting and the more so, avenging those, who due to my departure from Kwa Sizabantu, charged me with all kinds of accusations. The Word of God says it not unjustly, "*Beloved, never avenge yourselves, but leave it to the wrath of*

God; for it is written, "Vengeance is Mine, I will repay," says the Lord" (Rom.12:19)[53]. If we get even with someone, perhaps, for a moment we will receive a temporal satisfaction, but will never achieve peace at heart. The good example of it was left for us by King David. Being chosen by God, he did not even the score with Saul, who pursued him to take his life. Yet when Saul was in David's hands, the latter, having fear of God in his heart, said, *"The Lord forbid that I should do this thing to my master, the Lord's anointed, to stretch out my hand against him, seeing he is the anointed of the Lord"* (1 Sam. 24:6), because, David said, *"who can stretch out his hand against the Lord's anointed, and be guiltless?"* (1 Sam. 26:9).

I thank God for such words written on the pages of the Holy Scripture by *"a man after God's own heart"*. May the Lord keep me from passing a judgment onto someone whom only God can take care of! He has the right to execute such judgment, and only His ruling will be just and true. I too am guilty before God, therefore, how can a guilty one judge the one who is in the wrong? Even this chapter is written only because some of the readers of my trilogy hearing about my departure from Kwa Sizabantu wrote back to me and called from everywhere demanding an explanation of my action. But how can I explain to everyone that, which leaves me yet with a lot of questions?? All I know is that in time God Himself will dot all the "i's" and cross all the "t's".

After leaving Kwa Sizabantu I positioned myself between two fires. On one hand all who regarded themselves faithful devotees of this revival movement, turned away from me, advising others to avoid any possible contact. I am a betrayer in their eyes. On the other hand those who separated from KSB also shunned me, thinking that by continuing to distribute the trilogy about revival, I kept winning souls for Kwa Sizabantu and therefore, continued to support it.

Humanly speaking, each of them was right in their own eyes and therefore, I could identify with both groups very well. If I were in their shoes, perhaps, I would have looked at it the same way. However, there is another side to the matter, which God only knows. As it had been mentioned earlier, the idea of writing books did not belong to me. In this situation I have merely carried out the will of God, which, to be honest with you, is not especially clear to me even now. Besides, the books were written not to glorify Erlo Stegen, myself or the South African revival, but with a single objective – to help Christians independently of their notions or denominations to understand the reason for their spiritual warmness and recognize that sins and our loyalty to them separates us from God, preventing Him to do what He desires.

---

[53] Taken from ESV Bible.

Judging by many statements made by people whom I met during missionary trips as well as by thousands of letters received from everywhere in past years, the objective has been achieved fully. God's children told and wrote that they had not had a book that would have had spoken to their hearts in a way those three books had. As a result, thousands of Christians began a much more serious approach to their Christianity. They have changed their lives in many aspects, and put in order their relationship with God and others, receiving deliverance from spiritual oppression. The Lord only knows how many souls repented because of them finding the way to salvation, and this work of the Holy Spirit continues until now. How can one cross it off? The Lord can use what He likes and whom He likes in order to add to the Church those who are being saved[54]. Addressing common people Jesus had once said some remarkable words, which concerned His spiritual enemies – Pharisees, *"Therefore whatever they tell you to observe, that observe and do, but do not do according to their works; for they say, and do not do"* (Matt. 23:3). Therefore, what Pharisees taught the people was accurate and founded on the Holy Scripture. For that reason, in spite of the fact that this teaching came out of the mouths of seemingly unworthy men, Jesus still recommended doing and observing all they taught. The Word of God remains effective and powerful Word of the Living God, even when it is coming from undeserving lips. In Russia they have a saying "When there is no fish, crawfish is just as good"[55]. So, not having anything better, God can employ that which is available, although it may be far from perfect. Something, which from a human standpoint can look doubtful, in His hands becomes a powerful and useful tool.

We are living during the last days of which Christ and later, His apostles spoke. It is the time which is characterized by spiritual decline, loss of the first love, cooling off, permissiveness of sin, powerlessness and apostasy among God's people. Worldliness enters Christian churches and congregations more and more, but the fear of God, reverence and awe before the Lord gradually become things of the past. From the church pulpits you could hardly hear firm warnings and denunciation of sins, and as a result, false peace, self-satisfaction and spiritual sleep sneak in the midst of the people of God. Before the first coming of Christ took place, God had given His people a forerunner – John the Baptist. He was a man without fear of men who spoke openly and directly about their sin and departure from God. And only after Israel accepted it and deeply repented, Christ has come. I think we, Christians of the last times, are in great need of such "John the

---

[54] Ref: Acts 2:47 (NKJV).
[55] Equivalent of "half a loaf is better than no bread".

Baptists" and "forerunners". But where are they? Where are the ones who can courageously and decidedly call things by their names and show modern people of God the way out of spiritual stagnation? Where are the ministers who can not only correctly teach and preach the truth, but show by personal example that Bible does not require the impossible from us? Today Christians of all denominations are in need of such preachers! There is only one important detail – you must have a right to preach that way, because the unworthy life of a speaker puts the heaviest lock on his lips.

Every fresh breath of God's Spirit, each revival known to Christian history, were preceded by direct and non-negotiable sermon about sin, about righteousness of God and His judgment; sermon which led men to the realization of their sins, repentance, purification and sanctification. As an outcome, the new wave of the working of God's power was taking place, which became a great blessing not only to those who lived then, but also to all future generations. Books describing the events of revivals of the years long gone are being read with joy even today, kindling a fire of love towards God in the hearts and causing a yearning, which awakens the desire to draw near to the Living God. Unfortunately, up until now the devil has always succeeded in bringing all the blessed beginnings to zero; however, departing from the scene of Christian history, they left a good residue behind. This is where I see the value in revival trilogy, because it carries a message about things which many children of God need today. As far as those who, like Pharisees, teach and preach correctly but do not consider it a priority to live by that, may it be on their conscience. The Lord has no partiality and will ask of each one not according to his words, but his deeds. The Apostle Paul understood that very well and therefore, was concerned about it, *"[. . .] lest, when I have preached to others, I myself should become disqualified"* (1 Cor. 9:27).

Thus, the books have served their purpose and continue to do so, helping those who need help. No doubt, one day they will become a history and sink into oblivion, just as it happened with their predecessors; however, the footprint of their accomplishment will last till eternity, where all that is dimmed now, will be revealed.

As for me personally, I thank God from the bottom of my heart that He sustained me and helped me to walk through a very difficult time of despondency and despair. In the toughest moment when all seemed lost, the Lord poured His balm of consolation and encouragement upon my soul using the lips of William MacDonald who had said the following, *"There comes a time in life when we must stop mourning over the past and get on with the work of the present [. . .]. This has a voice for us in our Christian life and service. Sometime it may happen that a ministry might we wrenched away from us and given to someone else. We grieve over the death of an avenue of service. It may be that a friendship or a partnership is severed, and that, as a result, life seems empty and flat. Or that we have been cruelly disappointed by someone who was very dear to us. We mourn the death of a valued relationship. Or it may be that some life-long dream is shattered or some ambition is frustrated. We mourn the death of a noble aspiration or vision. There is nothing wrong about mourning, but it should not be prolonged to the extent that it cripples our effectiveness in meeting the challenges of the hour [. . .]. We must not be forever inconsolable over circumstances that cannot be changed"[56].*

And besides, I am absolutely convinced that it was God's will for all I have experienced, because at the end it served for good, forcing me to investigate, re-evaluate and discard the things which were wrong in my concepts and ideas. And under no circumstances do I want to blame anyone for my mistakes and sufferings, because in order to teach me something, God has certainly needed to use others. As I have mentioned before, a man tends to blame others for his misfortunes, misery and wrong decisions, considering himself only a victim, an innocently suffering unfortunate sheep, which has gotten into wolves' teeth. But is it really so? How often what we go through is our own fault, since knowing all too well the warnings and exhortations of the Bible, we neglect them.

For instance, we know very well the commandment, *"You shall have no other gods before Me"* (Exodus 20:3). However, we incredibly often deify someone, attributing to him something which he doesn't possess, and then later on, with frantic zeal dethrone and oust that person from the place we put him on. We are also familiar with another commandment, *"You must not make for yourself an idol of any kind [. . .] You must not bow down to them or worship them, for I, the LORD your God, am a jealous God"* (Deut.5:8-9).[57] Well aware of that, we nevertheless get idols for ourselves, and after encountering God's jealousy, unmercifully crush the images of our imagination, pouring out anger and hatred on the subject of our recent worship. The Word of God warns us, saying that, *"Cursed is the man who trusts in man and makes flesh his strength"* (Jerem.17:5). We know these words by heart; however, it doesn't stop us from finding another human being in order to make him the model and the example to follow, forgetting that any man remains only a human and therefore, liable to err. Deep in frustration about someone we once hoped in, we become his worst enemy and want nothing to do with him. The Lord says, *"My glory I will not give to another"*[58] and *"you shall give glory to the God of Israel"*[59]. But we have no fear in glorifying

---

[56] Excerpts from May 6 of "One Day at a Time" by W. Macdonald, page 131.
[57] Taken from a New Living Translation Bible.
[58] Isaiah 42:8
[59] 1 Samuel 6:5

those who are being used by God in His vineyard and when our admired ones fall into pride and collapse spiritually, we "sit with the same broken wash-tab as before"[60].

One can be thoroughly amazed how a man who loves to blame others is completely unwilling to admit his own mistakes. I had listened to many people who left Kwa Sizabantu as they retold with astonishment that they couldn't understand how in the world they could have become so deceived. And only one woman, a teacher in South Africa, said some very sober words, "It is true that Kwa Sizabantu has two faces, one of which only a few are able to see. In the hearts and minds of these people there is not even a trace of a thought that the leaders of the revival can possibly do something wrong. And there is no method by which such human way of thinking might be corrected. The believers assume that the leaders must be perfect and it can't be otherwise. Glory and magnificence of Kwa Sizabantu is based on such flawlessness. I think our problem is that we are just a very proud people. We take pride because we can belong to such a glory. But this is not a Kingdom of God, but a human kingdom. The Bible says that, "*Cursed is the man who trusts in man and makes flesh his strength.*"[61] It seems to me that it talks about a man who doesn't even allow himself to think of another person to be able to err. That's why we were totally shocked when we saw all the errors of Kwa Sizabantu. However, it would be definitely wrong to blame the leaders for everything. The fault is ours! The things we were supposed to entrust to God, we entrusted completely to men. From the beginning we should have never forgotten that people do make mistakes, and there are no faultless people and never will be. Just recently I was able to visit one of the Kwa Sizabantu branches in Germany. As I was there, I saw like in a mirror the same thing we used to have in South Africa. You could have called it a pinnacle of magnificence of people's lives fused together by one cause. The majority of sermons, no matter who preached were nothing less than the continuous polishing and making that glory shine even brighter. There were youths, who exercised self-control and kept up their purity, the European Choir, the purchasing of building for Kwa Sizabantu center, a sacrificial giving of its members, etc. As I was listening, I looked back and evoked our sermons, at Kwa Sizabantu of South Africa, especially when Erlo Stegen preached. I recalled how everything was presented to us, how many stories were told, main idea of which was to underscore the

---

[60] Refers to a fairy tale by the famous Russian poet Alexander Pushkin "The Fisherman and The Goldfish" with its literal meaning corresponding to an English expression "to be no better off than before".
[61] Jerem 17:5

190

splendor of the job being accomplished here. Then I realized: that's why when someone started criticizing our work, our answer was not in line with what in fact the Word of God taught, but an advice to critics, which usually went something like this, "You should go and see for yourselves what the Lord does **here by us**. Come and you will see the magnitude of the work. Doesn't that prove to you that **we have the Truth**. . . ?" In my opinion, it reflects what the Apostle John calls "the pride of life". When my eyes had opened, I understood that we longed to be a part of the best. I remembered what our reaction was when children saw the visitors who came to us adorned in jewelry, dressed up in contemporary fashion and wearing make-up on their faces and asked one and the same question, "Are they Christians, too?" Usually, our response was this, "Yes, they are Christians, but **they don't have the same light we do**. God hasn't shown them **the better way**." Only now do I realize how much pride there was in such answer. In other words, it sounded like, "They don't have **what we have**."

While listening to this woman, I thought to myself, "Why, she is right, indeed! Isn't it true that it seems appropriate to feel superior, peculiar and exclusive after we have experienced blessings? We so easily forget where we were dug out from and how much we have been forgiven! How swiftly we become teachers, instilling in others something in which we ourselves are way far from being perfect! It is conceivable to take upon yourself something which you have no moral right to do, and teach others the truth, which has no bearing in your own life. In doing this we are likened to those of whom it is said, *"While they promise them liberty, they themselves are slaves of corruption [. . .]"* (2 Peter 2:19).

If you believe in your own elitism and exclusiveness, a conviction will come unnoticed that God now looks leniently at us in things which would be unthinkable for others. Then, we confidently allow ourselves to commit sins against which so fervently preach from the pulpit. And when people listen to this seemingly "uncompromised" Gospel they can't even imagine that the person, condemning sin "in God's power", is guilty of it, and the one calling all to perfection is far away from the mark. Unwillingly the words come to mind spoken by Jesus about the Pharisees, *"[. . .] for they say, and do not do. For they bind heavy burdens, hard to bear, and lay* them *on men's shoulders; but they* themselves *will not move them with one of their fingers"* (Matt. 23:3-4).

Chapter 13

What We Must Be Aware Of

We live in such a time when there are more and more of new doctrines keep popping up and competing with one another. A lot of them based on some precious Biblical principles; however they are subtly twisted, so that people are enamored by their doubtful teachings. The cunning falsehood has taken up an enormous size and leads away from the course even those who spiritually started out extremely well. Painfully or not, but we must admit that the seeking, sincere, God-loving souls get into the nets of new doctrines especially often. Getting tired of a superficiality and formality of the nominal Christianity of many traditional churches, they look for something that would satisfy their spiritual needs. However, in their quest they begin not with the personal contact with the Lord or with the diligent Bible study, which certainly require a lot of patience. They follow an easier path, turning towards the contemporary new teachings, whose leaders zealously offer them "chewed-up-and-ready-to-swallow" spiritual food, which often looks quite appetizing and attractive. Thus, being engrossed in something new and fascinating, believers completely forget the warning words of the Holy Scripture, *"O My people! Those who lead you cause you to err, And destroy the way of your paths" (Isa.3:12).*

Deception has many faces and most of them, in fact, do look quite piously being based on certain verses of Scriptures. By resorting to religious philosophy, unintelligible and refined interpretations, using their eloquence and ability to convince others, the new spiritual leaders achieve incredible results. Unfortunately, many Christians do not trouble to occupy themselves with a deep and serious study of the Bible, preferring to spend their free time in relaxation, entertainment and earthly needs. They think that for their souls and spiritual nourishment they have Sundays and preachers at the church, whose task is to bring the Word of God to them in a comprehensible form. This has been craftily utilized by so-called "men of God", who openly state that there is no real necessity to examine the Holy Scriptures, because God puts into the mouths of "His anointed ones"- who they are, indeed, - everything that their souls may possibly need. Therefore, gathering for worship services, people mindlessly gulp down everything that is presented from the pulpit without any pondering and healthy critique.

Most certainly, I am not trying to tell that an unhealthy spiritual food is being served from all of the church pulpits; nevertheless, such cases happen much more often that we may like to think. The Word of God unequivocally addresses us individually and Christians as a whole,

"Search the scriptures; for in them ye think ye have eternal life: and they are they which testify of Me" (John 5:39, KJV). The searching and the scrutinizing of the Holy Scripture is a requirement for every Christian and an obligation, too. In eternity no one will be able to say in a validation attempt, "Lord, I did this and that because such and such admonished me to do so." Oh, no! We should not be lead and controlled by other people, no matter who they are, but only by God and His Word. If we turn to a false way, the reason for it lays in the lack of knowledge of the Bible. It wasn't unjustly what Jesus had once said, *"You are mistaken, not knowing the Scriptures nor the power of God"* (Matt. 22:29).

One of the most precious Biblical principles that devil has much success in subtly thwarting and using to his purposes, is the issue of sanctification, however strange it may sound. I think there is not a Christian who would argue about the necessity and importance of sanctification in our Christian life. The Word of God tells us fairly plain, that *"[. . .] this is the will of God, your sanctification [. . .]"* (1 Thess.4:3). Sanctification, holiness, purification and breaking the bondage of sins are terms that are all very similar to each other in their meaning and are tightly bonded together. We all know that there hasn't been a single revival or a great work of God which happened throughout the history of Christianity without manifestation of these crucial Biblical truths. God is holy, and the Holy Spirit is called "Holy" because He cannot stand anything unclean. Christian life is unthinkable without sanctification and holiness. The words "sanctify", "sanctified", "sanctuary", "holy", "most holy", and "holiness" speckle throughout the pages of the Bible. However, they must not remain something we just read about, but that, which we apply in our own life daily, if we truly are the children of God.

Unquestionably, this is a subject which we should more often meditate, talk and preach about, "[. . .] to stir up *our* pure minds by way of reminder"[62]. Nevertheless, doing that we must not fall into another extreme, because, we can unnoticeably lead people to thinking that we get saved through our own holiness, which is nothing else but the greatest heresy. We are saved by grace through faith, receiving righteousness through Christ just as it's written, *"For by grace you have been saved through faith, and that not of yourselves; it is the gift of God, not of works, lest anyone should boast"* (Eph. 2:8-9). Without a doubt, the grace that we have received does not take away our responsibility for our own walk with the Lord, because if we consciously commit sin, it may deprive us of grace, and therefore, of salvation. We find the affirmation of this statement in the passage of Scripture from the letter to Hebrews 12:15-16 and 28-29, *"[. . .] looking carefully lest anyone **fall**

---

[62] Paraphrase of 2 Peter 3:1
194

short of the grace of God; *lest any root of bitterness springing up cause trouble, and by this many become defiled; lest there* be *any fornicator or profane person like Esau, who for one morsel of food sold his birthright [. . .]. Therefore, since we are receiving a kingdom which cannot be shaken,* **let us have grace**[63], *by which we may* **serve God acceptably with reverence and godly fear**. *For our God is a consuming fire."*

Therefore, we are saved only by grace through faith in Jesus Christ, but this is not something immovable. According to the passage of Scripture above we can lose grace and consequently, lose our salvation. That is why the widely spread idea of "who has been saved once is saved forever" can hardly stand the test of the Word of God. The same thought is confirmed in the words of the Old Testament in the book of Ezekiel 3:20 and 18: 24, 26.

Besides the issue of our sanctification, there is one more point where Satan can easily attach himself, and it is a matter of confessing sins in the presence of a counselor. This method is also founded in the Bible. In the Old Testament after committing adultery, King David confesses his sin in the presence of Nathan, the prophet, and receives forgiveness right away (2 Samuel 12:13). When John the Baptist performed baptism in Jordan, many came there *"confessing their sins"* (Matt. 3:6, Mark 1:5). In Acts we read about an occasion when after hearing about the embarrassment of seven sons of Sceva, a Jewish chief priest, people became fearful and *"many who had believed came confessing and telling their deeds"* (Acts 19:18). In the Epistle of James 5:16 it says, *"Confess your sins to each other and pray for each other so that you may be healed. The earnest prayer of a righteous person has great power and wonderful results"*[64] In German translation it sounds a little different, *"Confess your sins one to another"*[65]. Based on that, one may say that bringing sins to light in front of another person corresponds with the Bible and in certain cases can become a great help to a sin-battered soul. However, it does not say anywhere in the Bible that a Christian must have a single counselor, who he should go and confess to constantly. If a man from time to time willingly goes to a minister who has a life of experience and is spiritually mature and able to help and instruct him, it is wonderful. But the practice of regularly going out of obligation

---

[63] In Russian translation of the Bible, the meaning of the verse is emphasized by using the verb "to keep" and therefore, it is read: "...let us **keep** grace, by which we may serve God..."

[64] Scripture quotations marked (NLT) are taken from the ***Holy Bible,*** **New Living Translation,** copyright © 1996. Used by permission of Tyndale House Publishers, Inc., Wheaton, Illinois 60189. All rights reserved.

[65] Same as in KJV Bible, "Confess [your] faults one to another, and pray one for another, that ye may be healed. The effectual fervent prayer of a righteous man availeth much".

and for each and every little reason has no Biblical foundation. Moreover, it may conceal a great danger, because it can be abused to gain a continuous control and manipulation over people, which, in fact, is widely spread among cults and sects.

When a person being prompted by the Spirit of God wishes to cleanse his heart in the presence of a counselor, naming each and every sin by its name, it is commendable; however, if he keeps doing it over and over again, forced by the preaching where confession of sins is overemphasized, it becomes something quite different and more likely is called psycho-emotional influence. In the Bible there is also no direct indication that if someone does not reveal his sins in front of another human-being, he will necessarily go to hell. Counseling[66] is a very precious ministry which can bring blessings and much needed help to many under the condition of not going outside the boundaries of the Holy Scripture and becoming an instrument of power, control and manipulation of people.

The next bullet point of the spiritual life which Satan always targets is our behavior towards leaders, pastors, counselors and other kinds of ministers. Christians know very well that the Bible calls to respect and revere those in spiritual authority, established by God. Thus, it says in the Letter to Hebrews 13:17, *"Obey your spiritual leaders and do what they say. Their work is to watch over your souls, and they know they are accountable to God. Give them reason to do this joyfully and not with sorrow. That would certainly not be for your benefit".*[67] Unfortunately, a situation with this issue in many churches and congregations is far from being perfect. More often than not one can hear the words of reproach than that of esteem from the mouth of ordinary church members addressed to their pastors and other ministers. However, there is another extreme, when a leader or pastor is exceedingly praised and almost worshipped.

The Bible forbids creating idols, exalting, glorifying and practically deifying any people, even if they are clearly being used by God. The most severe words about it are spoken in the book of Jeremiah 17:5 which we have mentioned earlier, *"**Cursed** is the man who trusts in man and makes flesh his strength."* It's frightening, when a man becomes a rabid admirer of another person, bringing down a curse on both,

---

[66] In Russian language, the meaning of "counseling" goes far beyond a simple advice-giving strategy. It literally is translated as "taking care of souls" which is more of a spiritual parenting, where a counselor really shares the burdens of the person in need, carrying them together to the cross of Jesus Christ and fighting spiritual battles if needed, while helping him to obtain true freedom in Christ from prevailing sins.

[67] Scripture quotations marked (NLT) are taken from the *Holy Bible*, **New Living Translation**, copyright © 1996. Used by permission of Tyndale House Publishers, Inc., Wheaton, Illinois 60189. All rights reserved.

because God is a jealous God, Who will not give His glory to anyone else. In the letter to Hebrews there are most sobering words, *"Remember those who rule over you, who have spoken the word of God to you, whose faith follow,* **considering the outcome of their conduct**"[68] (Hebrew 13:7).

Do you see when we should imitate other people's faith? – When the path of their life have come to an end, and after parting with this earth they have left a good legacy in the hearts of people and their name remained without a blemish. It is not in vain the Word of God says that, *"The end of a thing is better than its beginning"* (Ecc.7:8). It is important for a Christian to spend his life blamelessly until the end, and more so, for a minister. The nice beginning is precious, but it remains yet a beginning. If a mentor of souls looses his vigilance at the last span of his life's road, then a fog of dishonor will cover up the glory of former days. Therefore, one must never rush to praise or imitate people. It's necessary to wait until the end of a person's life course, - exactly what a man cannot do. Dashing from one extreme to another he causes much grief, trouble and disappointment and then, not willing to admit his own fault and disobedience to God's Word, doggedly looks for the one to blame.

Out of senseless adoration of people, sects and cults are born and their existence became a curse for many people, proving the startling truth of the words of the Lord, *"For the leaders of this people cause them to err; and they that are led of them are destroyed"* (Isa. 9:16, KJV). If ministers and leaders begin to accept people's worship of them and abuse their position, sooner or later they will get into Satan's trap and will have to leave their calling.

I totally agree with Erlo Stegen who numerously preached that "there are three things which Satan successfully uses to shoot off the men of God, making them incapable of further ministry, and such are **pride, women and money.**" One can confidently say that many revivals and great beginnings of God suffered and came to a halt due to these reasons. And we can add two more – lies **and guidance by a false spirit**, which artfully masquerades as a Spirit of God.

---

[68] A RSV Bible carries the closest translation to the Russian Synodal text in this passage and reads as follows, "Remember your leaders, those who spoke to you the word of God; **consider the outcome of their life**, and imitate their faith." Transcribed from: The Holy Bible: Revised Standard Version containing the Old and New Testaments, translated from the original tongues: being the version set forth A.D. 1611, revised A.D. 1881-1885 and A.D. 1901: compared with the most ancient authorities and revised A.D. 1946-52. — 2nd ed. of New Testament A.D. 1971.

Having met with the last two reasons in my own spiritual search and having read a lot of literature about spiritual revivals which happened before, I've come to a conclusion that lies and guidance by a false spirit can be named the core causes after pride which lead to obliteration of God's work. Thus, they are **pride, lies, guidance by a false spirit, women and money**. Let's look at each of the five one by one.

Pride is a widely spread human vice, going hand in hand with arrogance, haughtiness, conceit, presumptuousness, and self-assurance. Knowing the danger that pride hides, the Bible talks a lot about it on its pages, for instance, "[. . .] *pride, and arrogancy, and the evil way, and the froward mouth, do I hate.*" (Proverbs 8:13, KJV), "*When pride cometh, then cometh shame [. . .]*" (Proverbs 11:2, KJV), "*Pride goeth before destruction, and an haughty spirit before a fall.*" (Proverbs 16:18, KJV), "*The pride of thine heart hath deceived thee [. . .]*" (Oba. 1:3), "*For the day of the LORD of hosts shall be upon every one that is proud and lofty, and upon every one that is lifted up; and he shall be brought low*" (Isa. 2:12), "*God resisteth the proud, and giveth grace to the humble*" (2 Peter 5:5), "*Behold, I am against thee, O thou most proud, saith the Lord GOD of hosts: for thy day is come, the time that I will visit thee. And the most proud shall stumble and fall, and none shall raise him up: and I will kindle a fire in his cities, and it shall devour all round about him*" (Jerem. 50: 31-32). All of these and many other passages of the Holy Scripture are affirmed by scores of examples, recorded in the Old and the New Testaments. Devil was the first one who became proud and therefore, was cast down from heaven leaving the position of the once covering cherub. Another vivid example of pride and fall was the King Saul, who began so well, yet finished his God-given course so poorly. The lives of a whole cue of kings, such as Hosea, Hezekiah, Nebuchadnezzar, Belshazzar, Herod, Nero confirmed the truth of eternal and unchanging words of the Scripture, that "*God resists the proud*".

However, man hasn't changed. The same thing by which people perished during Old Testament times continued to lead them to fall in New Testament era up until our days. The great beginnings blessed by God and spiritual revivals sooner or later came to nothing as soon as these thoughts formed in the minds of their followers, "We are the special people! We are exclusive! We have the revival! God has revealed the higher and holier way to us! God leads us in a special way! We are the champions and heralds of the truth! God uses us to speak to the world and Christianity decaying in its sins and vices!"

We are. . . .We have. . . . Us. . . . To us. . . . By us. . . . When our own exclusivity is advertised and underlined in such a way, then a calamity is near, because the words of the Scripture, "Pride goes before the fall" will certainly verify themselves. I got personally convinced of that when I was on the peak of my popularity, so that the Lord had to permit not one but a few shocks to humiliate and humble me in order to get me to the right state again. Ah, if only He would give me grace so that these bitter but important lessons help me and guard me from pride until the end of my life!

Lies are something which we strongly detest in others; however, easily excuse and justify it in ourselves, so that it doesn't look all that bad after all. No need to persuade anyone that the father of lies is the devil, and where there are lies, there Satan does his work. We, Christians, are aware of that without additional explanations. However, that which we clearly know in theory, believe it or not, does not get to put into practice of life and ministry. It may seem rather strange but there are ministers who don't think it sinful to employ direct lie in order to keep and protect the work of God, as they say. This kind of lies they call "wisdom" and to prove their way of thinking, they find an argument on the passage of the Holy Scripture where it tells the story of Rebecca who together with her son Jacob deceived old blind Isaac, and therefore, received the blessing of a firstborn (Genesis 27:1-35). Without going into further details about this episode of their lives, I can only say that, personally, I really doubt that the Holy and Righteous God needed such "help" to accomplish His purposes. To tell you the truth, I don't have a heart to call obvious lies wisdom. There is absolutely no excuse to lie in the Bible, but on the contrary, it reproaches it in all and every form, for instance, "*Lying lips* are *an abomination to the LORD, But those who deal truthfully* are *His delight*" (Proverbs 12:22) KJV; "For *the sin of their mouth* and *the words of their lips, Let them even be taken in their pride, And for the cursing and* **lying** which *they speak*" (Psalm 59:12); "*Through Your precepts I get understanding; Therefore I hate every false way*", "***I hate*** *and abhor* **lying**, But *I love Your law*" (Psalm 119:104, 163); "*A false witness will not go unpunished,* **And he** who **speaks lies will not escape**" (Proverbs 19:5); "[. . .] no lie is of the truth" (1 John 2:21); "*Therefore, putting away lying, "Let each one of you speak truth with his neighbor,"for we are members of one another*" (Eph 4:25); "*But there shall by no means enter it anything that defiles, or causes an abomination or a lie, but only those who are written in the Lamb's Book of Life*" (Rev. 21:27); "[. . .] *and all liars shall have their part in the lake which burns with fire and brimstone*[. . .]*"* (Rev. 21:8).

As one reads these lines, he can hardly agree with a statement that there is a wise lie, forced lie, justified lie and a lie needed for the sake of protecting and keeping the work of God, because God is able to protect His work without lies. Any embellishment and every little lie, when it is carefully hidden, will grow into a monster which will cause us to get into trouble sooner or later. Half-truth and exaggeration in order to make a better impression and influence people are also lies and may not have any part in the true work of God. By using fraud and lie without thinking we turn to the father of lies – devil, condemning a work we perform to a total fiasco. Lies and true spiritual revival are incompatible.

Guidance by a false spirit, masquerading as a working of the Holy Spirit, in my opinion, is the most often occurring reason which led many of God's beginnings and spiritual revivals to a complete destruction. This is a finesse method of Satan, because with its help he can direct to a false way many a congregation and even the strongest men of God. It is especially widely spread among those Christians who indulge in all kinds of revelations and spiritual guidance, and trust them with ease. By the way, they also seemingly have some biblical foundation under it, building on the passage of the Holy Scripture where it describes events which will take place before the coming of the Lord's Day, *"And it shall come to pass afterward That I will pour out My Spirit on all flesh; Your sons and your daughters shall prophesy, Your old men shall dream dreams, Your young men shall see visions. And also on My menservants and on My maidservants I will pour out My Spirit in those days. "And I will show wonders in the heavens and in the earth: Blood and fire and pillars of smoke"* (Joel 2:28-30).

Well, what can I say? It looks like an impressive proof to the validity of indulging in such spiritual phenomena. Although, let's not be hasty with conclusions, because in the same Bible there are many more reminders about similar manifestations of power, only in conjunction with warnings about them, *"And He said, "Take heed that you not be deceived. For many will come in My name, saying, 'I am He,' and, 'The time has drawn near.' Therefore do not go after them."* (Luke 21:8), *"For false christs and false prophets will rise and show great signs and wonders to deceive, if possible, even the elect"* (Matt 24:24), *"And the LORD said to me, 'The prophets prophesy lies in My name. I have not sent them, commanded them, nor spoken to them; they prophesy to you a false vision, divination, a worthless thing, and the deceit of their heart"*(Jerem. 14:14), *"Behold, I* am *against the prophets,"* says the LORD, *"who use their tongues and say, 'He says.' Behold, I* am *against those who prophesy false dreams,"* says the LORD, *"and tell them, and cause My people to err by their lies and by their recklessness. Yet I did not send them or command them; therefore they shall not profit this people at all,"* says the LORD" (Jerem. 23:31-32). As far as the signs in the sky and on earth in the last days, it also says about the known to us beast with his number 666 that he will make great signs before all people and will cause fire to fall down from heaven to earth, and will deceive the inhabitants of the earth (refer to Revelation, Chapter 13). There are many similar warnings throughout the Bible. That's why it is amazing that in spite of them all Christians so easily fall under the influence of various revelations, prophecies, visions and signs.

Getting a goal for myself to elucidate the reason for ending of spiritual revivals in the history of Christianity, I flipped through much of different literature. Unfortunately, the majority of books telling about revivals describe only the events in the beginning and during the blooming season of these revivals. But only a very few authors, just a handful, write how they ceased and what was the reason for their termination. However, even that little what I could gather from the sources, has stunned me. It appears, the most often cause for revival to be brought to an end was a deviation from the truth and committing of sin by that man or those people who were at the roots of revival. It usually happened in connection with the work of a false spirit which entered while masked as an acting of the Holy Spirit, craftily deceiving and leading away the children of God farther and farther from the truth. We should never forget that Satan can imitate any work of God: repentance, spiritual gifts, other tongues, healing, miracles, deliverance from fear and demonic powers, - in other words, he can practically counterfeit anything.

In the history of railroad transportation there were often many tragic occurrences, when for some reason the points of the railways were moved incorrectly, and the whole train went to different direction, causing a catastrophic death. Something similar happens in the spiritual movement of any revival. Devil patiently waits for an opportune moment, and using various errors, neglects and oversights of Christians, unnoticeably wedges into God's work, and in time completely destroys it. The easiest way for him to accomplish that is if a man, by whom revival got started begins excessively trust different spiritual revelations and guidance received from others or by his own accord. In the beginning such leadership may look quite truthful and cause no doubts, being confirmed in deeds. However, devil knows how to wait. He is also a spirit and therefore, knows a lot. He will supply the revelations where 98% of them will be true in order to mask another 2% of added lies, which if goes unnoticed, in years to come will conduct its ravaging work and bring everything to zero.

It is equally dangerous when a leader who is on the forefront of God's work starts to get carried away with the statistics of the revival, for example, the number of opened branches, the quantity of people repented and turned to God, the amount of those being baptized, the number of attendees at the worship services, the figures for members of the congregation and new co-workers, the amount of revival campaigns, conferences, congresses, mission trips and so on. This is a devil's bait, and many bite into it. The more there is a publicity, advertisement and parading, the less likely it is a true work of God's Spirit.

When they speak about **women** as a reason for the falling of men of God and the annihilation of great spiritual beginnings, it is meant in the sense of **adultery and fornication** among those, whom the Lord uses for His work. One can stand amazed at how subtly and cunningly "the weaker gender" is used by Satan to strike at "the stronger gender"[69]. Although, I believe there isn't anything new. In all ages since the beginning of the earth, devil had successfully managed to use this kind of weaponry. That's why the wise king Solomon after fully experiencing its strength chose the following words to portray it, *"I applied my heart to know, To search and seek out wisdom and the reason of things, To know the wickedness of folly, Even of foolishness and madness. And I find more bitter than death The woman whose heart is snares and nets, Whose hands are fetters. He who pleases God shall escape from her, But the sinner shall be trapped by her"* (Eccl. 7:25-26) This aphorism has words that especially strike at the end, *"the sinner shall be trapped by her"*. All of this sudden a question comes up: but wait a minute, how can this be? How can you call them sinners, those who teach others spiritual and physical purity, who hold a banner of moral and self-control way up, putting high moral standards in hearts and minds of listeners? Is it even true, that this kind of preachers, the strong men of God, passionately guarding others from defilement of the flesh, are able to sin in the same manner?? Alas, it is true, though it doesn't fit in with our human conscience. And the following words from Psalm 50 will serve as a proof of it, *"But to the wicked God says: "What right have you to declare My statutes, Or take My covenant in your mouth, Seeing you hate instruction And cast My words behind you? When you saw a thief, you consented with him, And have been a partaker with adulterers. You give your mouth to evil, And your tongue frames deceit. You sit and speak against your brother; You slander your own mother's son. These things you have done, and I kept silent; You thought that I was altogether like you; But I will rebuke you, And set them in order before your eyes. "Now consider this, you who forget God, Lest I tear you in pieces, And there be none to deliver"* (Psalm 50:16-22).

Whom does the Lord address here and who does He call "the wicked"? (*In German translation of the Bible a word "godless" is used in place of the expression "the wicked" or "the sinner" as in Russian translation. – The author's comments*). No matter how strange it seems, but those heart-breaking wrath-filled words are addressed towards those who preach to others, teaching people the commandments and decrees of the Lord. Because God knows that which is concealed and carefully

---

[69] "A weaker gender" and "a stronger gender" are the phrases typically used in Russian language to compare female and male abilities in their relation to physical strength, yet often quite opposite in spiritual traits (Translator's note).

hidden and what we even fear to suspect them of. Once Jesus nailed the conscience of the teachers of His time, the Pharisees, with a short phrase when they had brought Him a woman caught in adultery. "Who of you is without sin", said He (perhaps, meaning their own sins of fornication and adultery), "let him cast the first stone". What an insight! What knowledge of the dark side of their lives invisible for others! It is no surprise that a little earlier He characterized all Pharisees, lawyers and scribes in these words, "*Woe to you, scribes and Pharisees, hypocrites! For you are like whitewashed tombs which indeed appear beautiful outwardly, but inside are full of dead* men's *bones and all uncleanness*" (Matt.23:27), "[. . .] *Woe to you also, lawyers! For you load men with burdens hard to bear, and you yourselves do not touch the burdens with one of your fingers*" (Luke 11:46).

And so, one can preach the truth to people, yet not live by it. One can teach others godliness, but be far from it in his own life. One can call to self-control and abstinence, severely condemning for even a slightest manifestation of feelings towards the other gender, while secretly doing things which are inconceivable to a sound mind. Life proves that the one who ardently gets on against all adulterers and fornicators is the one who himself is not free from that. In Russia there used to be an old saying with a question, "Who shouts louder 'stop a thief'? The thief does." Therefore, in order to distract everybody's attention from oneself, it is necessary to direct it to others. Who will ever think that a preacher lives in sin of adultery or fornication, if he inveighs against these sins from the pulpit and excommunicates the guilty ones from the church?? By listening to such "teachers" the ordinary believers make all the efforts to live pure and holy lives, truly becoming a model and a blessing for others; while at the same time their mentors don't burden themselves with putting into practice things they preach about. No, it wasn't in vain that Jesus said, "[. . .] *unless your righteousness exceeds* the righteousness *of the scribes and Pharisees, you will by no means enter the kingdom of heaven*" (Matt. 5:20).

Speaking of this, I, by no means, presume that all preachers and ministers are like that, because it would be a greatest tragedy of Christianity. However, it is of no secret to anyone, that not a few ministers were disqualified [70] for their ministry because of women, whom devil used as his mightily performing weapon. That is why the regular church members should seriously pray for their ministers, begging the Lord to keep them from the fiery darts of the lust of the eyes and the lust of the flesh. Satan knows all too well that if he plunges a leader of the church into that sin, he will bring irrevocable damage to the whole congregation.

---

[70] Literally "shot off" in Russian – to show the fatality of such sin. (Translator's note)

And finally, one more weapon, a strong one, which the enemy readily uses to destroy the work of God, is **money**. It is obvious for all of us that any missionary service and evangelical campaign entail financial expenses. The God of Israel not for nothing determined for His people a tithe, which remains effectual in our days. When the lots were established among the tribes of Israel, the Levites and priests were not given any land or cities. The Lord announced to them that He was to be their lot and therefore, would care for them (Numbers 18). In the New Testament one can also be convinced that God takes care of those who serve Him and His children, by saying, *"Let him who is taught the word share in all good things with him who teaches"* (Galatians 6:6). Nevertheless, Satan was able to penetrate even this fine instruction. Out of gratitude or at times, prompted by their own desires, known just to God and to them, people start making presents and give substantial amounts of money to the ministers not suspecting that they are digging a pit for them. Not infrequently, instead of using these monies for the Kingdom of God, they spend them on buying expensive houses and obtaining other things which have nothing to do with God's work. Thus, devil succeeds not only in destroying the souls of the ministers, but also the once blessed spiritual revivals. This is why the Holy Scripture says that *"[. . .] the love of money is a root of all kinds of evil, for which some have strayed from the faith in their greediness, and pierced themselves through with many sorrows"* (1 Tim. 6:10).

In many fairly new, recently born contemporary movements the collection of monetary contributions is given too much of attention. Certainly, it is being done under the banner of collecting the means for "the work of God" with citing the specific passages of Scripture and a clear emphasis that the sacrificial spirit is tightly connected with the receiving of blessings from the Lord. How sad it is, that the Bible is being misused to disguise far from being godly mercenary ends!

Unfortunately, even in matters such as construction of prayer houses, money collections played not so insignificant role in destruction of previously blessed churches and congregations. Many times during mission trips I heard groans and complaints of Christians telling how they lost peace and unity while building a house of prayer. In Western world there have been a number of cases when the church clergy was put on trial for manipulation of money and misappropriation of large financial assets, collected from credulous believers for the so-called "work of God". The Holy Scripture teaches us to add knowledge to virtue[71] (2 Peter 1:5). And this is a valuable

---

[71] In Russian text for the word "knowledge", a word "discretion" is used, indicating caution and sound judgment when a good deed is to be done.

advice to those who generously give to God's work, not bothering finding out if it really is such.

It is necessary to say that the above listed five points which lead men of God to spiritual blindness, weakness and falling away from the truth, simultaneously are the main reasons for infringement of the most blessed beginnings of God, including spiritual revivals, of which we should talk a little more.

Unfortunately, the word "revival" is often used inappropriately, loosing therefore, the real meaning of it. In his book *Opened Windows* James A. Stewart in regards to that writes the following, *"The majority of Christians today confuse revival with the work of evangelism. Such confusion is easy to understand, since revival results in a great wave of evangelism and ingathering of souls. Revival includes evangelism, but evangelism may not include revival. Evangelism always follows revival, but revival does not necessarily follow an evangelistic campaign.*

Evangelism seeks the resurrection of sinners who are dead in trespasses and sin. Revival is a spiritual quickening of the life of the redeemed. The aim of evangelism is to reach out after the lost souls, while that of revival is to bring new life and vitality to the saints of God through a renewal of the presence and power of the Holy Spirit. Revival means a fresh incoming of the Divine Life into a body threatening to become a corpse."[72]

"Revival is not God's standard for the Church but is the process through which the Church is restored to its former splendor and glory: "Wilt thou not revive us again: that thy people may rejoice in thee?" (Ps. 85:6). In days of revival there is a great time of heart-searching, when believers are smitten by the Holy Spirit as they realize afresh how far they have departed from the Lord. This spirit of brokenness results in deep humiliation, repentance, confession and restitution."[73]

"This spirit of brokenness and repentance in sackcloth and ashes must now be followed by a definite act of deliverance from defeat and failure and a renewed life of holiness and power."[74]

"It is not only possible, but it is the will of God that every redeemed soul should attain to and maintain such a standard of Christian living throughout this entire life, from the day of his salvation to the day of his translation."[75]

In many translations of the Bible to European languages, revival means "awakening from slumber", consequently, while praying for revival, we plead for cold, disheartened, sleeping Christians who fell

---

[72] "Opened Windows" by James Alexander Stewart, copyright ©1999 by Revival Literature: page 17
[73] "Opened Windows" by James Alexander Stewart, copyright ©1999 by Revival Literature: page 35
[74] "Opened Windows" by James Alexander Stewart, copyright ©1999 by Revival Literature: page 36
[75] "Opened Windows" by James Alexander Stewart, copyright ©1999 by Revival Literature: page 44.

away from God, to be awakened from their spiritual slumber. If a church is in need of revival it speaks of its degradation, apostasy, weakening and falling away. The tragic reality of our days is that the majority of Christians live a poor, powerless, defective spiritual life. The spiritual level of an average Christian has gotten so low, that the glory which revival brings to church seems abnormal to him. We got to the point that we consider our usual low stage of spiritual life a standard, and a blessing of revival which comes from the Spirit of God – a strange and extreme phenomenon.

In spite of the fact that the Lord always uses certain ministers in revival, its true Instigator is the Holy Spirit with the Son of God in the lead. While they both occupy the first place, the revival goes on. However, as soon as a man or something else takes the front seat, it starts smothering and slowly dies down. That's why the revival often ends when there are things like the cult of the leader's personality and ambitious self-confidence which claims that the blessings of the Lord will continue without the further search for God and walking in holiness. It must be admitted that in Christian world many revivals which began in the power of the Holy Spirit and gave a mighty impulse to believers in many countries, after a few years and decades started to die down, becoming merely a tradition. And this happens not only after the death of a founder of this work of God, but, alas, not too seldom during his lifetime. Obviously, it may seem too hard for the leaders and followers of these movements to agree to this fact, and they do everything within their power to make the rest of the people believe that the work of God goes on. However, no human efforts can hold onto something, if the Holy Spirit has already left it; and sooner or later, it will become evident. Well, there is truly nothing permanent on this earth. And no matter how sad the fact is, we need to reconcile with it, whether we like it or not.

But this is not the worst thing yet. The matter looks more serious when something which has no dealing with God is actually offered as the working of God's power. Speaking of that, I signify the various sects, cults and false teachings, presenting themselves as something unique and pretending to be exclusive and super spiritual, - of which, alas, there popped up quite a number today. I repeatedly confronted them in my own life and heard many sorrowful stories and testimonies during the mission trips to different countries of the world. Besides reading the mount loads of literature on the subject I also witnessed an excruciating pain of souls, despair and disillusionment from the spiritual crash people have experienced. Therefore, I feel it is my duty to warn Christians about a possibility of making these dangerous mistakes, to tell them of the main symptoms and typical features of sects, cults and false teachings in addition to their tactics in catching the unsuspecting souls into their nets.

In our world there is a mass of people, who in the middle of their quest for meaning of life try to find answers to the questions, concerning the innermost things of their souls. Many of them lost trust in their churches and have turned to small groups, cults and sects, to which they commend themselves simply and carelessly, accepting all without proper reasoning and sober, sound approach. One thing is unclear, though. Why do people who can't tolerate the admonishments of church pastors, so easily rely on leaders of sects, supplying them with an excellent opportunity to be manipulated as they like? As soon as they become followers of a sect or a false teaching, people begin to feel at home. They become especially susceptible to the influence of a sect while experiencing critical life circumstances or suffering from loneliness, misunderstanding or inner isolation for various reasons. As the newcomers get inside the sect, they are enveloped in love and understanding. This continues until a full trust of a soul is gained as well as willingness to do anything out of gratitude for received help and support. More than ever it occurs among those who have been disappointed in their former religion, hunger to finally find **the true Christianity**. As a German professor, doctor of theology Klaus Weber from the University in Koblenz, Germany, put it in expressing his opinion of the matter, "*cults and sects indicate not a crisis of the faith but **the crisis of its worthiness**.*"

According to any dictionary, **a sect** is a religious entity, which broke off from a dominating church; or a group of individuals engrossed in its own trivial interests and narrow-minded ideas. Based on this definition, **sectarianism** means isolation and narrow-mindedness, peculiar to people limited to their petty group interests. Inside the evangelical believers, a sect is a group which differs from others in the key matters of faith. For example, the Jehovah's witnesses do not think Jesus Christ to be God, which is the main foundation of all evangelical churches. **A cult** is a religious group which admires a certain person; stays under his influence and follows him more often without realizing it. Thus, the Jehovah's Witnesses organization possibly in the beginning of its movement was a cult, but currently, it represents a sect. Therefore, it is rather difficult to draw a precise line between the two definitions of a "sect" and a "cult" or find the exact borders, because a cult of personality of its leader could be clearly maintained inside a sect, and within a cult there may be seen the apparent features of a sect.

Typically, all cults, sects and false teachings have something in common, but it is really impossible to talk about all of their characteristics here, since it would require writing another book.

Therefore, I would like to settle now only on their most striking distinctive indications, which are founded on dangerous manipulations of people, leading towards profound change of their identity and all kinds of dependency. **Manipulation** is a desire to bring people to a certain way of thinking, feeling and behaving, which they would not have had under different circumstances. At that time they are provided with the information in such a way that it becomes the foundation for person's new way of thinking and shapes a different personality within him to change it as desired. Usually such "brainwashing" is performed so subtly and shrewdly that a man looses his ability to a sound, sober, critical analysis of what is happening and doesn't discern that he is being manipulated. Manipulation of people in sects, cults and false teachings is not a single case but a constant ingredient of their doctrines and system. Let's look at the signs of a typical manipulation, defining a group or an entire movement as a sect, cult or false teaching.

1. **A desire to achieve a total internal isolation**. It is expressed in a one-sided approach to the matter of discernment between good and evil. Here the whole world is divided to black and white. Everything and everyone belonging to this group is part of good, and the rest is all evil. Therefore, this artificially cultivated way of thinking spells out a principle: people are either enemies or friends. The members of the assembly see themselves as the elect, and try to make the remaining part of the world their mission field. The time is preferably spent with the like-minded ones. The followers of the group are being instilled with a feeling that here is the only place where they will find a true happiness, love, protection, security and stability. It is very important for their leaders, because this is why their supporters will remain with them. The consequences of such internal isolation are broken marital ties, pulled apart and divided families, torn away relatives and lost friendly connections, although they publicly preach the necessity to love their enemies and to pray for them that they be enlightened and their spiritual blindness lifted. It is not recommended for group members to communicate with those who don't accept their teaching, in order not to defile themselves or get infected by such, thus bringing much harm to their own souls. This destruction of social bridges with those who don't share the same notions and convictions, more and more limits all the contacts to the members of their organization.

2. **Convictions about their uniqueness and exclusivity as especially chosen ones**.

Usually, all leaders of sects and cults claim to possess an exclusive knowledge, persuading their followers that God revealed them a singular, high and holy way, and that only they know the truth hidden from others. This totally contradicts the Bible, which is infinitely far from stating that this or that confession or denomination, this or the other church, congregation or fellowship is the only representative of the true Christianity on earth. Nowhere in the Holy Scripture will you find a criterion for determining the authenticity of this or that earthly organization. Jesus has always known **who** His people were, because, *"[. . .] He calls His own sheep by name and leads them out"* and *"[. . .] My sheep hear My voice, and I know them, and they follow Me"* (John 10:3, 27). More or less, all cults, sects and false teachings make announcements about revelations received outside the Bible, i.e. about new divine truths unfamiliar to others. These revelations find their expression either in writings of their founders and leaders, or in unspoken laws and regulations which a group strictly adheres to and delineates their way of thinking and approach to vital questions according to the already existing experience of walking in their "extraordinary, high and holy way". In other words, such a group has its own additional authoritative source of truth, which is presented by all sorts of different revelations, dreams, prophecies, visions and other experiences of God's presence, and deception of the latter manifests only in a course of time.

Certainly, one cannot deny that revelations, visions and prophesies are listed in the Bible as some of many various methods God used to speak to His people from old. However, there is a danger to regard a vision or a prophecy as sent by God without testing it by the exact standards of the Word of God. In the Old Testament such manifestations were subjected to an examination as we read, for instance, in Deuteronomy 13:1-4 and Jeremiah 28:9. God severely reproached those who claimed to receive a vision and made false predictions, *"They speak a vision of their own heart, not from the mouth of the Lord"* (Jerem. 23:16). As we can see, God always prepares a test to those who get revelations, and very often, time is the indicator to be used. The Bible strictly condemns the one who adds anything to the Holy Scriptures, *"Do not add to His words, lest He rebuke you, and you be found a liar"* (Prov. 30:6). All of the so-called revelations that contradict that which was made known earlier, are guilty of adding to the Word of God and do not deserve to be acknowledged.

3. **A cult of personality within a movement, whether of its founder, teacher or leader.**

The Latin word "cultus" literally means "to worship" or "to be devoted to someone or something, to admire someone"[76]. Practically,

---

[76] The term "cult" first appeared in English in 1617, derived from the French *culte*, meaning "worship" or "a particular form of worship" which in turn originated from the Latin word **cultus** meaning "care, cultivation, worship," originally "tended, cultivated," also the past participle of *colere* "to till the soil". The meaning "devotion to a person or thing" is from 1829. Starting about 1920, *"cult"* acquired additional six or more connotatively positive and negative definitions. In Roman Catholicism,

all false teachings, sects and especially cults are characterized by a presence of the central figure of the leader who considers to be a messenger or the one anointed by God with unique access to the Almighty. Because this person has a very special personal relationship with God, he can dictate a theology and manners to all members of the current group or movement. Such a strong leadership, whose power is almost limitless, brings all the followers of the false teaching into a complete bondage in questions of faith, behavior and way of life. The unconditional surrender to the teacher or the leader of the sect, cult or false teaching goes without saying and is an unwritten law. In one of the LDS (Latter Day Saints) magazines *Improvement Era* under the section entitled "Ward Teachers" from June 1945 it is explained very directly and in unambiguous manner: "*When our leaders speak, the thinking has been done. When they propose a plan, it is God's plan. When they point the way, there is no other which is safe. When they give direction, it should mark the end of controversy. God works in no other way. To think otherwise, without immediate repentance, may cost one his faith, may destroy his testimony, and leave him a stranger to the kingdom of God*".

The teachers and leaders of the sects go so far in their power of influence that arrange marriages as they like and later manipulate them, impudently meddling in marital relationships and family lives. You cannot stop being amazed how can such leaders and teachers calmly hold the Bible in their hands, where the Lord speaks to them in wrath through the lips of the prophet Malachi, "*For the lips of a priest should keep knowledge, And* people *should seek the law from his mouth; For he is the messenger of the LORD of hosts. But you have departed from the way; You have caused many to stumble at the law. You have corrupted the covenant of Levi,*" *Says the LORD of hosts.*

"*Therefore I also have made you contemptible and base Before all the people, Because you have not kept My ways But have shown partiality in the law*" (Malachi 2:7-9).

4. **Prohibition of internal criticism.** Attention of sect followers is constantly directed at how dangerous the independent thinking is for them. No criticism is tolerated in regards to organization or leadership as well as the certain aspects of teaching, even if it is totally appropriate and fair. In order to preserve "the holy purity" they watch with a vigilant eye so that no treacherous thought, which may cause a doubt in their doctrine, penetrates the system. Being (as they think they are) surrounded by foes and enemies of the true God, they are obligated to keep watch so that no adversary may break through and impact the

---

cultus or **cult** is the technical term for the following and devotion or veneration extended to a particular saint. (Cited from Wikipedia, the Free Encyclopedia. Wikipedia® is a registered trademark of the Wikimedia Foundation, Inc)

minds of group members, having them changed. In these organizations and the likes, an internal control and surveillance one of another are widely practiced. Every member has to report mistakes and faults of others in order to safeguard the group from alien tendencies and improper way of thinking. Otherwise, those who keep silent about it will themselves fall into a category of suspects. People within the same group, often even the married couples, are afraid to share their own unfavorable questions and doubts out of fear that it will be told to their leaders or "counselors". Usually, it is followed by a "brotherly talk" in order to bring the wanderer to his senses, but if it doesn't work, to break him by embarrassing him in front of the others or by some sort of punishment, up to and including a segregation from the fellowship. For criticizing question some members are stopped from ministering and deprived of an opportunity to preach, while others are forced to be quiet; and yet others are subjected to complete collective embarrassment, making them an intimidating exhibit for the rest of the group. The purpose of it all is to avoid any criticism and questions which make dubious the truthfulness and purity of doctrine or forms of organization.

5. **Cult of confession of sins.** Just about all sects, cults and false teachings are authoritarian and have a strict hierarchical system. Approval, condemnation, punishment, fear and continuing feeling of guilt help to keep people in constant dependence and manipulate them as they wish. One of the surest means to achieve that is counseling or to say it more correctly, a meticulous confession of sins in front of one and the same counselor. In this case, this is not a counseling assistance that a sound Christian goes to from time to time, being prompted by the Spirit of God in most difficult physical and spiritual situations in order to find help and a subsequent joint prayer. No, here we are talking about the continuous, halfway mandated confessions when a person almost runs to his counselor for any smallest reason under the influence of stern, reproaching sermons   which   are   essentially filled with constant themes of sin and sinfulness. Having such incorrect exaggerated approach to this matter, the valuable counseling ministry becomes a cult of confession of sins and is used for a subtle invisible control over a person's soul. The distinctive feature of sects, cults and false teachings is that they usually do not maintain a confidentiality of confession. In contrary, the collected facts received in this way are used as needed for the purposes of leadership.

6. **Acknowledgement or refusal of right to fit in the group.** The group or rather its leadership determines whether a man may have a spiritual right to belong with them. All of those that don't come under the established criteria somehow are required to perfect themselves. If someone makes no progress, he is excluded or is placed

under the unbearable conditions which force him to leave on his own. If a man loses conviction in correctness of the offered teaching, it will carry consequences not only for him; it is expected from other members that they will severe or strictly limit their contacts with this person. Such a breach causes pain on both sides. Those remained in the group suffer from a thought that according to their opinion the departed person practically loses salvation, which he undoubtedly would have had by staying in the organization. People who have left the sect or the cult also experience a lot of hurt, because with their leaving all friendly and even kindred ties are broken, which is very hard to endure. Right after the separation the individual feels lonely, unwanted and cast out. It takes time and energy to make new friends and build social bridges. In sectarian organizations, a lot of attention is paid to nourish the idea of persuading its members in truthfulness of the taught doctrine. After breaking with them, a vacuum occurs in this place. The person is tormented by a question, "Where is the Truth?" Disappointment and despair cause him a long-lasting poignant emotional pain.

7. **The isolation from outside critics.** In any criticism, a false teaching sees a threat for itself. Critics outside of a cult or a sect, typically, presented as liars, slanderers and informers. Thus, everything is done to slander and humiliate such people in the eyes of sect members, who are told that all submitted arguments and facts are not worthy to start discussions about them. More often than not, outside critics are simply ignored or a method of intimidation is used to attack them with a mass of accusations while searching for the darker sides of their lives, even including the exposure of things that had once been revealed in a secret confession.

8. **The manipulation of facts and their own history.** Always, when a teaching of a sect goes against the reality, those facts are either concealed and veiled or transferred to some people exclusively, so that certain members cannot see the entire picture, and therefore, unable to form their own opinion about them. It reminds of an action of a magician, who masterfully uses different tricks. Moreover, the viewers would be greatly disappointed if only they knew what his "art" was. In the same way, it is difficult to discern and follow through similar tricks used by leaders of false teachings, sects and cults. Besides, a history of origin of such movements is told and used very selectively, especially when after looking back, certain things, which present a problem currently, are realized. While the leader is being idealized as a person without mistakes and blemishes, everything that may in one way or another cast a shadow on the history of the group or its leadership is silenced, shaded and modified in every possible manner. Facts are garbled, and the most different pious explanations and justifications

are found for the errors and deviations, which had occurred. In the process, various suggestions are offered why God might have permitted certain things (for example, for the purpose of testing and verifying His children to assure their faithfulness). In short, everything possible is done to calm members and instill confidence in them that all is well and therefore, no need to look back, searching for mistakes and, not to mention, listen up to the enemies of their teaching who try to cause damage to "the work of God". Any exhibit of independent thinking, critical analysis of the current events, speaking out of doubts regarding the trustworthiness of the movement entail unfavorable consequences for those who dare to stand up against the universal belief.

9. **The discipline by moral pressure and physical stress.** Any and every freethinking in a sect or a cult is cut off at the root. The person guilty of trespassing the accepted norms of thinking and behavior is disciplined by methods of moral pressure, which is created by humiliating him before others, by accentuated watchful treatment, unflattering comments, ignorance, malignant gossip behind the back, openly displayed distrust, unequivocal statements from the pulpit, removing from a ministry and so on. The goal is to break any resistance inside the soul, to destroy person's identity, to make him an obedient and a weak-willed slave of his leaders. Besides moral strain, everything is done by the group to fill the spare time of its members entirely by work and different tasks, often bringing people to physical exhaustion and total fatigue. Therefore, it becomes practically unfeasible to think through, evaluate, and assess that which is happening in the organization.

In the beginning, when a novice comes to a cult or a sect, he experiences a phase of euphoria. He is literally showered with attention, love and special favor. Therefore, he gets under the impression that he found himself in especially harmonized, filled with love group of people which is sharply distinguished from the evil and corrupted outside world, and is totally opposite of the surroundings he has come from. The showering of love makes him unable to criticize, and he closes his eyes to some confusingly feeble sides of the system he notices at the start. In order to display harmony, the leaders compel the older members to make sure that "love" always arrests one's attention in the group. Many supporters of the sects unceasingly tell others how happy they are, although in reality it all looks quite different, because a life under a totalitarian system is the life filled with hurt and many sacrifices. Deep within their soul they suffer and know about it, but being under control they cannot recognize that it causes them such harm. Without realizing it, the followers of the false teachings, cults and sects live in surreal world, created by their leaders;

213

however, they are confident about possessing the absolute truth. Children, who grew up inside the totalitarian sect, later suffer throughout their whole life. In some groups, children are beaten and severely punished for a smallest offence in order to promote the "right" discipline.

10. **The requirement to comply with impeccable cleanness and holiness.** In view of the fact that cults, sects and false teachings pretend to be so exclusive, they especially emphasize in their sermons and appeals, the necessity of observing the impeccable cleanness and purity in all aspects of human life. That concerns the appearance, clothing, manners of behavior, contacts between the opposite genders, the observance of strictest self-control before marriage, the expressions used during conversations and others. At a first glance, it looks positive and quite right, because in our filthy and corrupted age these human values are bluntly trampled. Nevertheless, the problem is that members of some cults and sects are presented with such overstating requirements that it becomes practically impossible to accomplish them. As a result, a fear of God's judgment develops and deepens in the souls of people, as well as a feeling of guilt that they are unable to achieve all, which is necessary for their organization, its leader or the salvation of humanity. When doubts come or a promised "healing" or "liberation" from sin hasn't occurred, they are told that the reason lies with them and it's their fault that they lacked faith, or didn't fully devote themselves to the common cause or weren't firm and uncompromising enough in regards to old connections and relations, having not severed them with absolute determination.

11. **Masking its religious activity.** If a cult, sectarian organization or false teaching movement fear to inevitably impair its activities due to a negative attitude towards them or ill-disposed rumors, then it masks its pursuits, trying to do everything in neutral form. Alternatively, it opens its branches under other names, using them as a cloak for further pushing of its doctrine and the same old ideas.

12. **Financial interests and camouflage of its business activity.** Practically all sects, cults and false teachings use diverse methods of collecting funds to finance their existence. Some groups do that in apparent and open manner. At the end of each worship service or even during the one, especially prepared "preachers" literally make people give money even above their affordable potential by manipulating with artfully selected passages of Holy Scriptures and cunning psychological techniques. It happens because from the pulpit they are constantly being told that blessings of God are poured in proportion to the spirit of sacrifice. Other cult organizations do that in a much more subtle and secret way. On the surface, they avoid talking

about it and especially emphasize that they bring all their needs only before the Lord, Who in a wonderful way responds to them, reaffirming His good will. The third kind does everything in their power to advertise their material prosperity and wealth, and there is quite a number of sincere but naive Christians who believe that it proves the validity of their teaching, God's approval of it and His presence. If we were to take that approach, then Jesus and His apostles were the biggest losers. They were unfamiliar with the doctrine of wealth and prosperity.

Religious cults and new teachings are the masters to mask their business activities. Many of them, their leaders in particular, own different enterprises, including large plants, monopolies, concerns, gold and diamond mines, oil refineries, great publishing houses and more. The existence of them is kept under low profile from the ordinary cult members or is being explained as a necessity to finance the work of God. The fact that the lion's share of the profit falls to the bottom of personal accounts of the leaders becomes evident only when a company goes into bankruptcy or gets in the midst of a scandalous situation. Wealthy people with monetary means enjoy a privileged attention, accentuated treatment and all sorts of benefits within the organization.

The above-mentioned twelve out of more than thirty indications of totalitarian groups described, as I have said, are only those that have to do with manipulation of people. And should you find any of them in your own circumstances, beware, should you happen to be a follower of the doctrine that is a false teaching. Someone who is familiar with work methods of such totalitarian systems has to come to conclusion that in reality, we are all in danger, because the secret of progressive success made by the leaders of those groups lies in keeping human conscience under control. Millions of people are subjected to psychological manipulation without realizing it. This inability to discern it can be explained by two reasons. First of all, a man caught by the system can only realize the existence of this type of control of his conscience when he is helped from the outside, because the main goal of such people management is to make sure the one controlled by it doesn't get a slightest idea. Secondly, incapacity to recognize manipulation is founded on lack of knowledge of **what** exactly the control of conscience really means, since only someone who truly knows how it works, can preserve him from its influence.

Today, many congregations and denominations open their doors to all kinds of falsehood and therefore, it shouldn't surprise anyone that their spiritual condition leaves much to be desired. If fact, the most alive, spiritually flourishing churches are the main targets of Satan. Moreover, what can be better for him than to effectively trick those who make decisions for a whole church? In order to destroy a congregation, deception does not have to turn into a kind of horrendous heresy. It is enough to guide the leadership to a single narrow, maybe even, right direction because any **lop-sidedness and narrowness** eventually will end up as sectarianism. If a leader of movement or a group of its directors get misled in interpretation of God's will then Satan easily takes power in his hands. Collective delusion is only possible when certain people get confused first and it happens to each one of them separately. Our problem is that we all tend to think that it is somebody else who can get deceived, but never ourselves. Although, the fact remains that due to either lack of knowledge, carelessness, self-confidence or simple human foolishness we are capable of becoming guilty to aiding and abetting the devil. To avoid it, it is essential:

a) To beware of self-confidence and spiritual pride, which blinds our mind and instills a false feeling of security;

b) To avoid personal preference and admiration of man, because both of them can lead us away from the Lord;

c) Never to hide the truth and never to speak a lie, since keeping silence about problems and using even a smallest lie can carry quite unfavorable consequences;

d) To be very careful in matters of following various kinds of guidance: prophecies, visions, dream interpretations and such, because all of them do not exclude a possibility of Satan's involvement.

e) Not to rush into accepting any type of event or manifestation as a sign from God, since it may very well be a simple coincidence.

f) Not to beg from God anything that He has already said His "no" to, because this is a way, which will easily lead to delusion.

g) Not to do anything if there are doubts regarding the right understanding of God's will, but to sort out the reason for hesitancy;

h) To be prepared to honestly admit your mistakes and deviations not only before yourself, but also before God and other people, then leave the delusion and start over.

This approach is crucial and very important for every church in general, as well as for each individual Christian, no matter whether he is an ordinary member or a pastor of a congregation.

Unfortunately, it must be mentioned that even though any cult or sect is considered a unit, which has separated from a main, leading, recognized church, still within the large churches you can find things, which are typical for cults and sects. Always, when the cult of the leader is practiced inside a church or a healthy sober criticism is ignored; when any discontent and argument against ways and methods of indoctrinating or leaning toward fundamentally narrow guidance in teaching and real life are suppressed, then a danger exists that certain sectarian-like tendencies have found a place in such congregation. Often enough inside big churches one can locate groupings which are situated, so to say, at the intersection of being "still a church" and "yet a sect".

And the last point I would like to mention is a question whether leaders of sects, cults and false teachings really believe in what they tell others. I am afraid that it is beyond our ability to look inside any man in order to understand what he actual thinks. It cannot be precluded that some of them are not too sure about their own teaching; however, undoubtedly many leaders sincerely believe in what they preach. It especially often happens in those cases when they fully depend on, as it seems to them, divine revelations, in which there is a constant message of confirming that they are chosen by the Lord, guided by Him, kept from error and are on the right track. Humanly speaking, one can somewhat understand this kind of leaders, because they deceive others by being sincerely deceived themselves. Nevertheless, there are situations when leaders of totalitarian systems know very well that they direct people to delusion, yet continue doing so for reasons known only to them. This is scary indeed, because it reminds the actions of a one widely recognized famous politician-Satanist, who had once said, "My task is to entice as many people as possible to hell and then laugh at them there." This approach is truly satanic, and entails the most dreadful punishment in eternity.

In conclusion I want to say a few words to those who became victims of cults, sects and false teachings. It is absolutely obvious how difficult it is to make a decisive step, since you are in the midst of a forceful, wretched situation. On one hand you have already began to doubt the truthfulness of your organization, but on the other hand, are still afraid of the consequences of your departure from there and disengagement of contacts with it. If your family or all of your friends remain in the group, then your parting with it will mean a complete solitude for you, because no one will desire to have anything to do with a traitor and apostate. In a similar circumstance many of those like you, members of cults and sects spend days and nights in tormenting thoughts of what they should do. In the end you have only two opportunities: either to continue playing your game, even if it goes against your conscience, or break from the group and its teaching, no matter what it costs.

Chapter 14

A Search for the Living God

Before I begin a new subject, I would like to say that more than once I was condemned and accused simply for applying the phrase "to seek God". Some believers expressed to me with indignation, "How can you even talk about some kind of searching for God?? We are called Christians for the very reason that we have found Him! How can you look for the One, Who is already found?? This is a pure delusion!"

Well, I will not argue about it. I know one thing, that this expression is not strange to the Bible. And to back up these words I will refer to several passages of the Holy Scripture, where it's employed along with other phrases similar in their meaning. In the First Book of Chronicles David commands his son Solomon, saying, "*If you* **seek Him** (God), *He will be found by you*" (1 Chron. 28:9). In the Second Book of Chronicles we find these words addressed to **God's people**, "*The LORD* is *with you while you are with Him.* **If you seek Him,** *He will be found by you*", and then later, "*[. . .] and whoever would not* **seek the LORD God of Israel** *was to be put to death, whether small or great, whether man or woman*" (2 Chronicles 15:2, 13). By the mouth of prophet Isaiah God tells **His children,** "*Seek the LORD while He may be found, Call upon Him while He is near*" (Isa.55:6). The prophets Amos and Zephaniah confirm these words, "*Seek the LORD and live*" (Amos 5:6) "*[. . .] Seek the LORD, all you meek of the earth, Who have upheld His justice*" (Zeph. 2:3). The anointed of God, the sweet singer of Israel King David says in his Psalms, "*For You, Lord, have not forsaken* **those who seek You**" (Psalm 9:10); "*The Lord looks down from heaven upon the children of men, to see if there are any who understand, who seek God*" (Psalm 14:2); "*When You said,* "*Seek My face*", *my heart said to You,* "*Your face, Lord, I will seek*" (Psalm 27:8); "*O God, You* are *my God;* **early will I seek You;** *my soul thirsts for You; my flesh longs for You in a dry and thirsty land where there is no water*" (Psalm 63:1); "*In the day of my trouble I sought the Lord [. . .]*" (Psalm 77:2). Echoing the psalmist David, prophets also spoke about seeking the Lord, "*With my soul I have desired You in the night, yes, by my spirit within me* **I will seek You** *early*" (Isa. 26:9); "*[. . .] and you* **will seek Me** *and find Me,* **when you search for Me** *with all your heart*" (Jeremiah 29:13); "*The Lord is good to those who wait for Him, to the soul who seeks Him*" (Lamentations 3:25). In the New Testament, Luke and the Apostle Paul reminds us of the reason **why** God created the human race, "*so that* **they should seek the Lord** *in the hope that they might grope for Him and find Him, though He is not far from each one of us*" (Acts 17:27). Also, "*There is none who* *understands; there is none who seeks after God"* (Rom. 3:11), *"He is a rewarder of those who diligently* **seek Him***"* (Hebrews 11:6).

I think there are enough of quoted verses to be convinced that a necessity of searching for God is not simply far from contradicting the Holy Scripture, but is confirmed by it. *"Seek the Lord while He may be found"*, the prophet Isaiah prompts us, *"Call upon Him while He is near"*. It tells us that time of mercy is not endless. We love to repeat nowadays, that we live in times of grace. Well, praise God for that! However, the question is do we draw on this period of grace and appreciate the given opportunity to seek the Lord? And if we do, is it a wholehearted devotion on our part?

By the mouth of prophet Jeremiah the Lord addresses us by saying, *"[. . .] you will seek Me and find Me, when you search for Me with all your heart"*. This servant of God, who had experienced much and went through countless sufferings, knew too well about the indispensable condition which was essential in order to find the Lord, *"[. . .] when[77] you search for Me with* **all your heart***"* (Jerem. 29:13). Is this what we do? How often in our faith and our love towards God, in our search for Him and our service before Him we are only half-hearted!

In my youth I had a favorite hymn[78], which has rendering lyrics. I think we should really ponder upon their meaning,

> *I do not want a half-truth,*
> *I do not want a half-aim,*
> *I do not want the strings*
> *Ring in my heart in vain...*
>
> *I do not want a half-faith,*
> *Pathetic, blinded judgments*
> *I do not want to feel*
> *Powerless heart's hunger...*
>
> *If I surrender, then — wholly.*
> *If I should serve, then — completely,*
> *So that my heart shall burn*
> *With a blazing fire of victory.*

---

[77] In Russian text, a word "if" is used to emphasize the condition of finding the Lord (Translator's comments).

[78] You will not find this hymn among the typical classical Christian English or American hymns. It was born in times of persecution and sufferings of Christians in the former Soviet Union, when believers knew the price of following Jesus and desired to be worthy of their Savior. We have tried our best to translate it into English without changing much of the true heartfelt meaning behind the words of this song. (Translator's comments).

I do not want a half-life —
So timid, pale and depressing.
I do not want my death
Be fruitless and void in essence.

Then let my sinful "Ego"
Die in the kiln of suffering
To bring a flame of a new life
Inside a heart set free!

I do not want a half-faith
I do not want a half-aim,
Let all my strings be torn -
They didn't ring in vain!

There is a revelation of a whole, fulfilled, realized and fruitful Christian life in this hymn. What a pity that today so many Christians do everything only half-way. They accept Christ as their Savior with double feelings and then, serve Him only half-heartedly, torn between love towards God and thirst for this world, between a call of their soul and desires of their flesh. That is why there is only half-truth in their ministry, half-aim in their aspirations, half-faith without joy, half-life without meaning, and half-death without fruits for eternity. Such a "half-way principle" brings no satisfaction to us, neither does it to God. Therefore, He says, "[. . .] *No one, having put his hand to the plow, and looking back, is fit for the kingdom of God*" (Luke 9:62).

Many years ago there was another hymn with lyrics my heart couldn't reconcile with. It went like this, "It is easy to search for God! It is easy to find God!" Even until now my soul cannot agree to it, because it was difficult for me to seek and find the Lord. You won't find easy ways of searching for God on the pages of the Bible, either. From the recount of the Holy Scriptures we know how difficult it was for King David to seek and find God again, after he had sinned with Bathsheba. This was a blessed man of God, of whom God Himself said that He found a man according to God's heart. David couldn't withstand a temptation, so God left him; and from that moment on sorrow, trouble, grief, drama in his own family always followed him. Then, David began to search for the Lord. We read that at nights he washed his bed with tears. His bones waxed old from daily roaring[79]. Nowhere and nothing could bring him rest and joy. David poured out his soul before God, confessed his sin, and longed with all his heart a restoration of a close communion with Him, "*Have mercy upon me, O*

---

[79] Psalm 32:3

God, according to Your lovingkindness; According to the multitude of Your tender mercies, Blot out my transgressions [. . .] Against You, You only, have I sinned, And done this evil in Your sight—That You may be found just when You speak, And blameless when You judge…Create in me a clean heart, O God, And renew a steadfast spirit within me. Do not cast me away from Your presence, And do not take Your Holy Spirit from me. Restore to me the joy of Your salvation, And uphold me by Your generous Spirit" (Psalm 51:1, 4, 10-12).

What a supplication! What a groaning! What a cry from a soul which departed from God! What a thirst to find the One, Whose intimacy cannot be supplemented by anything! What a shocking example for all who also lost their contact with the Savior! Intimacy with God doesn't simply return, especially if you lose it deliberately. And we should never forget that. As a husband who in his human jealousy leaves his unfaithful wife, so the Lord does not turn His face back easily, if we purposely betray Him. The one who has ever experienced it in his life needs no persuasion of this fact.

We, Christians of the last days, love anything and everything to be easy, and therefore, widen our paths as much as we possibly can. However, Jesus didn't promise us effortless ways. He spoke of a difficult, thorny road leading up to His Kingdom, and that's why only a few wish to follow it. Why, it is so simple just to believe Him, accept Him as your personal Savior and then, without any complexes about some finicky searching, mindlessly go with a flow, guided by superficial motto, "Praise God! Halleluiah! Hooray! Move on!" Unfortunately, this is what Christianity looks like among way too many believers. After meeting the Lord for the first time or so to say, barely getting acquainted with Him, for the rest of their lives they remain in the stage of shallow association, continuously abiding in spiritual infancy. It wasn't like that with the Apostle Paul, who can be a model for each of us. Addressing Corinthians he explained to them, *"When I was a babe, as a babe I was speaking, as a babe I was thinking, as a babe I was reasoning, and when I have become a man, I have made useless the things of the babe"* (1 Cor. 13:11, Young's Literal Translation). Seeking God, searching for personal contact and intimacy with Him always lead to growth in faith and the spiritual maturity which many Christians of our days lack.

It is not easy to seek the Lord. This exercise is not contained in something external. God most often reveals Himself to man during a quiet time alone with Him and frequently in a sound of a gentle blowing. Do you remember the prophet Elijah, with whom the Lord had made a kind of appointment?[80] This man came to the appointed

---

[80] The closest translation which corresponds to Russian text of 1 Kings 19:12 is found in NASB (New American Standard Bible and reads as follows, *"After the earthquake a fire, {but} the LORD {was} not in the fire; and after the fire a sound of a gentle blowing"*.

place and time, and waited. Then, there was *"a great and strong wind* [. . .] *rending the mountains and breaking in pieces the rocks"* (1 Kings 19:11, NASB), but there was no God in this wind. After the wind an earthquake started, however, God wasn't there either. After the earthquake there was fire, but the Creator wasn't in the fire. After the fire a gentle whisper came, calm, and the Lord revealed Himself there. This was how the man met with God – in isolated place, in trembling and reverence. And how often do we have such meetings? Is it often that we remain alone with Him in a quiet room, filled with fear of God, trembling and admiration? If not, then we shouldn't be surprised that we can't find Him.

One can get under impression that modern Christians tend to think that the Lord does not reveal Himself in a quiet whisper, as it was before, but particularly, in the wind, storm and earthquake. It manifests, of course, not in correlation to the weather elements, but in a loud noise and rumble, which frequently accompany our Christian worship services. In some congregations while praying, believers shout so much that it reminds you of a four hundred and fifty prophets of Baal on Mount Carmel. In others, a so-called Christian music goes together with a thundering noise of drum sets and makes you feel that you are about to witness a real storm. Yet in the third ones, one becomes an observer of so much stomping, clapping, dancing and other wild scenes that unwillingly thinks of an earthquake. Have we truly consigned to oblivion the words of the Lord spoken to us by the prophet Malachi? *"A son honors his father, and a servant his master. If then I am the Father, where is My honor? And if I am a Master, where is My reverence? Says the LORD of hosts to you priests who despise My name"* (Malachi 1:6). It looks like we have forgotten the meaning of the word "reverence", and therefore, have no shame to act unruly before God, without any fear calling it "worship". Can you imagine this behavior in the first apostolic church? I don't think so.

Once and again the questions come up, "How do we, children of God, seek the Lord today? Who is Christ for us, anyway? Is He a one-time random passer-by? Is He just a distant acquaintance who we contact from time to time? Or rather, has God really become a purpose of our life, a Father, a Counselor, a Friend Who is the closest of all in the whole world? What is the essence of our Christianity? Is it only in church-going? Is it in being a member of some local congregation or fellowship? Or, is it in the intimate relationship with the Lord, and in constant personal contact with Him, in that unduplicated closeness, sweetness of which is incomparable to anything?" This is what makes us His sheep, which hear the voice of their Shepherd.

Those particular children of God who had personal contact with the Lord left the deepest and inerasable trace in my heart and mind. Holding my breath I could spend hours listening how God led someone in a most wonderful way, how He taught her, convinced, reproached, warned, stopped and, literally, saved from a certain death, reaching out with His helping hand in the most critical moment of time. There is something in a face and a whole appearance of such people that draws to them with an overwhelming Him leave a special mark in a man, similar to what happened to Moses, whose face radiated glory after his meeting with God on the Mount Sinai. The life of a true child of God presents a reflection of a calm and strong inner health, which the Lord gives to one who abides in a close communion with Him.

Unfortunately, for many Christians a notion of "seeking the Lord" is inseparably linked to a desire of getting more knowledge about Him. This precludes a certain danger, because you can have the deepest knowledge of Christ's teaching, yet know not the Lord Himself. In the recent decades there seems to grow a tendency among believers of the former Soviet Union to acquire a theological education. New theological schools open one after the other. Well, it should seemingly cause a lot of joy: the young people seek God! The new personnel is being brought up, who will take the Good News to other people! This is great! In Russia and Ukraine, and in the entire former Soviet Union where there had always been a deficit of religious education, a new generation of spiritual workers is being raised up prepared to labor on the ripened and ready for harvest God's field! It is all fine and looks really attractive, except for one "but", namely - a substitution of a personal contact with God for theological knowledge about Him.

Till the end of my life I will remember my encounter with a young Christian man after his graduation from a Bible school. I had known him for several years. In my first acquaintance with him you couldn't help but notice his blazing love towards the Lord and a child-like trusting attachment to Him. There was something irresistibly attractive, light-giving, pure and unspent about this young person. What made most impression was his inward thirst and his searching for a personal relationship with God. And now, three years later after our first contact, a graduate of the Bible school sat in front of me and I couldn't recognize him anymore. He spoke in a composed manner about all the famous theologians from all over the world that were his professors, in what way the lectures were presented, which departments of theology they studied and how he received the more insightful knowledge of God's Word and of the Christian doctrine and so on. In between he mentioned also that while studying the Bible he was able to "reshuffle" all imperfections, vices and mistakes of the forefathers of faith, and now he looks at them with completely different eyes. While attentively listening to him, I looked closely at his facial expression and was inwardly terrified. Where did all his zeal and burning of his first love go?? Where was his spiritual freshness and attractiveness? In front of me there was sitting a modern Pharisee type: calm, educated, self-confident, outwardly very pious, however, somewhat colorless, uninteresting, lacking life person.

By telling this story I am not trying to say in any way that obtaining theological knowledge is a bad idea, not at all! It is quite an excellent thing. We are all aware that many blessed men of God and widely known evangelists and missionaries have had some kind of theological education. I am not against knowledge, and there was time when I too yearned to acquire it, spending seventeen years of my life doing that. Nevertheless, it is very important that everything is balanced out concerning this kind of desire.

Once I had an opportunity to be at one of the famous Bible colleges of the former Soviet Union, where we had a meeting with a rather extensive student body of listeners. As I was looking into their young faces beaming with a good enthusiasm, I suddenly remembered another young man whom we get familiar with on the pages of the New Testament. His name is Saul. He also was a kind of theology student of his time and received the highest religious education, being taught at the feet of the most respectful teacher of the law Gamaliel. But when under the most amazing circumstances he personally met the Lord, he left all that was precious to him before. Do you remember his words? *"But what things were gain to me, these I have counted loss for Christ. Yet indeed I also count all things loss for the excellence of the knowledge of Christ Jesus my Lord, for whom I have suffered the loss of all things, and count them as rubbish, that I may gain Christ"* (Philip. 3: 7-8).

Humanly speaking, it's hard to understand. How could you count loss all the acquired knowledge and achievements of theology of that time and compare it with rubbish, which is thrown away as something needless?? How is it even possible? How can he treat something to which he, perhaps, devoted years of his life with such disregards? To take the best of Gamaliel's teaching and call it a waste??

Yes. This great Apostle of Gentiles counted all, which he acquired by paying a price of great efforts, as trash, for the sake of gaining Christ, in spite of saying later in his life, *"[. . .] but I laboured more abundantly than they all"*.[81] A question comes up involuntary, "Hadn't he known and had God before?" No doubt, he had. Moreover, he was

---

[81] 1 Corinthians 15:10

"being more exceedingly zealous of the traditions of my fathers".[82] However, when he experienced his **personal** special wonderful encounter with the Son of God, Saul who later became Paul, realized that all his previous knowledge and wisdom could not make him a child of God. His mind was filled with the knowledge about God, but He was not in his life and heart. As he became conscious of it, Paul dropped everything else in order to grasp the One, Who was now his own Savior, being radically changed for the rest of his life. From the abstract, imaginable, known only by the books of the Mosaic law, God had become for him real, living, revealing Himself as his Father, Teacher, Counselor and Friend.

Therefore, all of you who strive to obtain the deeper knowledge about the Lord! Do get a hold of it and take the Word of God to those who are in dire need of it, but...remember one thing: you will not be able to give others more than you yourself have. If you only grab the theory and "dry theology", then while preaching you will hardly be able to bring people the living God Himself, with Whom each real child of God should experience an encounter. The knowledge is beautiful. Nevertheless, while getting at it one must be careful that it doesn't grind the whole grain of the Holy Word of God into a dead flour unable to give any life. Yet what we sow, we shall reap. All great ministers of God, all vessels used by the Lord to His glory were only able to become such after they experienced **the personal encounter** with the Savior and realized **what** it really meant. It would be sufficient to recall Moses and his forty years spent in a scorching desert. What was he thinking about while there? What did he experience there? How did the Lord speak to him? The Scripture doesn't tell us about it in much detail, but one thing is clear – Moses, the way he was before, and Moses who came back from the wilderness, were too different men. Personal contact with the Lord and intimate relationship with Him are the two things that radically change people at the root and what in fact makes a man a child of God and there isn't anything that can replace it.

But how do you achieve this intimate contact with the Lord? How is it practically done? This question tormented me until the Lord put it on my heart to read the Holy Scripture from Gospel of John beginning with the first chapter, verse forty-five, *"Philip found Nathanael and said to him, "We have found Him of whom Moses in the law, and also the prophets, wrote—Jesus of Nazareth, the son of Joseph." And Nathanael said to him, "Can anything good come out of Nazareth?" Philip said to him, "Come and see." Jesus saw Nathanael coming toward Him, and said of him,* **"Behold, an Israelite indeed, in whom is no deceit!"** *Nathanael said to Him, "How do You know*   me?"*

---

[82] Galatians 1:14

226

*Jesus answered and said to him, "Before Philip called you, **when you were under the fig tree**, I saw you." Nathanael answered and said to Him, "Rabbi, You are the Son of God! You are the King of Israel!" Jesus answered and said to him, "Because I said to you, 'I saw you under the fig tree,' do you believe? You will see greater things than these."*[83]

When many years ago I read those verses, one phrase spoken by the Lord to Nathanael answered the cry of my soul, "Lord, what are You? Reveal Yourself to me! Answer me, how do I find You?" These simple and seemingly unimportant words: *"Before Philip called you, **when you were under the fig tree**, I saw you"*, helped me to find an answer to the question 'how to seek the Lord in order to find Him'. God doesn't talk as much as, alas, we, people, do. However, when He does, His Word becomes living and acting, piercing through the depths of a soul. As He pointed at this passage of Scripture, the Lord asked me a question, *"Tell Me, how often have you been under your "fig tree" and what have you been thinking while there?"*

What could I say to that? Of course, I have had my quiet moments with the Heavenly Father, when I forgot about everything else as my soul conversed with Him. But it happened rarely and was more an exception than the rule. In general, my Christianity consisted of attending church services, periodical Bible reading and all the rest of the stuff that is considered "a Christian life". As far as that kind of personal encounters with the Lord, solitary talk with Him, intimate communion between my soul and her Shepherd. . . . How many times have I experienced it: two . . . three . . . five . . . seven? Perhaps, I could use all fingers of my hands to count them down. But I had years and decades of Christian life behind my back! Then I understood where the most intimate contact begins, when a Father and a child, a Shepherd and His sheep, a soul and the Maker and Creator Who breathed life into her, meet each other. There a conversation begins when one asks and another answers.

Who knows how long Nathaniel had sat under the fig tree and how often he sought this solitude. One thing is clear; Philip knew where to find him. What was he thinking about under that tree? What was the concern of his heart? Which questions bothered him? How did he communicate with the Heavenly Father? Ah, that I might be able to penetrate his world of thoughts and his secret of communion with God in order to grasp the reason of Jesus' attention to him! What kind of man was he, if the first words addressed to him stated an amazing definition of his nature, *"an Israelite indeed, **in whom is no deceit**"*. As I read these words, I suddenly realized how much deceit I had had in my life. How much of hypocrisy and piety just for a show there were in

---

[83] John 1:45-50 NKJV

my so-called Christian life, although I was considered a seeking and sincere Christian! The Lord came with the answer without a delay to a man who had no deceit. However, He did not hurry to respond to me.

To Nathaniel's question how Jesus knew him, a reply came, *"Before Philip called you,* **when you were under the fig tree**, *I saw you"*. Extraordinary, is it not? God sees and hears His child when the latter is seeking communion with Him. In solitude of man with God there lays a mystery known only to those who know what it means. Nathaniel who sat under the fig tree had this type of contact with God and therefore, in the One saying to him: "I saw you", he immediately recognized the One Whom he just recently talked to. At this the words filled with revelation escaped his lips, *"Rabbi! You are the Son of God! You are the King of Israel!"* This man knew that only the Messiah, only the Son of God and God Himself could know his hidden thoughts and so incredibly respond to them. His soul has encountered the One, Whom it sought and identified Him instantly.

At once another similar occurrence from the Old Testament comes to mind, which happened with a different young man, whose name was Gideon. He, too, was deep in his thoughts alone with the Lord when in his heart a question was born, "Where is God?"; *"And where* are *all His miracles which our fathers told us about?"* (Judges 6:13). While beating out wheat Gideon pondered upon these things and his soul cried out to God in such a way that He answered without delay by sending an angel to him, who announced the will of God telling him to free the people of Israel from the hands of the Midianites.

Unwavering, sincere seeking of God will never go unanswered. The question remains, though, how often and in what way we are doing this. How do we talk with God and what is our relationship with Him all about? Do we really have confidential conversations with our Shepherd and if, yes, how often in a course of our Christian life? How often do we remain alone with the Lord under our "fig tree"? As I ask this question, I don't mean a prayer when we are dead tired of our daily duties, cares, troubles, work and many other things, kneel by our bedside in the evening and say, "Lord, thank you that You have protected me today and gave me all I needed. I ask You to give me this and that and bless me in this and that, and also keep me safe during this night. Amen." After that, not knowing what else to say we crumple into our bed, basically, telling God "good-night". Or early in the morning, while rushing to work and trying to start our "to-do" list, we hurriedly read a verse or two from the Holy Scriptures to quiet down our conscience, then, kneel before God with a variety of needs and requests for the upcoming day and dive into a whirlpool of an everyday life. Or we groan before God when there is trouble on every corner, pouring out our problems and asking His help in solving them.

You have to agree that we have had enormous amount of such prayers, and generally, it's good and right. But the question is this: how often did we have prayers, talks and meetings with the Lord after which we got up from our knees absolutely confident that God was there, beside us, that He stood, listened and responded? Did we have a lot of prayers like that? As I had once realized what was missing in my communion with the Heavenly Father, I was deeply grateful to Him that in His mercy He pointed it out to me. Since then, I seek and crave for that intimacy with Him and lose peace and calm when I don't experience it for a long time. I am not trying to say that attending church services cannot be a blessing and that God cannot speak to us through this or the other preacher, not at all! Of course, He may help us in a different way for He has many ways of doing things. Nevertheless, only close, intimate relationship with the Lord under our spiritual "fig-tree", known just to us, make our Christianity especially priceless and full of meaning.

The man of God Oswald Chambers wrote about it in these words, "The *one sign of discipleship is intimate connection with Him, knowledge of Jesus Christ which nothing can shake.... Is my knowledge of Jesus born of internal spiritual perception, or is it only what I have learned by listening to others? Have I something in my life that connects me with the Lord Jesus as my personal Savior? All spiritual history must have a personal knowledge for its bedrock. To be born again means that I see Jesus.... Never allow the dividing up of your life in Christ to remain without facing it. Beware of leakage, of the dividing up of your life by the influence of friends or of circumstances; beware of anything that is going to split up your oneness with Him and make you see yourself separately. Nothing is so important as to keep right spiritually.*"[84]

When I finally got this, then much of my Christian life had to be re-evaluated. With the Bible in my hands I asked God to show me what in particular my Christianity was in His eyes. The answer to my call was sent through the first chapter of the Book of the prophet Isaiah. As I opened the Holy Scripture to find the indicated verses, I frightfully read, "*To what purpose is the multitude of your sacrifices to Me?" Says the LORD. "I have had enough of burnt offerings of rams And the fat of fed cattle. I do not delight in the blood of bulls, Or of lambs or goats. "When you come to appear before Me, Who has required this from your hand, To trample My courts? Bring no more futile sacrifices; Incense is an abomination to Me. The New Moons, the Sabbaths, and the calling of assemblies— I cannot endure iniquity and the sacred meeting. Your New Moons and your appointed feasts My soul hates; They are a trouble to Me, I am weary of bearing them. When you spread out your hands, I will hide My eyes from you; Even though you make many prayers, I will*

---

[84] Excerpts from "My Utmost for His Highest" August 15, 16, 19 on line provided by http://www.myutmost.org/08

not hear. Your hands are full of blood. "Wash yourselves, make yourselves clean; Put away the evil of your doings from before My eyes. Cease to do evil, Learn to do good; Seek justice, Rebuke the oppressor; Defend the fatherless, Plead for the widow. "Come now, and let us reason together," Says the LORD, "Though your sins are like scarlet, They shall be as white as snow; Though they are red like crimson, They shall be as wool. If you are willing and obedient, You shall eat the good of the land; But if you refuse and rebel, You shall be devoured by the sword"; For the mouth of the LORD has spoken" (Isaiah 1:11-20).

This response from the Lord shook me to the depths of my soul. Then, that's what my former walking before Him and my Christianity was in His sight! And I have been so absolutely sure about my salvation; and in my confidence, unfortunately, I wasn't an exception but rather a typical specimen of a Christian of end times. Why? Simply, because the only positive characteristics of many Christians are not to drink and not to smoke. Of course, it is good they don't. However, if this is where our Christianity starts and ends, and in all other aspects we don't differ from people of this world, then our hope for a blissful eternity is in vain. Many believers have this notion that if they don't drink and don't smoke plus belong to a local Christian congregation or a church, it affords them a heavenly paradise. Alas, it is a dangerous self-delusion of which Jesus warned us by pronouncing these words, *"Not everyone who says to Me, 'Lord, Lord,' shall enter the kingdom of heaven, but **he who does the will of My Father in heaven**"* (Matt.7:21). To be counted a member of a church and regularly attend its services does not mean to be a Christian. That is why God talks so strictly to His chosen people through the prophet Isaiah. He was not satisfied that the believers outwardly complied with all religious rituals that were commanded; went to God's temple, brought the gifts and sacrifices appropriated by the law, celebrated religious holidays and lifted their supplications and prayers to heavens, that is, did all as it was appointed to them, to the letter. Nevertheless, after leaving the temple, they also left their God behind.

Three thousand years have passed since, but very little changed in the life of God's modern people. It looks like we feel responsible before God only for performing regular church attendance, praying and making money offerings to the work of God. But by treating our Lord like that, we aren't only not glorifying Him but also becoming a heavy burden to Him. When one starts looking into the depth of the words of the Lord spoken through prophet Isaiah, then one gets under impression that the worship of God's people in its essence was made into an outer form of tradition, which consisted of determined times of worship, following of religious rituals and holidays, bringing sacrifices as directed and so on. In the eyes of people it sure looked like important service to the Lord, whereas, in God's sight it was no more than a futile "trampling of God's courts".

Oh, how deceived the children of God were then! But, what about us? Aren't we just as deceived today when we are so confident that by all we do for the Lord we serve Him? May He not repeat the same words to us, *"Your hands are full of blood"!* You will ask, why? Well, because *"Whoever hates his brother is a murderer"*. And there is such a great deal of malice, hurt, grudge and open enmity reign in the midst of God's people nowadays! There is so much blood shed, spiritually speaking! But everything remains 'behind the scenes'. And on the stage a pious spectacle is still being played out. There are beautiful and harmonious choirs continue to sing, there are calming, comforting and lulling sermons about God's love, grace, redemption, forgiveness, salvation and future eternal dwelling in paradise continue to be preached. The mass evangelization campaigns are being held, and summits and conferences are getting organized, as well as all kinds of exciting trips, incredible meetings and other interesting and fascinating arrangements.

In other words, the modern people of God are full of various initiatives and activities at the same time when from the pages of the Bible a cry is heard, *"Wash yourselves, make yourselves clean; Put away the evil of your doings from before My eyes. Cease to do evil, Learn to do good; Seek justice, Rebuke the oppressor; Defend the fatherless, Plead for the widow [. . .]"* However, in the din and clamor of our Christian life, filled to the brim with activities, we are unable to hear this voice of the Lord. We don't have time to stop and calm down before Him, like Mary did. We are more like a squirrel spinning a wheel - on and on, and on. . . . We have become so blind and deaf that while seeing, we don't see, and while hearing – don't hear what, in reality, is happening with us and around us. And one is ready to cry out, "Have mercy on us, o Lord! Be gracious to us, sinners! Turn us to Yourself and we will turn to You!" Thus, I too groaned, crying out in my soul when God showed me my state of affairs, bringing about repentance and the seeking of His face. As I began doing that, I asked the Lord to show me a person in the Holy Scriptures, whose life and searching would be worthy of imitating. God answered by pointing at the Apostle Paul who said, *"But what things were gain to me, those I counted loss for Christ. Yea doubtless, and I count all things [but] loss for the excellency of the knowledge of Christ Jesus my Lord: for whom I have suffered the loss of all things, and do count them [but] dung, that I may win Christ"*[85]. The way of his searching and fighting, achieving the goals he set for himself, served me a great example, showing the steps which he gradually took one by one, attaining the

---

[85] Philippians 3:7-8 NKJV

person he consequently became. He had a life which may without hesitation be called "**a life of constant searching for God**". Observing the Apostle Paul's walking before God one starts to understand that the resource of his unfading strength in ministry was the Lord Himself, in whose communion and intimate relationship he learned what he could later pass onto others, "*For I received from the Lord that which I also delivered to you* [. . .]" (1 Cor.11:23). The older I get, the more I realize that the whole school of life is given to us in order to learn how to enter into a close association with our Savior. And fruit-bearing is a direct progression of such relationship. Therefore, Jesus confirms it by saying, "*As the branch cannot bear fruit of itself, unless it abides in the vine, neither can you, unless you abide in Me*" (John 15:4). As we enter into a close, intimate relationship with the Lord we stop feeling lonely and have no need to be comforted and pitied. Nearness to Christ brings us the best enduring innermost health, which a Christian needs very much, indeed. And such intimacy we should have all the time, not just every now and then. It doesn't matter how long ago we have believed and how many years we are living with God. Spiritual health is determined not by church attendance and daily prayers each morning and night, but by intimacy with the Lord. When we walk further away from Him even for a short time, we inevitably begin to stumble and fall. While neglecting the reading of the Word of God and genuine communion with the Lord in prayer, we quickly forget what we live for and wander aside to where we shouldn't have, which brings us to falling. The Bible serves as a stoplight for us, and it is necessary to learn reacting to its signals aptly. All of its warnings are a yellow light; all of the sins listed there are the red light, and all the good deeds are the green light. If the Holy Spirit, by means of our conscience, turns on the red light, showing us envy, malice, animosity, pride, lust, selfishness and so on, we must immediately "put on the brakes". And when the green light is on, we should make haste and act kindly, show humility, help others, love and pursue purity. As we obey the Holy Spirit, Who dwells in us and reproves us, we grow in holiness, which doesn't happen overnight, but steadily, little by little. It is necessary to ask ourselves more often, "Where exactly have I not shown God's holiness? Was it an unclean thought or rudeness and impatience towards someone; or was it a hurting word that I said without thinking, an unkind action or a conscientiously committed sin?"

Don't try to forget it at once, but better try and correct it at this instant, immediately. Come to the Lord in your penitent prayer. Ask your neighbor for forgiveness. Overcome your sin by the power of God. Say "no" to all unclean desires and impulses. Without doing that, it's impossible to restore the broken close relationship with God, though it is our main goal. The aspiration of a true Christian is to reflect Christ in his life. But in order to live like Christ one must live with Him, which means, gradually, step by step expelling "unholiness" out of one's soul, seeking the Lord with all the heart and getting closer to Him. There can be no better achievement for a human being. Therefore, **true faith, self-discipline, purity, holiness and obedience to the Spirit of God** are the crucial conditions for having a close intimate relationship between a Christian and his God. That's why it is written, *"Who may ascend into the hill of the LORD? Or who may stand in His holy place? He who has clean hands and a pure heart, Who has not lifted up his soul to an idol, Nor sworn deceitfully. He shall receive blessing from the LORD, And righteousness from the God of his salvation.* **This is Jacob, the generation of those who seek Him, Who seek Your face.** *Selah"* (Psalm 24:3-6).

To seek, find and keep unvarying closeness to the Lord must become the aim and the purpose of our Christian life. While achieving that, it is important to be persistent, acting upon it the way Jacob did when he fought all night trying to receive what he desired, *"I will not let thee go, except thou bless me."*[86] And the result was – a new name given to him by God and a new heart. During this spiritual fight, just like in sports, you can't loosen up and slack off. If a sportsman gives himself a time off between finals for a couple of months and totally stops practicing, he shouldn't think of winning in the next competition. We can't allow ourselves any breaks as Christians. The life of a true child of God who is burning with love for the Lord is a continuous battle, incessant keeping up in shape and constant going forward.

In track and field athletics there are different running distances. There are short, one-hundred-meter tracks, when it is very important to make a first strong dash forward and without slowing down, reach the finish line in shortest time. There are longer running distances, like two-, four-, eight-hundred meters, and then, it is necessary to spread out your strength. But there is also a particular type of long distance foot race, which is measured in kilometers and called "a marathon". In this race the winners aren't the strongest who made the best charge forward in the beginning, but the ones who endure and persevere, and though sweating out, keep running without quitting, on and on, an on. More often than enough the one who has spared his strength to the end of the long distance, becomes the winner. And so the running of a Christian is a marathon, and only the persistent, enduring and persevering ones complete it by getting to the finish line, which asserts the truth of famous words, "The end crowns the matter, not its beginning" and "[. . .] *many* who are *first will be last, and the last first"*[87].

---

[86] Genesis 32:26 NKJV
[87] Matthew 19:30 NKJV

As we begin our Christian walk or, in other words, our running towards the goal, we should not forget that it will cost us something. It is a long, weary, exhausting, and, at times, insufferable path, indeed, where many things will be encountered and must be overcome. Unfortunately, we often get the impression that spiritual running for many Christians is made of many 100-meter distances. They jerk forward, get out of breath and stop. Again, dash on and sit down to rest. Then, another jerk and one more: up and down, flying up and falling down, a victory and a complete defeat and so it goes on and on for the rest of Christian life. It is no wonder that our spiritual state is as poor as it looks.

In spiritual life and in the seeking of the Lord we must learn to set goals and achieve them no matter what. In our physical life we can aim at getting an honorable occupation and make good money. We can attain profound knowledge in any field of science and become a famous scientist, a renowned singer, musician, artist, or in other words, establish our life the way we desire. But it may happen that something unexpected comes to pass and with all our achievements we are suddenly left alone at a "broken wash-tub"[88], not knowing what to do next. During my missionary trips I had met with a lot of people who impressed me with their erudition, education and amazing accomplishments and abilities. They, for sure, were able to succeed at large. But suddenly, out of the blue something happened in their lives and literally destroyed all they had gained. Now they think only of their daily bread and a roof above their heads. Though, this is only an earthly life, which sooner or later will have to end, but not so with our spiritual life. . . .

Our earthly life is too short to spend it wastefully, and eternity is too long to treat is carelessly. Therefore, each one of us must ask himself a question: "How do I live here, on this earth? How do I run spiritually? Being still in my body, how much have I been able to know the Lord and had He been able to know me intimately close?" This will determine our place in eternity and whether we will be there with Him, or not. Was our Christianity a continuous ascend and a victorious fight or taking it from Apostle Paul[89], had we only "beaten the air"? Perhaps, we had "beaten" it with the words of our ritual prayers, or with hymn singing which had no connection with our own life; "beaten" with our outward piety and our superficial barren Christianity that had no light in it. If this is true then we are in danger that once standing before the

---

[88] Referring to a famous Russian fable by A.S. Pushkin "The Tale of the Fisherman and the Golden Fish"

[89] "Therefore I run thus: not with uncertainty. Thus I fight: not as *one who* beats the air" (1 Cor. 9:26)

Lord, we may hear His shocking words, "*You wicked and lazy servant!*"[90] When you are starting to think about it, it sure frightens. And then you undeniably begin to cry out with your whole heart, "O Lord, help me to walk through this life in such a way as to come to abide with You in eternity, so that things I consider "the right Christianity" don't turn out to be a self-delusion!"

As a physician-therapist I had to hold dying people in my arms more than once, when there wasn't anything else that could be done for them. O, if only every person would have been able to see their eyes! There is a horrifying fear before the inevitable. These face-to-face death encounters are the blessing in themselves, because they remind us how fragile and temporal we are. They show us foolishness and emptiness of all worldly values and teach us that the poem of our life is not that long after all, and can be stopped short on a half-word. And no one will escape the last minutes of his life. Only imagine, how frightening we would feel, if in a moment before the end we suddenly realize clear as a day, "I've lived my life in vain and my Christianity will not save me. I believed, hoped, thought and expected that I had found the Lord and lived with Him; however, He is not with me right now. In my Christian life and walk there was something important missing; something, that made a man a true child of God. Now I am departing into eternity...but where? And who will I be there with. . . ?"

To avoid this and to safeguard ourselves from false hopes; to evade an overdue repentance in the last minutes, when there is no more chance to change anything, let us **seek the Lord** now, while we are on this earth and still have an opportunity, strength and time to do it. "***Seek the LORD*** *while He may be found, Call upon Him while He is near*" (Isaiah 55:6). May this advice which was left for us on the pages of Scripture become our yearning and our goal for the rest of our lives. Then, we will be able to elude conditions mentioned in the beginning of this chapter, which are: half-truth, half-aim, half-faith, half-life and half-death. After tasting the sweetness of God's presence and of the close relationship with the Lord we will always look for it and will not be able to satisfy ourselves with anything less.

∽⟨⟩∾

---

[90] Matthew 25:26

Chapter 15

I Have No Regrets About Anything

Dear Reader, I have shared with you the experience of my own Christian life on the way of spiritual searching. Now you know that these pages contain not only blessings I have had, but also the mistakes I've made, deviations and even delusions. I have told you how God taught, instructed, admonished, reproached and stopped me through His Holy Spirit and by His grace when it was necessary, He exacted and punished me, for He shows no partiality towards anyone. As I conclude my story and sum up my narrative, I would like to express my deepest gratitude to my Heavenly Father that He enabled me for it and to explain at the end why I have no regrets.

The Word of God tells us, Christians, that "*all things work together for good to those who love God, to those who are the called according to* His *purpose*" (Rom. 8:28). There are no perfect people among those born of a human seed. We are all in school of life where we get to be taught difficult and sometimes even severe but precious and necessary lessons. All great men and women of God, prophets, apostles and ministers went through this school. They had also made mistakes and even were capable of turning aside from the truth and holiness of God. Nevertheless, God by His grace opened their eyes over and over again, making them listen, instructing them and returning them to His bosom. Thus, the psalmist David says, "It is *good for me that I have been afflicted, That I may learn Your statutes*" (Psalm 119:71). King Hezekiah in agreement with David resonates with him praying: "*Indeed* it was *for* my own *peace* That *I had great bitterness; But You have lovingly* delivered *my soul from the pit of corruption, For You have cast all my sins behind Your back*" (Isaiah 38:17). Apostle James writes, instructing us, "*Blessed is the man who endures temptation; for when he has been approved, he will receive the crown of life which the Lord has promised to those who love Him*" (James 1:12). Apostle Peter confirms this thought with his words, "*In this you greatly rejoice, though now for a little while, if need be, you have been grieved by various trials,* that the genuineness of your faith, being much more precious than gold that perishes, though it is tested by fire, may be found to praise, honor, and glory at the revelation of Jesus Christ [. . .]*" (1 Peter 1:6-7). Apostle Paul, whom I quoted often in this book also doesn't leave this question unanswered and comforts us by saying, "*No temptation has overtaken you except such as is common to man; but God is faithful, who will not allow you to be tempted beyond what you are able, but with the temptation will also make the way of escape, that you may be able to bear* it" (1 Corinthians 10:13). Finally, the Lord Himself sums up all the human expressions this way, "*For I know the* *thoughts that I think toward you, says the LORD, thoughts of peace and not of evil, to give you a future and a hope"* (Jerem. 29:11).

We all know very well that the life experience of a man is gained by him in difficulties, hurdles of life, in illnesses, during hardships and sorrows. In fact, very often our mistakes and miscalculations teach us good things. They, in particular, humble and subdue us, breaking the foundation of our pompous and proud "Self". And they especially compel us to reject our own "goodness" and search for the Lord's help, getting closer to Him. They also teach us to respect, value and consider other people's opinions. In Russia we used to say: "A smart man learns from mistakes made by others, but a fool learns from his own". I am not sure if it's always true, but perhaps, then I am in the "fool" category, since I mostly learned from my own mistakes. I don't know if you will appreciate my statement, but I can say that I have no regrets about it. Not only my mistakes but my misconceptions and deviations served for my good. First of all, they embarrassed me and brought low my haughty "Self", which I have described in details in the beginning. Secondly, they freed me from my self-confidence and were making me much more cautious in coming to conclusions and making various decisions. Thirdly, they aided me in gradually obtaining essential maturity and spiritual experience, which often is gathered one grain at a time and paid for with a price of anguish, search, disappointment, emotional pain and suffering. I recall when at the age of twenty-eight or thirty being low in one of my spiritual pits, I frantically called upon the Lord, saying: "Why?? But why do I have to go through something which others were able to escape without mistakes and fallings??" A clear answer came back to my heart, *"You won't understand it now. You will know it later."* It took not only years but decades of my life before I realized what the Lord was telling me then. In my soul-caring ministry as I met different people, I could understand them very well and share in their sufferings not because I was so kind and compassionate, but because I had walked that road myself. Surely, everyone knows the unquestionable truth that only the one who had experienced the same situation can really understand another man's sorrow. God makes no mistakes allowing certain things in our life. In time He turns them into blessings for us and for others.

I remember how much turmoil I had suffered during the time of departure from the truth within our former congregation in Estonia where I had experienced great blessings before. However, that which I encountered, mostly helped me to see something similar happening at another church, where my husband and I attended for three years, and later, in the case of Kwa Sizabantu. As I once suffered God's chastisement because of my extreme credulity and adoration of men I felt disheartened and wept for a long time. However, this bitter experience helped me later to quickly come to my senses and cast off devil's net he threw on me. The apostle Paul had expressed it very well when he said, *"Now no chastening seems to be joyful for the present, but painful; nevertheless, afterward it yields the peaceable fruit of righteousness to those who have been trained by it"* (Hebrews 12:11). Because of that, the words, *"As many as I love, I rebuke and chasten"*[91] and affirming consolation in God's promises given to us as His children, *"My son, do not despise the chastening of the LORD, Nor be discouraged when you are rebuked by Him; For whom the LORD loves He chastens, And scourges every son whom He receives" If you endure chastening, God deals with you as with sons; for what son is there whom a father does not chasten? But if you are without chastening, of which all have become partakers, then you are illegitimate and not sons"*[92] have become dearer, more precious and profound to me, now bringing joy to my heart.

Through my mistakes and digressions, looking back and remembering how patient the Lord had been with me, as never before have I realized His mercy, kindness and unconceivable to a human mind love towards men, which can only be explained by the enormous value of the blood of the Lord Jesus Christ shed for us, worthless sinners. How often I used to "write-off" those who thought, believed and followed the Lord in a different manner than I had! How much I was able to scorn others for their actions, surprised by their imprudence and disloyalty. Now, when I have seen myself very much capable of the same things, I learned to be lenient to mistakes and failures of other people, remembering that every man is competent to err and fall. That is why the Word of God warns us from condemning others by saying, *"Who are you to judge another's servant? To his own master he stands or falls. Indeed, he will be made to stand, for God is able to make him stand"* (Romans 14:4). These truths seem to be so simple and familiar to all of us, though, how hard it is for us to understand and implement them in our daily Christian walk!

As I work with people, having a close contact with their souls, I cannot stop to wonder how radical a person can be. How often he tosses from one extreme to another! Certainly, it is a lot easier if you get disappointed in something or someone, just to reject everything, trampled it all under your feet along with former blessings and having shaken off the ashes of the past choose a new path, which may of may not be the one where your soul find the desirable peace and rest. As you face something which hurt your heart and brought disappointment, it is a lot harder to follow the advice given to prophet Jeremiah by the Lord, *"If you **take out the precious from the vile**, You shall be as My mouth"* (Jeremiah 15:19).

---

[91] Revelation 3:19
[92] Hebrews 12:5-8

In connection with this I treasure and value the devotional thoughts of Oswald Chambers, "*Disillusionment means that there are no more false judgments in life. To be undeceived by disillusionment may leave us cynical and unkindly severe in our judgment of others, but the disillusionment which comes from God brings us to the place where we see men and women as they really are, and yet there is no cynicism, we have no stinging, bitter things to say. Many of the cruel things in life spring from the fact that we suffer from illusions. We are not true to one another as facts; we are true only to our ideas of one another. Everything is either delightful and fine, or mean and dastardly, according to our idea. The refusal to be disillusioned is the cause of much of the suffering in human life. It works in this way - if we love a human being and do not love God, we demand of him all perfection and all rectitude, and when we do not get it we become cruel and vindictive; we are demanding of a human being that which he or she cannot give. There is only one Being Who can satisfy the last aching abyss of the human heart, and that is the Lord Jesus Christ. Why Our Lord is apparently so severe regarding every human relationship is because He knows that every relationship not based on loyalty to Him will end in disaster. Our Lord trusted no man, yet He was never suspicious, never bitter. Our Lord's confidence in God and in what His grace could do for any man was so perfect that He despaired of no one. If our trust is placed in human beings, we shall end in despairing of everyone*" (End of quote)[93].

What a realistic understanding of our human nature, isn't it? What a correct description of us, the Christians of the end times! Indeed, how easy it is in our despair to negate everything and mercilessly blame everyone who is trying really hard to work for the Lord yet slips up and fails at times while at it. I think it is still much better to go wrong while serving the Lord than make no errors when doing nothing for Him! That's why we've had this saying in Russia: "Only the one who does nothing makes no mistakes". I believe that God will judge us not by mistakes we made during our work for Him, but for our lack of doing His work. As I look back I remember with a twinge all those who had lifted me up for a long time and, practically, adored. But when they didn't find me perfect and I failed their expectations, their malice, judgment and retribution had no boundaries. However, I thank the Lord even for that, because this way He taught me not to rely on people and therefore, not to lose my hope in Him when they

---

[93] My Utmost for His Highest, July 30th (Taken from "Our Utmost" website - My Utmost for His Highest by Oswald Chambers. (c) 1935 by Dodd Mead & Co., renewed (c) 1963 by the Oswald Chambers Publications Assn., Ltd., and is used by permission of Discovery House Publishers, Box 3566, Grand Rapids MI 49501. All rights reserved.

abandoned me.

Our life is filled with purpose not because of pleasant circumstances and recognition by other people, but through our faithfulness to God and His cause to which He has called us. To be faithful is to keep your promise and to follow through with your commitment. You can rely on a loyal person. He is dependable. The word "faithfulness" means also self-sacrifice, dedication and love. The antonyms of faithfulness are disloyalty and treachery, when someone if left in his trouble alone, betrayed and let down. Unfaithfulness is an exceptional mark of the end times that are filled with alienation and apostasy from God. First and the foremost attribute of faithfulness is patience. Faithfulness and patience grow out of love, of which the Scripture says that it *"never fails"* (1 Cor. 13:8). "Love" that fails exposes itself as artificial. It was rather not love but a disguised self-love. The same is true with faithfulness. If faithfulness is broken, it becomes evident that is wasn't genuine because time has no power over true faithfulness. Broken faithfulness has never been one to begin with, but most likely was a hidden self-interest. You cannot be loyal for ninety percent! The genuine love, patience and loyalty have no boundaries and are in fact the fruits of the Holy Spirit, if He indeed lives in us.

All of that and more I had to learn. To bring us to the depth of knowledge of vitally essential things in life God normally takes us through sorrows, pain and sufferings. Of course, as I said earlier these are the things we usually fear and do all in our power to avoid them. However, there are no other ways to spiritual maturity. It is quite interesting to note that with time we react to sufferings less and less painfully. In years I perceived that the more often I was "beaten", the much calmer I received the blows. Somehow they unobtrusively have become inseparable portion of my life and spiritual ministry, making me a different person than I used to be. And one can be certain of a single truth, that if we are with God, the blows of fate will not break us, but will make us strong. Fairly recently I read these words in a book: "If there was everything tip-top in our life, without a hitch, then any sort of Christian would be suitable for a ministry. But we live in a world where battles are fought to death. That's why we go through trials which prepare us for the service under the much more difficult circumstances".

As we follow the Lord in the way of searching we should get accustomed to the thought of inevitability of sorrow and suffering and just stop fearing them. Looking back I recall how often I cried out in my mind in the midst of difficulties and problems happening to me, "No! This is beyond my strength! Lord, I cannot stand it any longer! I simply can't . . . !" But time went on, difficulties stayed behind and I survived, although earlier cried I couldn't. We really don't know ourselves, and our abilities, and often forget the words of the Holy Scripture saying that God will never allow anything happen to us which goes beyond our strength of endurance (1 Cor. 10:13). Troubles, either physical or spiritual, always temper our character. Patience is taught in tough times. And under tight circumstances we receive free range for spiritual development.

The most difficult times we ever experienced become the most blessed time, too, and I have been convinced of that more than enough. Periods of sadness, pain and sorrow usually turned into days of joy and thankfulness to God when the true meaning of things He allowed was revealed.

How often as I faced the uninhibited injustice, seeing how wicked prospered and falsehood gained foot and was justified I cried to heavens, "Lord, how can this be? You are unbiased! How can You possibly let the lies triumph??" How often stunned in bewilderment and confusion before some tormenting bitter thing that happened to me I whispered in despair, "Why, Lord?? But why . . . ?!" But God usually kept quiet. I asked and demanded an answer from Him, but more often never got it; although, if it had been given to me I would have hardly heard it, because in all the turmoil and tempest of my soul I was unable to hear the still small voice of God.

Heavenly Father gave me time to calm down, accept the situation around me and then, He shed His light on what caused me to shake and lose balance. Then I was capable of understanding that the things He did were meant to be for my good. How great is the wisdom of God and how pathetically small our human mind is in order to grasp it! Therefore, my dear friend, if something happens to you which you cannot understand, please don't rush to conclusions but better, wait until the chapter is finished and all 'i's are dotted. The Lord had never been mistaken. When hour comes and you are able to observe the full picture of your circumstances, you will understand that our Righteous Judge has done everything just right.

These lessons don't come easily. But when you learn them, they become a priceless treasure. And this is why I want to repeat that I have no regrets about things happened to me. No matter how it hurts to recall some events at times, I can say with a grateful heart, "Lord, everything You did was right, and if I had an opportunity to start my life over I would have lived it the same way. Not because I have had an exemplary life, but because my experience proved to be for my good". Most certainly, I take no credit for it. All of that is by God's grace and His grace alone.

Speaking engagement in Russia about counseling ministry

During a Christian Conference in Romania

During women's service in Kishinev, Moldova

Broadcasting on Latvian Christian Radio in Riga

Speaking engagement at Lutheran church in Hamburg, Germany. The theme is "A Man is Born for Suffering"

Meeting with the readers at the Christian bookstore "Sirin" in the city of Moscow

Getting to know Christians from a Baptist congregation in Sidney, Australia in 2005

2000 people are gathered at the largest church of the Union of Evangelical Baptist Christians in Minsk (the capitol of Belarus) listening intently to the theme of "Personal Spiritual Revival"

I must state that three times in the course of my life I had to follow the Lord on a lonely road. I realize that some Christians think that the lonely way cannot be from God and when a person remains outside of the fellowship of believers it constitutes his or her poorspiritual condition. I cannot totally agree with such conclusion, since it doesn't concur with the Holy Scripture. Otherwise, we would have to call some great men of God and prophets of the Old Testament as well as the blessed ministers of the New Testament and of our days unfaithful to God. Moses, the eminent man, spent forty years of his life in the desert isolated from his people and in complete spiritual seclusion. However, God was with him and did His work, preparing him for the upcoming enormous ministry. Later, during the exodus he also was often alone in spite of the multitude of people with whom he lived. Righteous Job was left alone by all his loved ones and friends in the most trying times of his life.

More than once prophet Elijah whose endurance and bravery could amaze anyone had been in an absolute isolation. Of course, it wasn't easy for him, particularly since his solitude was accompanied by the constant pursuit of his countless foes. As he foretold the upcoming of a drought and famine he had to hide **all alone** by Cherith, a brook before Jordan where God took care of him, sending him ravens with bread and meat. Then, he was **alone** in the desert covering himself from Jezebel's wrath under a juniper tree and asking God to take his life. Or he stood by the cave where he met the Lord **one on one** and experienced His appearance in a gentle whisper. Then, we find him alone among the four hundred and fifty prophets of Baal on the mount Carmel surrounded by the unloving people of his, the people of Israel. In the direct sense of this word, he was a lonely prophet, whom nevertheless God had used mightily. For many years he had been **alone** before the Lord gave him a faithful helper and his successor Elisha.

Often, the prophet who wholly devoted himself to God, Jeremiah, remained alone. Being persecuted by his own people whom he dearly loved and whose apostasy he bitterly wept over, Jeremiah was continuously trodden on and rejected. However, the Lord was with him. Prophet Ezekiel hadn't been too popular nor accepted among the people of Israel, but the Lord made him His herald and a living symbol. Apostle Paul, the one who labored for Christ the most, had to suffer constantly from persecutions, pressure, rejection, charges and refusal. Once and again he was forced to write in his letters that he was left alone by his friends, "[. . .] *all those in Asia have turned away from me, among whom are Phygellus and Hermogenes*" (2 Tim.1:15); "[. . .] *for Demas has forsaken me, having loved this present world, and has departed for*

*Thessalonica—Crescens for Galatia, Titus for Dalmatia. Only Luke is with me [.
. .]. At my first defense no one stood with me, but all forsook me. May it not be
charged against them"* (2 Tim.4:10-11, 16). As he was abandoned by his
friends and coworkers, was Paul also forsaken by God? Of course, not.
On the contrary, during the most oppressive times for the Apostle the
Lord had been especially close to him, bestowing His protection, help
and abundant grace.

By saying this, I am not in any way trying to pronounce that
loneliness should be the norm of a Christian life for a child of God,
certainly not! Otherwise, it wouldn't be noted in the Word of God
numerous times about the necessity of fellowship between God's
children. See Acts 2:42, 1 John 1:3 and 7:2; 2 Cor. 6:14; Gal. 2:9; Heb.
10:25. Nevertheless, there may be some moments in the life of a
Christian when due to one reason or another he remains alone and it
doesn't mean at all that his relationship with God got flaws. Quite the
opposite, those days, weeks, months or may be even years of solitude
the Lord often uses for the intimate relationship with Him; for
preparation of a man to a certain ministry or to help him re-examine
his walk with God; perhaps, reassessing his Christianity in the light of
the Bible. Usually, this time of private seclusion with the Lord and
oneself brings out huge changes in one's life. Therefore, we must not
rush into human-based conclusions and, moreover, to reproach,
condemn and make thoughtless, hasty decisions. Just as not all of
those Christians who attend worship services are in the right spiritual
condition, not all who remain in isolation for a time have grown cold
and departed from the truth.

In the Word of God we find an excellent example of the right
reaction of the Apostles and disciples towards Paul's behavior who had
just become a Christian. After he had a personal encounter with the
Lord on his way to Damascus he didn't attempt to seek fellowship
with those who walked with Jesus but for the whole three years
remained separately from them. Having heard about his conversion,
the Apostles and disciples didn't try to investigate closer and elucidate
why he wasn't joining them. They did not judge him, nor
excommunicated him (although, humanly speaking, his behavior
looked suspicious). But they gave it all up into the hands of the Lord,
observing how He would lead further. Three years is no short period
of time, however, the true disciples of Christ were careful and wise,
having the patience to wait.

In the meantime, God was busy with Paul. And the Apostle later
on shared the following, *"But when it pleased God, who separated me from my
mother's womb and called me through His grace, to reveal His Son in me, that I
might preach Him among the Gentiles, I did not immediately confer with flesh and
blood, nor did I go up to Jerusalem to those* who were *apostles before me; but I*

went to Arabia, and returned again to Damascus. Then **after three years** *I went up to Jerusalem to see Peter, and remained with him fifteen days. But I saw none of the other apostles except James, the Lord's brother* [. . .]. *And I was unknown by face to the churches of Judea which* were *in Christ. But they were hearing only, "He who formerly persecuted us now preaches the faith which he once* tried to *destroy." And they glorified God in me. Then* **after fourteen years** *I went up again to Jerusalem with Barnabas, and also took Titus with* me. *And I went up* **by revelation**, *and communicated to them that gospel which I preach among the Gentiles, but privately to those who were of reputation, lest by any means I might run, or had run, in vain. Yet not even Titus who* was *with me, being a Greek, was compelled to be circumcised. And* this occurred *because of false brethren secretly brought in (who came in by stealth to spy out our liberty which we have in Christ Jesus, that they* **might bring us into bondage**), *to whom we* **did not yield submission** *even for an hour, that the truth of the gospel might continue with you.* **But from those who seemed to be something— whatever they were, it makes no difference to me; God shows personal favoritism to no man**—*for those who seemed* to be something *added nothing to me. But on the contrary, when they saw that the gospel for the uncircumcised had been committed to me, as* the gospel *for the circumcised* was *to Peter (for He who worked effectively in Peter for the apostleship to the circumcised also worked effectively in me toward the Gentiles), and when James, Cephas, and John, who seemed to be pillars,* **perceived the grace that had been given to me, they gave me and Barnabas the right hand of fellowship, that we should go to the Gentiles and they to the circumcised"** *(Galatians 1:15-19, 22-24; 2:1-9).*

I don't know what others get out of this, but to me personally this account by Apostle Paul sounds truly incredible. And this we read not in some obscure book but in the Bible! Can we possibly imagine anything similar happening within a Christian congregation or a church, no matter what denomination it belongs to? I suspect that such type of behavior by a young minister would have been considered extraordinary and carried some far lasting consequences for such a bold spirited free-thinker. Such a bizarre independency, going beyond any usual boundaries as it seems in the beginning, might not be easily forgiven or ignored by "those who seemed to be something" of our days.

As one reads the Apostle Paul's narrative it causes amazement not only about his own guts and courage, but also of a reaction by the spiritual pillars, especially revered key leaders and famous elders of the time. There was no indignation, no taking measures against "the one who dared", no attempting to subdue his unusual for others initiative. No, they simply listened to Paul, discussed his actions and, taking into consideration the fruits of his ministry, joyfully gave him the right hands of fellowship. What meekness! What readiness to receive another person in his service even if it doesn't agree with the traditional approach! What an amazing Christian unity and a brotherly love, indeed! Moreover, in that same letter to Galatians we read that Paul challenged to reproach the Apostle Peter openly by telling him **in front of the others,** *"If you, being a Jew, live in the manner of Gentiles and not as the Jews, why do you compel Gentiles to live as Jews?"* (Gal. 2:14). It's unbelievable to say this to someone who has been the most revered Apostle by all Christians!!

Can we imagine anything like that in our days? Personally, I am having a hard time imagining that and I guess you know why. Therefore, there is a burning desire to ask the former leaders and the great men of God the sore question: "Peter, James, John! What kind of ministers were you? How were you able in spite of your high spiritual position to preserve simplicity, approachability, humbleness, meekness and readiness to admit a dissimilar opinion and accept a ministry by others which differed from yours? Had it been Jesus Who taught you in various circumstances of which we read on the pages of the Bible, as recorded by the evangelists Mark and Luke? *"Now John answered Him, saying, "Teacher, we saw someone* **who does not follow us** *casting out demons in Your name, and we forbade him because* **he does not follow us."** *But Jesus said,* **"Do not forbid him,** *for no one who works a miracle in My name can soon afterward speak evil of Me. For he who is not against us is on our side"* (Mark 9:38-40). And there was another similar situation, *"But they did not receive Him, because His face was set for the journey to Jerusalem. And when His disciples James and John saw this, they said, "Lord, do You want us to command fire to come down from heaven and consume them, just as Elijah did?" But He turned and rebuked them, and said,* **"You do not know what manner of spirit you are of.** *For the Son of Man did not come to destroy men's lives but to save* them" (Luke 9:53-56).

What precious and significant lessons Jesus taught His disciples at that time, which they kept in their hearts to the end of their lives! But should we not just as well-being His disciples of the end times, obtain the needed lesson for ourselves?

There are some leaders who are not only incapable of admitting and respecting a different opinion and ministry of others, but do all in their power to isolate members of their churches from "dangerous", according to their estimation, people. In fact, they do that not because they care so much for their sheepfold but more out of fear to lose their sheep. By the way, it is especially true of groups, churches and congregations which display sectarian tendencies. Our common Shepherd, the Lord Jesus Christ wasn't like that. When seventy of His followers turned around and left, He hadn't even tried to return them but addressed the rest of the group with a question, *"Do you also want to go away?"* In reply Peter answered for all, *"Lord, to whom shall we go? You have the words of eternal life*". [94] So there is no need to be afraid to lose "your sheep". If the spiritual sheep know they are taught the true "words of eternal life" leading them to salvation from the pulpit, they will not go anywhere.

I only touched on these subjects because in real earnest I faced similar problems in the course of my own searching and spiritual ministry. It wasn't easy and I spent many nights crying into my pillow, repeating over and over again, "Lord, how can this be? Is it really written in the Bible??" However, all the grudges, misunderstanding, reviling and despising which I had to bear brought me closer to Christ, making me to take the Holy Scripture and look for the affirmation of truth or falsehood of the happening. I must admit, the Lord had never been partial with me, strictly punishing for smallest deviation, unfaithfulness and disobedience. Of course, it costs you something to experience it personally but looking back I thank Him all the more for it.

As many various difficulties and problems occurred, a lot of verses of the Scripture acquired for me much clarity, and therefore, the Word of God really became alive. For instance, had I not gone through tough financial hardship during the first years in Germany I would not have learned to humble myself and understand the amazing in their simplicity yet profound words of the Apostle Paul, "*I know what it is to be in need, and I know what it is to have plenty. I have learned the secret of being content in any and every situation, whether well fed or hungry, whether living in plenty or in want*" (Phil 4:12, NIV). In duration of my ministry the words of Jesus has become much more comprehensible, "*A prophet is not without honor except in his own country and in his own house*" (Matt. 13:57). In the midst of critical situations when it seemed the ground gave way under my feet, because those I especially relied on had suddenly rebelled and left, instead of showing support and understanding, the following words became alive and revealing to me, "*For it is not an enemy who reproaches me; Then I could bear it. Nor is it one who hates me who has exalted himself against me; Then I could hide from him. But it was you, a man my equal, My companion and my acquaintance. We took sweet counsel together, And walked to the house of God in the throng*" (Ps.55:12-14).

Much later, when after the publishing of all the books of the trilogy I had to experience a test by fame and trumpets of praise, and afterwards, once the first effect died down and more often than not all sorts of blaming and judging were sent my way, a characteristic made by the Apostle Paul to him and to his coworkers was becoming very precious to me, "*We give no offense in anything, that our ministry may not be blamed. But in all things we commend ourselves as ministers of God: in much*

---

[94] John 6:67-68 NKJV

patience, in tribulations, in needs, in distresses, in stripes, in imprisonments, in tumults, in labors, in sleeplessness, in fastings; by purity, by knowledge, by longsuffering, by kindness, by the Holy Spirit, by sincere love, by the word of truth, by the power of God, by the armor of righteousness on the right hand and on the left, by honor and dishonor, by evil report and good report; as deceivers, and yet *true; as unknown, and* yet *well known; as dying, and behold we live; as chastened, and* yet *not killed; as sorrowful, yet always rejoicing; as poor, yet making many rich; as having nothing, and* yet *possessing all things"* (2 Cor. 6:3-10).

Time and again, as I read those words which were recorded by a victorious child of God and penetrated the depths of my soul, I thought with sadness and heartache that along with some other statements of the Apostle Paul I couldn't also repeat, "*We give no offense in anything, that our ministry may not be blamed*". At this point I had no choice but to admit with embarrassment that, alas, it hasn't always been the case with me. Here and there mistakes were made; sometimes there was a divergence from the Bible; in other times, there was my own misunderstanding and even, on occasion, plain physical exhaustion, bordering with a complete fatigue, known only to those who labor to the limits, were the reasons of showing hardness, misunderstanding, impatience, indignation and lack of Christian love towards other souls. Much of this cannot be revamped and my heart wrings in belated remorse. However, I needed that, so that after soaring in heights of glory and being showered in streams of human gratitude I was brought low, realizing my imperfection and nothingness.

The Lord knows very well what we need, and appropriately uses either punishment or consolation. In those moments when it seemed best to fall into despair recognizing the errors made and throwing up quit everything, ending the whole ministry, a sobering voice of my conscience would say, "Fine. And then, what? Will you really be able to live in some other way, without all of this? After all you've experienced, can you even continue with pointless, pathetic and purposeless existence? No, never!! Well, then, what are you waiting for? Rise up and keep pressing on. Your lifetime is turning towards evening. Your head is covered with gray. It means you must hurry. Don't you know the summoning words of the Lord, with Whom you should also say, "*I must work the works of Him who sent Me while it is day; the night is coming when no one can work*" (John 9:4). Arise, Ludmila, arise! The night will come for you, too, and then, you will meet the Lord in eternity. What will you bring Him and what will you carry in your hands when you stand before Him? Beware, that it doesn't happen to you according to a Christian hymn we sing, "Others were bringing the golden sheaves, but I did just leaves . . . leaves . . . I brought the leaves"[95].

This type of conversation within myself helped me more than once to get up spiritually. And when, exhausted, I made just a step towards the Lord, He made three, and life went on along with the battle, which really is an inseparable part of a Christian life. However, in my search I was convinced many times that God surely never sends anything beyond our strength, giving us comfort, help and power to endure it in a timely manner. When I experienced the most critical, despairing moments in life, and my soul was under great pressure; as the stubbing, cutting blows of my fellow believers deprived me of my last strength and it seemed as if no one was near, in my heart I suddenly heard, *"Do not fear, I remain with you"*. In other times, from the pulpit of the church where I happened to be by chance, I would hear a sermon, which seemingly was prepared for me and got right on target, that would renew my strength to move on. Or a wonderful dream occasionally brought comfort and spiritual support, indwelling hope and shedding light on surrounding circumstances.

But more often the Word of God served as the best encouragement, becoming suddenly so indescribably alive that it seemed as if I heard a clear voice of the Lord – so familiar to me from my childhood – that brought peace and rest essential for that moment. Once as I spiritually "lay on the floor" having not the slightest will nor desire to get up, I took my Bible without thinking and opened it as it was when I read the words, *"Arise, shine; For your light has come! And the glory of the LORD is risen upon you"* (Isa 60:1). Another time, wrecked from all the false charges and accusations and not knowing where and how to find encouragement, again I opened the Word of God and through the lenses of my tear-fogged glasses read, *"Fear not, for I am with you; Be not dismayed, for I am your God. I will strengthen you, Yes, I will help you, I will uphold you with My righteous right hand.' "Behold, all those who were incensed against you Shall be ashamed and disgraced; They shall be as nothing, And those who strive with you shall perish. You shall seek them and not find them—Those who contended with you. Those who war against you Shall be as nothing, As a nonexistent thing"* (Isa 41:10-12).

This is our Lord. A mother cannot console her child the way He does. There is no better or more loyal friend than He is. Everything passes away, changes and disappears; yet He remains unchangeable and faithful forever. It makes complete sense to lay your life down to His feet; and there is no sacrifice that would be too much for Him. The One Who had given His life as a sacrifice for you and me is worthy to have our complete surrender in service to Him. And then, it won't

---

[95] An old Russian Christian hymn, well beloved by many believers and usually sang by church choirs.

matter that animosity of other people, their accusations and back-biting will become an inseparable part of your life. Thomas Jefferson had once said in his letters, "[. . .] *Were such things to be answered, our lives would be wasted in the filth of foldings and proving... After all, men of energy of character must have enemies; because there are two sides to every question, and taking one with decision, and acting on it with effect, those who take the other will of course be hostile in proportion as they feel that effect*".[96]

To hear the truth may be very painful. Instead of surrendering to it, people often begin to curse the ones who speak it. The genuine servant of the Lord must always be ready to pay such price and speak the truth, even if costs him his life – it will have to end sooner or later, anyway. Therefore, it is exceedingly significant where you invest your life while living on this earth. Frank William Boreham had said more than once to this effect that it is a duty of every person to find a suitable occupation for the time until his body is laid to rest.

However, we can't consider a grave to be our final destiny. Each one of us must build for eternity. There is a lot of different work and various activities which bring fruits for eternity, and therefore, it is good if we particularly concentrate our main efforts on them. First of all, we can classify as such a forming of Christian traits within, because this is something we shall take with us to heaven. Secondly, these are the souls to whom we were able to show the way to Christ. Thirdly, there is a precious ministry of providing spiritual help to the weak and the sick sheep of Jesus. The incredible enduring value must be allotted to labor of those who teach the Word of Truth, promote spiritual growth of young believers and nourish the souls of God's children. Parents who brought their children up in the fear of the Lord and gave them to God's service may be certain that their efforts will never perish. The prayer warriors who in quietness and solitude raise their voices to heaven for those who have pressing needs will not lose their reward in the Kingdom of God. The faithful servants of the Lord who give their money for Christ and His work carry out a ministry which will not be wasted. And the list can go on and on.

Soon before her passing away an old woman whispered with pain and bitterness, "I am already seventy, and I haven't even begun to live . . . ." Yes, it is true. A life lived for oneself is a wasted life. Many years ago I came across some amazing words, "A man begins to live only when he stops living for himself". This indisputable truth is what Jesus

---

[96] An excerpt from "Memoires, correspondence and private papers of Thomas Jefferson..., Volume 4" pages 309-310 – Internet file:
http://books.google.com/books?id=zpv0ilqHIYC&lpg=PA310 7OTS=z-6RkG9WAR&dq=Thomas%20Jefferson%3A%20there%20are%20two%20sides%20to%20every%20matter&pg=PA310#v=onepage&q&f=false

had in view when He said, *"For whoever desires to save his life will lose it, but whoever loses his life for My sake and the gospel's will save it"* (Mark 8:35).

God created us **for Him** and therefore, we may hardly find purpose in our life if we don't dedicate it to His service. The results of our toil for eternity can far outlive us. For that reason, I treasure a phrase by an American philosopher and psychologist William James[97] who had once said, **"The greatest use of life is to spend it for something that will outlast it."** One can't argue about it. When finishing your life on earth and nearing the eternity it is important to realize that you haven't lived in vain. But it is especially priceless if you leave a shining light behind it - your spiritual legacy. It sure is precious when things you've done continue to serve God and people whereas you dwell with the Lord! To wholly give yourself up to a work which has a surpassing value in eternity should become our only goal and the main purpose for our lives.

Believe me, it is worth living for!

ഇരുഇരുഇരു
ഇരു

---

[97] William James, US Pragmatist philosopher & psychologist (1842 - 1910). Internet file: http://www.quotationspage.com/quote/23543.html (c) 1994-2010 QuotationsPage.com and Michael Moncur. All rights reserved.

Bibliography

1. *My Utmost for His Highest* by O.Chambers. O.Chambers Publications Assosication Limited.

2. *One Day at a Time* by William MacDonald, Everyday Publications, 1999

3. *Grace of God* by William MacDonald, ECS Ministries.

4. *True Discipleship* by William MacDonald (Russian translation, published by CLV- Christliche-Verbreitung, Bielefeld, 1991)

5. *The Many Faces of Deception* by Florence Bulle, Bethany House Publishers, Minneapolis, 1994

6. *The Deceivers* by Josh McDowell (Russian translation, published by Protestant Publishers, Moscow, 1994)

7. *Is Christianity Bankrupt?* By Paul Taine (Russian translation, published by Keren Avhah Meshhit, Jerusalem, 1998)

8. *Opened Windows. The Church and Revival* by James A. Stewart, Revival Literature, Asheville, NC, 1999

9. *Je parle en langue plus que vous tous (I speak in tongues more than all of you)* by G.F. Rendal (Russian version translated from French was published by Peredaite Dalshe, Vancouver 2005) Originally published in Orbe, Switzerland, 1982

10. *Toedlicher Sekten-Wahn* by Luise Mandau, Bettendorf, Verlagsanstalt GmbH, 1995

11. *Sekten. 99 Fragen – Was heute jeder wissen muss* by Ulrich Rausch, Heyne-Sachbuch, Munich, 1999

12. *Warum faszinieren Sekten?* by C.Lademann-Priemer, Claudius-Verlag, 1998

13. *Religionen, Sekten, Seelenfaenger* by Hans-Otto Wiebus, Loewe-Verlag GmbH, 1997

14. *Die neue Zungenbewegung* by Kurt Koch, Bibel-und Schriftemission e.V. Aglasterhausen, 1985

15. *Die Geistesgaben* by Kurt Koch, Bibel-und Schriftenmission e.V. Aglasterhausen, 1986

Ludmila Plett
By Way of Searching

*To order the book in Germany or USA
send your inquiries to:*

*Wasser des Lebens Mission, e.V.
Kolomanstrasse 32
73527 Schwäbisch Gmünd
Germany
Phone: +49 (0) 7171-39734
Email: info@wasserdeslebens.org
Internet: www.wasserdeslebens.org
Or
Waters of Life Mission
Chicago, USA
Phone: 630-790-4937
Email: watersoflife2005@yahoo.com*

CPSIA information can be obtained at www.ICGtesting.com
Printed in the USA
LVOW071035080113

314789LV00018B/220/P

9 781603 834186